Nine Black Women

Nine Black Women

■

AN ANTHOLOGY OF
NINETEENTH-CENTURY WRITERS
FROM THE
UNITED STATES, CANADA, BERMUDA,
AND THE CARIBBEAN

■

Edited and Introduced by
Moira Ferguson

Routledge
New York and London

Published in 1998 by

Routledge
29 West 35th Street
New York, NY 10001

Published in Great Britain by

Routledge
11 New Fetter Lane
London EC4P 4EE

Printed in the United States of America on acid free paper

Library of Congress Cataloging-in-Publication Data

Nine black women : an anthology of nineteenth-century writers from the United States, Canada, Bermuda, and the Caribbean / edited by Moira Ferguson.
p. cm.
Includes bibliographical references (p.) and index.
ISBN 0-415-91904-5 (cloth). — ISBN 0-415-91905-3 (paper)
1. American literature—Afro-American authors. 2. Caribbean literature (English)—Women authors. 3. Afro-American women—Literary collections. 4. Bermudian literature—Women authors. 5. American literature—Women authors. 6. Women, Black—Literary collections. 7. Canadian literature—Women authors. 8. American literature—19th century. 9. Autobiographies—Women authors. 10. Autobiographies—Black authors. I. Ferguson, Moria.
PS508.N3N56 1998
810.8'09287'08996—dc21 97-26460
CIP

For Leola Bullock and Lela Shanks

Contents

Acknowledgments

IN THE COURSE of compiling this collection, I incurred several debts that are a pleasure to acknowledge. For excellent assistance with acquiring texts from Love Library, University of Nebraska, Lincoln, I thank Brian Zillig of the Inter-Library Loan Office, and Professor Debra Pearson, Supervisor of Circulation.

For information about Mary Prince, I thank the curator of the Bermuda Archives, John Aden, and Sandra Taylor Rouja for their unstinting expertise and attentiveness, and Sonia Grant and Arthur Hodgson, who arranged my visit to the archives. I also want to thank the numerous staff members of the British Library who aided me in this project and the late Audre Lorde for warm encouragement. For information about the Hart sisters, I thank the National Archives in St. Johns, Antigua, especially the curator, Mrs. Bridget Harris, and the assistant archivist, Mrs. Maudrey Gonzales, for invaluable assistance and for putting me in touch with other sources. I also thank numerous staff members at the Museum of Antigua and Barbuda in St. Johns, Antigua. I am especially indebted to curator Desmond V. Nicholson and assistant curator Michele Henry. At the London Methodist Missionary Archives in the School of Oriental and African Studies, University of London, I am grateful to Rosemary Seton, archivist, Jane Partington, library assistant, and Brian Scott, assistant librarian, all in Reader Services. For information about Mary Ann Shadd Cary I am warmly indebted to Joellen Elbashir, senior manuscript librarian at the Moorland-Spingarn Research Center, Howard University.

I thank students in several graduate seminars on African Caribbean and black female writers at the University of Nebraska, Lincoln, who participated in stimulating discussions of Elizabeth Hart Thwaites, Anne Hart Gilbert, Mary Prince, Mary Jane Grant Seacole, Harriet Ann Jacobs, and Harriet Wilson. I especially thank Suzanne Jenson, LeAnn Bracks, Amanda Putnam, Marla Styles, Stephen Moore, Lydia Kualapai, Aaron Petersan, Christy Traut, and Devon Niebling, as well as students in my undergraduate classes, who eagerly debated the experiences of Nancy Prince and Harriet Ann Jacobs. For helpful discussions of Mary Seacole, I am indebted to Eulanda Sanders and Ziggi Alexander.

I also owe a large debt of thanks to two anonymous readers, one of whom enabled me to rethink the inclusion of Jarena Lee.

Last, I thank Anthony Appiah, Michael Peterman, Marcus Wood, and Jean Fagan Yellin for invaluable conversations; and the Nineteenth-Century Colloquium, University of Nebraska, Lincoln, especially Jennifer Putzi and Heidi Jacobs, for an opportunity to talk about Mary Ann Shadd Cary. Most particularly, I thank Sharon Harris for information about editions and for rich, wide-ranging discussions.

For their helpfulness, skill, and care, I thank Angela Volzke, who typed early drafts, and Kristen James, who typed the final manuscript. Research assistants Lisa Cooper, Josh Motsinger, Jee Young Lee, Lisa Cooper, and Margie Rine provided fine assistance. I thank Christine Cipriani and Neill Bogan for expert readings.

And, I am grateful to William Germano at Routledge for ongoing, good-natured support.

Introduction

■

THIS COLLECTION DOCUMENTS the writings of nine of the earliest black women writers in the East and West Caribbean, Bermuda, Canada, the United States, and England. What links these diverse writers is a commitment to intellectual, spiritual, and physical freedom. Using their texts as tools of resistance, they use bold, double-voiced articulations about race and gender to question and undermine traditional concepts of inferiority and superiority. Their often firsthand accounts of bigotry and brutality constitute a politics of opposition. The text of each woman contributes to a collectively stunning list of "firsts."

As a whole, these nine African American and African Caribbean women established a new black female cultural politics that spans oceans and eras. Active agents in their own destiny, these intrepid pioneers led slave rebellions, traveled extensively, served as healers in war, raised families, evangelized, broke ground as journalists, taught school, and founded numerous societies—for political refugees, the infirm, children, and homeless people. Additionally, their knowledge of the Scriptures, religious conversion, and personal selflessness bestowed upon them an ineradicable dignity as they strove toward freedom and self-empowerment. They wrote energetically in a wide range of genres, from anti-slavery polemic, autobiography, religious testimony and history to editorials, biography, hymns, meditations, poems, travel, narrative, and a novel.

The collection opens with the texts of two sisters, Anne and Elizabeth Hart, who lived and worked as educators on the island of Antigua in the East Caribbean. They wrote in a variety of prose forms: history, letters, memoirs, and hymns. Born the same decade that Phillis Wheatley published her first volume of poems in 1773, and a quarter-century before Lucy Terry published the first known African American writing discovered to date, these sisters became the first black women in the Caribbean to write in English, to open Sunday schools, and to teach children and adults collectively, both free and enslaved.

In the following decades, many distinguished black women writers in North America, Bermuda, and the West Caribbean joined the Hart sisters in recording their diverse responses to a cross-cultural world turning upside down.

■ Having grown up in Bermuda in the late eighteenth century, Mary Prince penned the first anti-slavery autobiography by a black woman in English after she "walked away" from slavery in London.

■ Mary Seacole, born in Jamaica in 1805, traveled extensively around the world as a "doctress," crossing the Isthmus of Panama in the 1840s and nursing the wounded in the 1850s on the battlefields of the Crimean War. (She was the only black woman to record such experiences.)

■ Mary Ann Shadd Cary, born in Delaware in 1824, was the first black female newspaper editor in North America; she advocated emigration to Canada from the United States as a response to slavery and the Fugitive Slave Act of 1850.

■ Originally from New Jersey, Jarena Lee wrote a spiritual autobiography and became the first female preacher of the African Methodist Episcopal Church.

■ Nancy Prince, born in 1799 in Massachusetts of mixed African and Indian ancestry, published a fascinating account of her momentous travels in Russia during the era of the Decembrist uprising and then in post-emancipation Jamaica.

■ Harriet Wilson, born in New Hampshire some time in the early 1800s, was probably the first African American to publish fiction written in English that coded personal experiences with hypocritical white abolitionists.

■ Last, Harriet Jacobs from Edenton, North Carolina, wrote a unique, self-affirming autobiography that recorded the life of a fearless slave who avoided capture and finally escaped to a freedom often in jeopardy.

Having won the right to speak through necessary compromises with white editors and friends, all nine writers locate themselves in opposition to their societies. They adopt multiple strategies of resistance that include omission, displacement, false naiveté, evasion, and accommodation. For the most part, they had to conceal the unspeakable and subvert what might prove dangerous or unprofitable to reveal. Let me mention a couple of examples.

With their informally circulating texts, the Hart sisters counter racist mythologies about black inferiority. Through cultural representations of themselves as propagandists and educators, they display both intellect and altruism.

Since Mary Prince's brutalizing sexual experiences would be unacceptable reading for an evangelical (or any) audience, she can talk only of a master who forced her to wash him naked. In another case, asterisks pepper an unacceptably explicit anecdote. But, surprisingly, those lacunae are partially filled when Prince speaks in court. Like Harriet Jacobs, Prince forces her readers to learn the truth about black bodies and brutalization.

Moreover, Harriet Wilson and Harriet Jacobs had to resort to a title page and a pseudonym, respectively, to conceal their identities. Countering false representations and fragmentation, giving voice individually and in unison to the silent, the silenced, and themselves, they scripted a global resistance to slavery and an expanding colonial order.

Together, all nine women used their writing to carve out a place for themselves in an entrenched patriarchal society. Struggling to sound themselves and above all to be heard, they transformed marginalization into a site of power and agency. But not only were their personal experiences, their professions, and their generic span protean, their cultural identities and their roles as travelers were equally and unprecedentedly expansive. Some of them repeatedly voyaged across the Atlantic to London, Russia, and the Crimea, down to Jamaica from the United States, down to South America from Jamaica, across the United States itself, down the North Atlantic to Turks Island and the East Caribbean, and north to Canada. Hence they were sturdy forerunners of what Paul Gilroy has brilliantly characterized as the "Black Atlantic World," that vast arena of black culture that encompasses Africa, Europe, the Americas, and the Caribbean. Even Harriet Wilson, who never left the United States, and Anne Hart Gilbert, who always lived in Antigua (as far as we know), were engaged with international cultures and ideas, their lives rich, challenging, and politically, often physically global. In their exceptional mobility, furthermore, these writers suggest the lives of displaced or dispossessed peoples. They exemplify Carole Boyce Davies's superb phrase "migratory subjectivities." Collectively, these narratives about constant movement form a transcontinental, textual diaspora.

Through their collective endeavors, these writers constructed insurrectionary texts that offered alternative visions and oppositional vantage points, that exposed white duplicity and varied forms of colonial violence. They shared a vista on the future. In doing so, they often voiced subjugated communities' as well as individuals' experiences. Their texts spoke and still speak to one another across continents, forming a diasporic cultural interchange that bespeaks a collective refusal in the face of injustice.

■ ■ ■

Although this volume stands firmly on its own as a collection, it also doubles as a classroom text with multiple uses. For example, I sketch the comparative historical backgrounds of each writer and her text in the various countries where the women lived. I suggest correspondences and differences among the women that might be helpful in a number of courses in women's studies, black studies, history, English, sociology, and any course concerned with cultural diversity. Certain pairings of writers could work for distinct teaching units: for example, spiritual writers, featuring Elizabeth and Anne Hart together with evangelist Jarena Lee. The adventures of Mary Seacole and Nancy Prince, on the one hand, and the slave narratives of Mary Prince and Harriet Jacobs, on the other, are two further potential pairings. These four, moreover, were either voluntary or politically coerced travelers, as were Jarena Lee and Mary Ann Shadd Cary. In tackling journalism and fiction, respectively, for the first time, Mary Ann Shadd Cary and Harriet Wilson could also work as a classroom segment on black women writers as professional standard-bearers.

Finally, I want to mention my principle of selection. It was primarily but not exclusively based on a concentrated number of texts written by black female pioneers addressing a panorama of subjects, primarily in prose. For reasons of space, I had to omit such crucial pioneers as Zilpha Elaw, Charlotte L. Forten Grimké, Frances Ellen Watkins Harper, Ann Plato, Sarah Parker Remond, Maria W. Stewart, Lucy Terry, Sojourner Truth, and Phillis Wheatley.[1] The nine writers selected, however, are strongly representative of this long cultural epoch in their genre, geographical region, professional diversity, political perspective, and psychological depth, their social condition as free or enslaved women, and their economic status, which ranged from poverty to self-subsistence. Using their own words, I want to suggest the rich, cumulative cultural history that the first one hundred years of black women's writings embodied.

The Hart Sisters

■

INTRODUCTION

ANNE HART GILBERT AND ELIZABETH HART THWAITES lived their lives in Antigua, at the southern end of the East Caribbean. Sisters born a year apart to a black slaveholder father, Anne Hart Gilbert (1768–1834) and Elizabeth Hart Thwaites (1771–1833) were the first educators of slaves and free blacks in Antigua and among the first African Caribbean female writers.[2] Elizabeth Hart, moreover, was one of the first women in the Caribbean to agitate and write against slavery. Related to distinguished Wesleyan Methodist families, the Hart Sisters were prominent members of the religious and cultural intelligentsia in Antigua during the late slave period there, when the institution was under attack and the character of society was changing.[3]

For the most part, whites viewed the free colored (as the population of African Caribbean former slaves was known) as too insignificant numerically to make trouble. The Hart sisters were part of this free colored community. Unlike other islands, Antigua had given free colored men and women the rights of citizenship in the 1770s. This freedom to vote angered many whites, who tried to perpetuate ideas about racial superiority and maintain political hegemony. Voting rights, moreover, suggested how much the power of free coloreds was on the increase.[4]

For African Caribbeans in a slave society, becoming free men and women was a difficult process and usually came about through reward or purchase. Another factor in the anxiety the plantocracy manifested about the ascendancy of free colored men and women was the dilution of its own power. Members of the white professional class in Antigua,

> merchants, lawyers, doctors, government officials, and even clergymen made up some part of the membership of the Assemblies. This group was well represented in the Assembly at Antigua. At the general election of 1788, for instance, 12 professionals were returned out of a total of 25 members of the Assembly. St. Johns, the capital town, returned as its four representatives an attorney and three merchants; and the new Assembly also counted among its members five doctors and three lawyers—one of them the Solicitor-General of the Leeward Islands. At least some of this group were proprietors of

> land; most were probably substantial men of property. They combined with the planters to give the political system of Antigua its reputation for superiority to the other governments of the Leeward Islands, which lacked Antigua's advantages of settled population and property.[5]

The more slaves were freed, the more whites worried about their control and sought ways to keep the society divided. The subjugation of the free colored community guaranteed white supremacy. During the Napoleonic War, which offered opportunities for freedom, the plantocracy was very much afraid for its power. Yet slaveowners, caught in their own political contradictions, began granting civil rights to white men of little property and allowing Roman Catholics to serve on juries. Primarily, they wanted as many white representatives as possible among the ruling class.[6] The Hart sisters' Methodism was another tool of empowerment that angered the plantocracy.

Not surprisingly, becoming as "white" as possible was a goal for many free coloreds because only by crossing the racial line ("passing") could they achieve upward mobility. Increasing fairness of complexion through miscegenous relations was an almost guaranteed way of moving up the social ladder.[7] Free colored men thus sought free colored women; for social advantages, however, free colored women often sought out white men. Free colored men, then, often ended up marrying slaves, in turn augmenting the potential proportion of the free colored population.

Discrimination against free colored people provoked them to such dissatisfaction that in 1823 they presented a petition of their grievances; hence the desire of many African Caribbean women to associate with or (much less commonly) marry white men. This vigorous system of racial disparity meant that the most poverty-stricken and subjugated group consisted of black slaves. Clement Caines, one of the elected representatives of the general legislature of the Leeward Islands, encapsulates the abominable condition of field slaves as opposed even to house slaves: "They are also the most miserable creatures that we own, the most corrupt and the most dangerous."[8]

In such a society, Anne Hart Gilbert and Elizabeth Hart Thwaites occupied a special niche, both because they were respectable members of the free colored community and because, as members of a Methodist family, their religion and by extension their political values were opposed to nominally Anglican ruling-class values.

The Antiguan Methodist church to which the Hart family belonged was dominated in its early days by several households: the Clarkleys (also called

Clearkleys), the Cables, the Lynches, and the Gilberts, the last related to Nathaniel Gilbert, who introduced Methodism to the West Indies.[9] The Hart sisters were connected to all four families.

Their maternal grandmother, for example, was Frances Clarkley, an African Caribbean convert to Methodism under the ministry of Francis Gilbert, Nathaniel Gilbert's brother. "My grandmother," states Anne Hart Gilbert, "receiv'd her first [admission] Ticket [to a Methodist meeting] pinned in the rules of the Society."[10] Frances Clarkley must have been a free colored; otherwise her daughter would have been a slave. (In slave society the mother's status determined the children's.) The original membership of the Hart family within the free colored community may, then, have come from this marriage. The Harts' maternal grandfather was Timothy Clarkley. Their mother was Anne Clarkley, the daughter of Frances Clarkley, an African Caribbean Methodist convert. Their father was Barry Conyers Hart, an African Caribbean planter and slaveholder with an estate at Popeshead near St. Johns, Antigua, where Elizabeth wrote her early correspondence.[11] The sisters grew up in a racially divided society within a sophisticated family of evangelical Methodists who were respected members of the so-called free colored community, but who were nonetheless used to being in the political opposition, specifically against slavery. Their father rendered slaves free service in preparing their manumission papers.

After the death of her mother in 1785, twelve-year-old Anne Hart had staunchly acted as surrogate mother to her many siblings. When Anne married in 1798, her sister Elizabeth took over the responsibility for the next three years. Not content with instructing their siblings, both sisters also offered religious instruction to slaves and taught them to read, a courageous and conspicuous decision for any woman to make when slavery was being attacked on both sides of the Atlantic and societal values were shifting. Having been raised in homes where religion and culture—Methodist principles as well as the writings of John Milton, Edward Young, and William Cowper—were prized, they habitually involved themselves in philanthropic work.

Such remarkable pursuits, especially in women so young, discomfited the white Antiguan population, who politically feared the spread of nonconformity.[12] Successful conversions not only flouted religious hegemony but suggested manipulation of the vulnerable that could lead to social unrest, if not rebellion. Besides, at a social level non-Methodists looked down on the Methodist Society for its orientation toward the disadvantaged. Even more critically for the island elite, Elizabeth Hart's forthright views on abolition were repugnant. The idea that marginalized members of society were to be embraced as spiritual equals was deemed scandalous as well as injurious to white safety.

Any instruction of blacks challenged traditional views and indirectly undermined white authority. Thomas Coke, for example, was unequivocal in his view of African Caribbeans as people in a state of "heathenish and savage darkness," living in "all manner of uncleanness with greediness."[13] Black Antiguans had to be converted before they could be "civilized" and hence moral.

The Hart sisters had their work cut out for them with "fallen" slaves because their social order—let alone the much-bandied about assertion of "loose" sexual practices—made monogamy almost impossible. Husbands had no legal rights as family men. Males vastly outnumbered females. White men in diverse positions of power kept black women as concubines.[14]

By the time the Hart sisters began teaching, the slave system was expensive and becoming even more so as slaves got wind of efforts in London to pass an emancipation law. Sugar production had become much less profitable to planters and required a large slave population density, three hundred slaves to a square mile. The upkeep of such a population was enormous, especially after 1807, when no more slaves could legally be imported. Contrary to William Wilberforce's expectations, this led not to improved but to deteriorating conditions, a psychological as well as a financial consequence of abolition. The publicizing of atrocities intensified, helped by the establishment of the *Anti-Slavery Reporter* in 1816. One argument goes that only the sugar boom of the 1790s saved the plantocracy from financial disaster. But the writing was on the wall.[15]

Wesleyan Methodism was critical to the Hart sisters' spiritual and political development. John Wesley's encouragement of women preachers and teachers, coupled with his message of redemption for all, deeply attracted them. These tenets seem to have matched their own political vision.[16]

The church activities in which the Hart sisters and other women engaged removed them from an exclusively domestic sphere, physically and emotionally. But whether they viewed themselves as God's instrument rather than as individual writers is hard to say. Certainly, they were keenly concerned about salvation by grace and bearing witness.

1

Elizabeth Hart Thwaites (1771–1833)

■

Biographical Narrative

Born in May 1771 in Antigua, Elizabeth Hart, a committed, publicly vocal abolitionist and educator, wrote the first known prose in English by a black woman in the Americas.[17] She is the first known black woman in the Caribbean to write against slavery in English. Her grandmother was Frances Clarkley, probably a free woman of color and an African Caribbean convert to Methodism under the ministry of Francis Gilbert, Nathaniel Gilbert's brother. Her mother was Frances Clarkley's daughter Anne, who married Barry Conyers Hart in 1766, a local black plantation owner, poet, and trouble-shooter who died in 1808.

After several bids in her youth to join religious communities and some painful backsliding, Elizabeth Hart was "convinced" or converted to Methodism in 1786 by the Reverend Thomas Coke, having finally discovered "the Sinfulness of my nature and deeply to feel the plague of my own heart" (p. 93). After that conversion, Elizabeth Hart dedicated herself to lifelong spiritual and political pursuits. Following her mother's death in 1780, she and her elder sister, Anne Hart, gave religious instruction to their siblings but soon expanded their teachings to slaves. At the turn of the century, after Barry Conyers Hart's plantation began to fail and he moved to Trinidad, the family gradually split up.

Elizabeth Hart's long early letter to a male friend in 1794 condemns slavery. This bold polemic was unprecedented since slavery was virtually a taboo subject in the colonies—particularly for women—where plantocratic feelings understandably ran high.[18] Writing from her father's slave plantation, she decries the institution of slavery as "the will and work of corrupt, fallen men" (p. 109). Africans, she argues, "are not so depraved as the generality of the Europeans, but more especially the West Indians" (p. 109; white understood.)

In Elizabeth Hart's short *History of Methodism* (1804) a decade later, written in response to a request by the Reverend Richard Pattison, a new Methodist missionary, she reiterates her abolitionist views. She compares the impact of religious ideas to explosive natural disasters and acts: they have "the same effect upon my mind as Earthquakes, Thunder and lightning" (p. 91). Parallel to *The History,* Hart wrote hymns and verse that express her religious convictions. She cries to Jesus for help, regrets worldly corruption, and craves redemption: "Let me love my God and die" (p. 98). Dedicated to the conversion of laboring and enslaved people, she aims to live honestly and decently and help others, especially disadvantaged people, to do likewise. Sparing no personal pain, she gives up meat to be able to distribute more funds to the needy, laying out "upwards of twenty dollars cash from my own pocket since Christmas" for children who need clothes (p. 113).

Elizabeth Hart married a white evangelical educator named Charles Thwaites, who had a similar selfless commitment. In 1805, they moved from St. Johns to English Harbour to be near her sister Anne, who had married John Gilbert.

Four years later Elizabeth Hart Thwaites and Anne Hart Gilbert co-founded the first Caribbean Sunday school for boys and girls, open to any class or race. Their defiant commitment to the education of slaves suggests how unprecedented a space the sisters were creating for themselves as educators in Antiguan society, far beyond just the establishment of Sunday schools. Their actions also stressed both the necessity and the importance of educating all black Antiguans. To improve her educational skills, Thwaites visited the island of Montserrat, where the well-known Lancastrian teaching system was in effect. Using a self-progressing monitoring system, pupils could become instructors and teach one another. Still known in the Caribbean and throughout the world to this day, the motto of the system sums up its practice: "Each One Teach One."

After seven years, Thwaites co-founded another society, this time for the orphans and children of "fallen and depraved relatives"; it was later called the Female Refuge Society. Over the years, she became a familiar figure in the Antiguan educational system, at one point teaching two to three hundred children daily in a schoolroom built by slave volunteers (p. 15).[19] One of her goals was to help slaves become productive salaried citizens. In her view, "Enlightenment is next to religion for the prevention of crime." Slavery allows the "indulgence of every diabolical disposition" (p. 109). Distinguishing between negative and worthwhile work, she opposes the "work of instituting slavery," but advocates work in general as a means to keep the "devil" at bay. Always advocating conversion and literacy, she sought to right the wrongs perpetrated against black women by attacking forced concubinage and other abusive practices.

Alongside this spiritual-educational program, her political struggles continued; her busy domestic missionary schedule included battling against slavery at diverse levels. British abolitionists had already organized a campaign on behalf of Antiguan slaves, a fact that infuriated island legislators. This situation precipitated one of the major crises of Thwaites's life. Because she had disbursed funds to the needy, Elizabeth Hart Thwaites was called to testify before a committee of the House of Assembly. Unafraid of controversy and personal calumny, she refused to name "the estates, the proprietors, the slaves, the kind of relief, whether money, clothes, or food." In testifying before the investigating committee, that is, she intrepidly followed what she called her "path of duty" and refused to "name names" (p. 21).[20] In Britain she was the target of a notorious plantocrat, James Macqueen, editor of the *Glasgow Courier*. He referred to Thwaites as the "bosom crony" and "tool of anti-colonial faction and rancor" (p. 22). The attacks on her in the British press also included attacks on Mary Prince, whose memoirs had just been published. Macqueen, notoriously pro-slavery, cast serious aspersions on both Joseph Phillips and Elizabeth Thwaites in the famous *Blackwood's Magazine*. His attack shows that Elizabeth Thwaites's opposition to slavery scandalized those favoring slavery on both sides of the Atlantic:

> In his [Joseph Phillips's] capacity as second secretary to the deluding society entitled, "The Society for the Relief of Old Worn-out and Diseased Slaves," the Assembly of Antigua, in the name of the colony he had unjustly attacked and basely calumniated, thus speak of him in the Report of their Committee appointed to examine into his charges against the colony:—"Previously to dismissing his evidence, your committee cannot help remarking upon the character of this second secretary of the Society, which unfortunately ranks equally low with that of the former one, so much so, as scarcely to leave a worse in the whole community!!"
>
> Time, space, and circumstances, compel me to quit this miserable tool of anti-colonial faction and rancor, and his bosom crony, Mrs. Thwaites. . . .
>
> By tools like Mary Prince, and Joseph Phillips, Pringle, and the band of which Pringle is the tool and the organ, mislead and irritate this country, browbeat the Government, and trample upon, as they

> are permitted to trample upon, our most important transmarine possessions, the value and importance of which I am bound to shew to your Lordship and the public.[21]

In fact, Thwaites's vigorous anti-slavery perspective was no longer championed in Methodist circles, as it had been when Wesley was alive. Hence her interrogation in the House of Assembly amounted to punishment for suspected pro-emancipation talk and actions, however concealed. The economic situation in North America figured large in this policy shift against emancipation in Methodist circles, which further marginalized Thwaites and her views. In defiance of the fierce attack against her lifelong commitment to education and social justice, many Antigua residents paid warm respects to her political vision and courage after her death at Willoughby Bay, Antigua, in 1833, on the eve of the emancipation that she had championed for decades.

■

Chronology

1771	Born in St. Johns, Antigua, to Barry Conyers Hart and Anne Clarkley Hart, who married 1766. Introduced to Moravianism by an aunt, Grace Clarkley Cable, at a young age.
1780	Mother, Anne Clarkley Hart, dies.
1786	Converted to Methodism.
1794	Writes letter to a male friend attacking slavery.
1798	Her first classes instructing slaves and siblings begin, following her sister Anne's need to give up these responsibilities after her marriage.
1804	*History of Methodism.*
1805?	Marries Charles Thwaites, a white Antiguan educator; they move to English Harbour.
1809	Establishes, with her sister Anne, the first Sunday schools in the the Caribbean for boys and girls, without regard to class or race.
1809–1813	After she visits Montserrat to study the Lancastrian system of education, she and her husband introduce that innovative system in the English Harbour educational venues where they teach.

1813	By this year, the couple institute a plan to teach five hundred children from neighboring plantations to read. Slaves voluntarily build a schoolroom for the purpose; Thwaites names it Bethesda. She teaches two to three hundred children and adults daily.
1815	Co-founds, with her sister Anne, the Female Refugee Society.
1831?	Refuses to give testimony before a committee of the House of Assembly about disbursing funds to the needy in Antigua; refuses to name names.
1831	Attacked by James Macqueen in *Blackwood's* Magazine.
1833	Dies at Willoughby Bay, Antigua, on the eve of emancipation.

■ ■ ■

FROM *HISTORY OF METHODISM*

St Johns, May 5th 1804

The Reverend Richard Pattison
My Dear Sir,

I am induced by two considerations to a compliance with your request, one is, that I would be obedient, and the other, that in so doing in this case, I afford myself a fresh opportunity of making mention of that goodness and mercy which have followed me, the most unworthy, all my days.

Knowing the interest you take in the concerns of Immortal Souls, I would give you a more circumstantial detail of my spiritual course, and for your satisfaction, add some account of others with whom I am acquainted, but time will not at present admit, I hope to write you again on the subject.

I am as you know, a native of Antigua. My deceased Grandmother, who was converted to God by the ministry of the Rev. Francis Gilbert and who died in the Faith, with my Dear Mother (gone to Glory) were united to the Methodists and trained up the younger branches of the Family, myself among them, in the fear of God and the observance of religious duties. I was also blest with an affectionate Father who ever watched with the tenderest solicitude over the morals of his Children, as did others of our near Relations, who by their kind attention prevented our feeling the want of Mother's care after her death.

Having soon imbibed a great regard to the Duty of Prayer, and believing in its efficacy, I never omitted the performance of it without feeling some compunction, and upon all occasions of danger or difficulty, I would either retire to prayer, or at the moment, lift up my heart to Heaven for assistance or direction, notwithstanding this, I was from my earliest days, subject to many painful temptations concerning the being of a God and of a future state, and would often be led into such labyrinths of inward reasonings on some parts of scripture and things that I could not comprehend as have made me wretched.

After my Mother's death, I principally attended the Preaching of the United Brethren at St Johns; the retirement of their situation, together with the simplicity of their manners and Preaching, greatly pleased me, and their Preachers used to dwell in such a pathetical manner on the sufferings and death of the Savior, has never failed to affect my heart. I thought they were happy, and in the midst of my Childish follies, often wish'd that I was of their communion. About this time, one night several severe Earthquakes were felt all over the Island. . . . [Fervid fears and praying; reassured by atonement given by Savior.]

Some time after this, Mr. Lambert, a Methodist Preacher came here from America; curiosity led me to go and hear him, his preaching was alarming and impressive, and always had the same effect upon my mind as Earthquakes, Thunder and lightning, rousing me to greater seriousness, to pray and read my Bible more, and it operated in like manner on some of my relations, yet did we not submit to the truth, but contrived after all, to hold fast our own Righteousness. Mr. Lambert returned to America, and I remained destitute of the power of Godliness, and for the most part, content with the form, Yea, a Lover of pleasure more than a lover of God. I continued my attendance at the Methodist Chapel, the Established Church of that of the Brethren, experiencing more or less of the strivings of the Spirit and the restraints of conscience, but none of all the preaching which I had heard produced any lasting or saving effects upon me, 'till the arrival of the Rev. Doctor Coke and the Missionaries which accompanied him. I heard the Doctor's first sermon with a sort of delight, yet, because it was Christmas, I went into the country for the purpose of amusement, and spent the evening in dancing. The next day, I was restless and very desirous to get back to Town, to attend the Preaching. I did so, and was made really ashamed of my conduct by the sermon which the Doctor Preached on my return, and in which he mentioned the evil consequences of Dancing in particular. I heard him eagerly and all his Brethren in turn, and my heart was now powerfully attracted to the truth. . . . [Temporarily resists the religious Society.] Every

Sermon which Mr. Warrener preached, that I heard, entered my heart, enlighten'd my darkness, and showed me the path of Life. I was at last stript of my fancied goodness, beat out of every false refuge, made willing to be saved on the terms of the Gospel and brought humbly to seek for Pardon and Salvation. In this state, I joined the Society, and some months after, one night, in private Prayer my Soul was set at liberty, my prayer was suddenly turned into Praise, and with the eye of Faith I viewed a smiling Savior. It is not possible for me to describe the transports of my Soul on that glad hour, and so much the more did I rejoice in this clear manifestation of his favor, because I had so often been told that I was not to expect it, nor any who had lived morally.

My beloved sister Anne Gilbert, joined the Methodists at the same time that I did. She was brought to God in the same way, and first found peace. This was a Providential circumstance for me. She was the only Person to whom I could communicate my Joys and Griefs. . . . [Acceptance, grace of Society, distracted by skeptics; conversion.] I now began to discover the Sinfulness of my nature and deeply to feel the plague of my own heart; though I think I had power over Sin for more than three years. The doctrine of Sanctification was not preached and enforced as I have since heard it, but happy would it have been for me had I gone on to perfection and obtain'd a complete victory, but alas! I loitered, and almost imperceptibly lost ground. Company, conversation and Books which did not tend to the Glory of God, together with Music's charms and Worldly attachments, bewitched, and in a measure stole my heart from God. . . . [Variously tempted, she thinks, away from God.]

While in a comfortless and discouraging situation, that chosen messenger of the Lord Mr. McDonald arrived here, his first Sermon came with indescribable power to my heart. I was, as it were broken to pieces and all my bones were out of Joint. My ingratitude stared me in the face and every instance of my unfaithfulness; the anguish of my spirit was very great, and I could have wept my Life away for having grieved his Love. A few nights after Mr. McD's arrival we had our Covenant meeting, and while all around me were repeating the solemn words after the Minister, the language of my desponding heart was:

> My solemn engagements are in vain,
> My promises empty as air,
> My vows I shall break them again
> And Plunge in eternal despair.

Mr. McDonald preached soon after. I really thought that someone had told him my case, or that he could discern spirits and this made me ashamed to look toward the Pulpit. The word Preached by this servant of God, to my diseased and helpless soul brought life and liberty. It seized on all my powers. I was again enabled to venture on the Sinners friend, my bands were burst; the Captive was Delivered, and I could once more say, "O Lord, I will praise Thee! tho' thou wast angry with me, thine anger is turned away and thou comfortedst me.". . . [Continues praising McDonald until his death; personal experience of goodness of preachers/salvation abstracted to congregation.]

Having to meet upwards of 160 in Class, affords me an opportunity of knowing several who have a hearing ear, and understanding heart, two of them are Whites who have a saving knowledge of the truth, the others are Black and Coloured from 13 to 60 years of Age. Some of the poor Africans can particularize such parts of a Sermon as they felt most, and one of them told me a few Sundays ago, after Preaching, "Massa open me poor sinner heart. He tell me every thing me do," with many of such expressions. I rejoice in the certainty that there are many real converts in St. Johns, both of young and Old. I am inclined to think, that one reason why so many of the poor Slaves upon the Estates, cause you trouble and discouragement is, that they are in general received into the Society, as Catechumens, and not convinced Sinners, and if a genuine work of Grace does not take place, they soon relapse into those Sins, which habit and custom have rendered as their meat and drink, particularly Quarreling and Unchastity.

You know, Sir, that very, very few are brought up with any sense of decency or regard to reputation, with respect to the forming of their connections they are obliged to be governed more by convenience than affection and being bound by no Laws human or divine, their engagements are easily broken. It is mostly the case that when Female Slaves are raised to wealth, and consequence (may I not say respectability) it is by entering into that way of Life, that cause women in another sphere to fall into disgrace and contempt, I mean concubinage. Of this you have many Instances. Truly labour and want are not the evils of Slavery (horrid system!) though these, as well as the Oppressor's Yoke, cause many still to groan.

In my late visits to Parham, I have been very glad to see the prospect brightens there, and that it wears a very different face to what it did a year ago.

May the good hand of Our God, who brought you and your Dear Partner among us, enable you with patience and perseverance to continue your Labours of Love, among the Outcast of Men, and crown the same with abundant success, prays.

My Dear Sir,; your affectionate and respectful,
Sister and Servant Elizabeth Hart

■

Hymns[22]

[Untitled]

Weary world, when will it end,
Destined to be purging fire?
Fain I would to heaven ascend;
Thitherward I still aspire.
Saviour, this is not my place:
Let me die, to see Thy face.

O cut short Thy work in me;
Make a speedy end of sin;
Set my heart at liberty;
Bring the heavenly nature in:
Seal me to redemption's day,
Bear my new-born soul away.

For this only thing I wait,
This for which I here was born:
Raise me to my first estate,
Bid me to Thine arms return.
Let me to Thine images rise:
Give me back my Paradise.
For Thine only love I pant:
God of love, Thyself reveal.
Love, Thou know'st, is all I want:
Now my only want fulfil.
Answer now Thy spirit's cry:
Let me love my God and die!

Thy nature I long to put on,
Thine image on earth to regain.

And then in the grave to lay down
    My burden of body and pain.
O Jesus! in pity draw near,
    And lull me asleep on thy breast;
Appear to my rescue, appear
    And gather me into Thy rest.

O take a poor fugitive in;
    The arms of Thy mercy display,
And give me to rest from all sin
    And bear me triumphant away,—
Away from a world of distress,
    Away to the mansions above,
The heaven of seeing Thy face,
    The heaven of feeling Thy love!

[Untitled]

O Thou whose ear attends the softest prayer!
Redress our wants, our cries for Zion hear.
Resign'd we to Thy dispensations bow.
Nor tempt Thee more, nor ask Thee, "What Doest Thou?"
But on Thy Church a blessing we implore:
Thy servants save, nor thus afflict us more.
Regard our sorrow, for the Saviour's sake,
Nor all Thy watchmen from our Israel take;
But grant the blessed few who yet survive
May for Thy cause and to Thy glory live;
That every sacred precept they enjoin
With brightest lustre in their conduct shine.
O may they ever speak in Thy great name,
Thy glory and our good their single aim,
While they advance the kingdom of Thy grace,
United spread Thine everlasting praise!
And give, O give us eyes to see our day.
And hearts that may the glorious truths obey.
May all who hear (through Thee) by them be taught,
Nor spend their precious time and strength for nought!

Borne on our minds, to Thee their wants we bear,
While Thou for us regard'st their faithful prayer.
Protect by day, be Thou their guard by night,
Nor scorching sun no sickly moon shall smite;
Rest them secure beneath the Almighty shade,
Nor troubles nor untimely death invade.
And then, when each the appointed race has run,
Ready that "glory end what grace begun,"
In years and labours rich, their farewell give
To earth, and "cease at once to work and live,"
With rapturous joy receive the signal given
To 'scape from earth, and hail the friends in heaven,
There to remain in glory with the just,
Till life Divine re-animate their dust.

■

Poem

On the Death of the Rev. Mr. Cook

What mournful tidings these salute our ear,
Alarm our hearts, nor can our grief forbear?
Another Prophet from our church has fled,
And Cook is number'd with the happy dead!
Another dead! how doleful is the sound!
How sad the stroke! Our Zion feels the wound,
Awakens all her sons with awful call,
And makes us tremble, as her pillars fall.
How soon, alas! he gains the immortal shore,
And we shall hear his warning voice no more!

In tender years, ere sin, with treacherous arts,
Had spread its baneful influence o'er his heart,
The Saviour drew him with the cords of love,
Wean'd him from earth, and raised his heart above;
Commission'd him to spread the Gospel grace,
And offer mercy to the fallen race;
Nor in his native land alone proclaim

The saving power of Jesu's precious name:
But distant climes the adventurous youth invite,
His labour with the faithful few to unite,
Who, in obedience to the heavenly call,
And for our sakes, had left their early all.
The cost he counted; this his aim and end,
His health and strength in the blest cause to spend.
Nor now with flesh confers; the time was come,
When he should bid adieu to friends and home,
Himself, his friends, his all to Heaven resign,
Sail with new life and fortitude Divine.
With lively faith that Israel's God would keep,
He now encounters the tremendous deep;
Preserved o'er rocks unknown to him before,
At length is landed on the wish'd for shore;
With joy is welcomed to our favour'd Isle,
When soon he enters on his happy toil,
With strength Divine to sinners cries aloud,
And mercy offers to the listening crowd;
While we with pleasure heard the stripling bold,
With wondrous voice, the sacred truths unfold;
In all the warmth that language could express,
He urged repentance, faith, and holiness,
Was ever for this duty well prepared,
And the whole counsel of his God declared.

The season soon arrived when we should join,
As long accustom'd, in our feast Divine.
He by the simple board with pleasure stood,
A happy guest, partaking heavenly food;
With rapture heard the diff'rent tribes converse,
In Canann's tongue redeeming love rehearse,
And Afric's sable sons in stammering accents tell
Of Jesu's love, immense, unspeakable.
The grace that reach'd his heart, to all it came;
Their language, as their spirit, was the same.
Thankful he to our feast of love had come,
With heart elate, he left the sacred dome.

Like faithful Abram, call'd, he must obey,
Cross the great deep again, pursue his way,
Till reach'd a neighboring Isle, and there proclaim
His welcome embassy in Jesus' name.
They now conclude, and, as by God's command,
Once more embark'd, he seeks the destined land:
The haven gain'd,-but ah! some fell disease
Resistless on his youth and bloom did seize,
Nor could their prayers nor human art detain;
The struggling spirit press'd its home to gain;
Arrested by the ruthless hand of death,
No more does Cook here draw his labouring breath.

Mourn him, Tortola, and your loss deplore,
Who brought you light; but, ah! it shines no more.
Your Pastor and his flock united mourn;
Your gratulations into sorrow turn.
He living, would have taught you how to live:
An equal lesson from his death receive;
To the blest task your every heart apply;
His steps pursue, and learn of him to die.
His title clear to mansions in the skies,
He breaks from earth, and gains the glorious prize.
Repine not at this awful providence,
Nor ask, what urged his swift departure hence.
'Til Heaven has call'd its youthful favourite home
In mercy taken from the ills to come.
Let every murmur cease, no more complain;
Our loss is his unutterable gain.
No more shall gloomy clouds o'ercast his sky,
Nor the destroyer's piercing arrow fly:
His happy soul exempt, secure from harms,
It now encircled in the Saviour's arms.
'Tis there he rests, his griefs are all laid down;
He waves the palm, has won the glorious crown.
Let us ascend with him above the skies;
Let our rapt minds to that bless'd state arise.

Letter to a Friend[23]

Popeshead, October 24th, 1794

Dear Sir,—

Had I not promised in my last to say something concerning slavery, I should certainly have dropped the business; for I have since thought myself a very unsuitable person to write on controverted points; and were I equal to the task, I do not know it will answer any end that I should take the subject in hand: however, I am (and I believe you are likewise) on the side of truth. I have never declared my sentiments so freely to any person (except my sister) as to you on this head. I find none disposed to receive such hard sayings; and why: Because they are not disinterested, self is concerned; and I cannot, to please the best and wisest, lower the standard of right, or bend a straight rule to favour a crooked practice, I am, for the most part, silent.

I thank you for your kind intention to guard our minds against unnecessary solicitude at evils which we cannot remedy. In doing this, you first ask, "Is not the being so very anxious concerning it, in some measure, letting go our own work, and meddling with God's?" Undoubtedly it is, if I am very anxious. I acknowledge I am not easy about it; nor is it possible, as the matter stands, that I should feel that Christian indifference so necessary upon some other occasions. It is not the stoical, but submissive, spirit that should pervade our minds. Believe me, Sir, I do not leave my own work to meddle with God's. I do not pretend to scan His all-wise dealing with the children of men; nor am I bold to tempt the Lord, or ask Him, "what doest Thou?" Far be it from me.

I do not recollect that I ever made any objections to the merely being in a state of servitude, including much labour. This has been almost from the beginning, and perhaps subsists, more or less, in all parts of the world. Nay, were I obliged to provide for myself, I should desire no higher station than that of being servant: but Heaven forbid that I should be a slave! Nor have I said much about the shocking practice of taking the Africans from their native land, where—

> "The sable warrior, frantic with regret
> Of her he loves, and never can forget,
> Loses in tears the far receding shore,
> But not the thought that they must meet no more.
> Deprived of her and freedom at a blow,
> What has he left, that he can yet forego?

To deepest sadness suddenly resign'd,
He feels his body's bondage in his mind."

It is not, I say, the being merely placed in a state of subordination; for this is by choice the condition of many; but it is the black train of ills which I know to be inseparably connected with *this* species of slavery: such as may you never know, if it will give you needless pain,—such as my eyes see, and my ears hear daily, and makes my heart shrink when I write. When any thing is said like compassionating persons in this situation, it is urged by some, who seem wilfully blind, that they are much better off than the poor Europeans. Now, when things are clear to a demonstration, I know not what to say of such assertions, unless, as a good man observes, "it is sometimes in morals as in optics: the eye and the object come too near to answer the end of vision." I know that persons in a state of indigence, free as well as slaves, are exposed to many troubles; and are subject, especially if dependent, to every insult from those above them, who have little minds. These take every advantage of, and oppress, the poor. They have, however, laws made to redress their personal injuries. Slaves either have not, or they are never put in force; so that many of them suffer all these distresses, besides those peculiar to their situation. All who have their liberty, though servitude and penury may be their portion through life, have yet some of the greatest earthly joys within their reach; comforts such as give vitality to existence, and are really necessary to the being of man. They need not be deprived of those dear relatives,—

"Whose friendly aid in every grief
Partakes a willing share;
In sickness yields a kind relief,
And comfort in despair."

But, alas, how is it reversed with the others! It appears to me that pains are taken to prevent, or break, the nearest alliances, often in times of sickness and distress, and sometimes from the basest views. . . . [She describes slavery's ills and family separations.]

Christians who are not slaves, need only to be subject to the will of Heaven and of those they love; while most of those who are in bondage must either continually submit their wills to that of some irreligious, reasonable being, or undergo a sort of martyrdom. There are likewise others, who being endued with good natural understanding, aspire after refinement, useful knowledge, and sweets of social life, &c., &c.: were there a possibility of changing the colour of their skin, and emancipating them, with culture they would become ornaments to society. These are not permitted to emerge; they are bound down by some unenlightened, mercenary mortal, who perhaps has not a thought or wish above scraping money together. You may suppose such slaves find it a galling yoke:

> "And oft endure, e'en while they draw their breath,
> A stroke as fatal as the scythe of death."

. . . [Talks of slavery robbing labor of reward and taking virtue from slaves. Slave owning complicates the principles of Christianity.]

Now, Sir, I have only given you a specimen of the situation of the slaves in this part of the world. It does not suit me to say the worst I know concerning it: only I assure you it comprises a mystery of iniquity, an endless list of complicated ills, which it is not likely you will ever know. You will not, perhaps, find the sufferers disposed to complain of their case. Not many are capable of *explaining,* however keenly they may *feel,* their disadvantages. As to the opposite party, while blinded by self-interest, (and who among them are not more or less so?) they will not allow that they act unjustly. As I do not think it possible that those whose property consists in slaves can be persons of *clean hands,* must I not think you feel something on this account? And particularly for those who are dear to me, that have been so unfortunate as to gain this wretched pre-eminence. Those of them that are any way enlightened are themselves uncomfortable, and would be extricated. They are unhappy at their deviation from the golden rule, "Whatsoever ye would that men should do unto you, even so do ye unto them."

But you farther ask: "Is it not, at least, permitted by the all-wise Governor of the universe, and will He not do all things well? Might there not be some clue to it quite unknown to us, such as the sins of the Africans, as it was the case of the Israelites before their bondage in Babylon?" I readily allow their being in a state of servitude is permitted by the Almighty, and do not question but He *may* intend bondage for this race of men; but I account the abominations that follow to be purely the will and work of corrupt, fallen men, and displeasing to God. "He doeth all things well." But we cannot take upon us to say, "This is the Lord's doing." I agree with you, that there might be some clue to it quite unknown to us; but this does not strike me as being the sins of the Africans. . . . [Enslaved people no different from Europeans as human beings.]

Another thing to be observed is, that many of the slaves are not Africans; some white people sold themselves for a term of years, and shared the same fate with the blacks, being debarred their civil and religious rights; and many who now suffer as slaves, are much more nearly allied to the whites than to the others: so that I do not give full assent to your proposition at the conclusion of your queries, that the perpetrators of guilt, whether fair, black, or brown, are doing God's work. He has, and does still make use of the wicked (being most fit) as His sword to punish wickedness; but if these are in *this* case doing God's work they have mixed so much of their own with it, as at length to be bringing the same sort of punishment upon themselves. I have thought, that when the Almighty afflicts a people, *for sin* they repent and are humbled before deliverance is brought near. But I believe the Africans remained in their original darkness when He raised up men in Europe to espouse their cause. Nor have we reason to suppose the Negroes in St. Domingo, Martinique, &c., are one whit better than ever they were. Concerning these we have strange accounts, many of them having their masters' places; and the oppressors are now the oppressed. I believe, with a good man, that "present impunity is the deepest revenge."

But, lastly, you inquire. "Will all our solicitude make the least change in the matter? Have we not reason to believe that a brighter scene is approaching, and that this dark night will be the precursor of a brighter morning? Should we not by all means rejoice in hope, and be thankful that we are not in bondage, either in a literal or spiritual sense?" It is certainly wrong to be solicitous about these things, it ever makes bad worse; not do I suppose that any thing I may feel, say, or do, will make the least change in the matter, however the disposition of soul in inculcated by Him whose heart was tender; and pity is not apathy, but sensibility resigned; it is to this that I aspire, that while I feel my own and others' woes, I may recline on Heaven, and meekly and patiently say, "Thy will be done." I think with you, we have reason to believe that a brighter scene is approaching; and agree with the sentiments of a pious writer, (who has nothing in his book respecting slavery but what follows,) when he says, "I indulge myself in moments of the most enthusiastic and delightful vision, taking encouragement from that glorious prophecy, that 'of the increase of His government there shall be no end;' a prediction which seems to be gradually accomplishing, and in no instance more, perhaps, than in the noble attempt about to be made for the abolition of the African Slave-Trade." For what event can human wisdom foresee, more likely to "give His Son the heathen for His inheritance, and the uttermost parts of the earth for His possession," than the success of such an enterprise? What will restore the lustre of the Christian name, too long sullied with oppression, cruelty, and injustice? We should indeed rejoice in hope of this bright morning, be abundantly thankful that we are not in the chains of sin or *slavery,* and pray that God would hasten the time when "violence shall no more be heard in our land, neither wasting nor destruction within borders, but our walls be salvation and our gates praise." Then shall we:

> "Love as He loved,—a love so unconfined
> With arms extended will embrace mankind;
> Self-love will cease, or be delated, when
> We each behold as many *selfs* as men,
> All of one family, in blood allied,
> His precious blood, who for our ransom died."

I assure you, Sir, it is not any thing which I have read that has furnished thoughts upon the subject; I do not recollect to have seen any writing respecting it but Mr. Boucher's pamphlet, (which I think you have,) and a piece of "Charity" by Cowper, from which I have quoted a few lines in the first sheet of this letter. My mind was perfectly made up before these came into my hands. I was no sooner capable of thinking, than my heart shuddered at the cruelties that were presented to my sight; but more have I felt since I began to think seriously. I am, however, most concerned to have the evils within rectified, or rather cured; this will perhaps render some of those that are without less poignant, though I do not expect that religion will deliver me from fellow-feeling, nor do I desire it should; only I wish that I (and all who are in those things like-minded) may be enabled to live—

> "Unspotted in so foul a place, And innocently grieve."
> I am, dear Sir, Your Sister in Christ, E. H.

■

Excerpts from Correspondence with a Cousin, Miss Lynch[24]

[An unknown editor comments: "(The following) extracts convey an interesting view of the character of Mrs. Thwaites and of her multifarious and unwearied labours. In this pleasing task of teaching and training the young she continued till the year 1816, when a Society was established, denominated 'The Female Refuge Society,' designed to gather these orphans and others into an asylum, from the contaminating example of their fallen and depraved relatives. In this same year there was published in the Missionary Register a letter from Mr. Dawes, (then of Antigua, but formerly Governor of Sierra Leone,) agent of the Church Missionary Society in Antigua, showing the destitute condition of the young women growing up in the Island, virtuously and religiously, by means, under God, of Sunday-schools; at the same time pointing out the state of those children who lived with their guilty mothers, and earnestly requesting aid for the schools. This letter excited considerable interest in England, and the call thus made was promptly responded to by many benevolent Societies and ladies, who liberally sent aid in money and clothes from time to time; and afterwards the schools were patronized and supported by the Ladies' Negro Education Society."]

One of the bonnets sent has been bestowed on M.P. She attends our meetings whenever she can. Her poor mother called last week. On my asking how Marie behaved, she answered, "O ma'am, God bless the child! I don't know what I should do without her, now I am so poorly; she is a little mother to the young ones; she is quite content with her poverty.

—Many of the children are truly benefitted by religious instruction. I will give you an instance in P.O., the white orphan, who has to beg at the grog-shops, &c. I asked her, a few days ago, how her "mother," as she calls her, was: she answered with tears in her eyes. "She is very poorly, Ma'am, getting worse; but she don't pray; and when I beg her to pray to God, she swears at me."

—M.M. is about eleven or twelve years old; you would hardly think, from the modesty and rectitude of behaviour, that she lived in a house of ill-fame, the resort of the basest characters. Her mother, at present having no rest to the soles of her feet, and being miserably poor withal, sends every day to get her meal from a wealthy woman, of the most vulgar manners, who lives with Commissary D.

I hasten to inform you that our prospects brighten. Mr. Thwaites last Sunday invited the old country Leader, "Daddy Harry," to bring the poor little blacks he is teaching to read to our chapel, where we would furnish him with some of Lancaster's newly invented lessons, and put him in the way of teaching on that plan. The old man accordingly came in time to preaching with upwards of one hundred boys and girls. The chapel was very well filled when they came in, so that we would hardly stow them away. After preaching I sent them all away to our house, under the conduct of a careful person; for the old Leader went into the chapel cellar with Mr. Thwaites, and assisted him in meeting a large Class of men, while three female Leaders met above.

There are several children who cannot yet attend the school for want of clothes, and yet I have laid out upwards of twenty dollars cash from my own pocket since Christmas, exclusive of the seven dollars which you sent, and which have been well applied. I shall send the list to Mr Brookes, &c. I think, if he and some others could once be roused to consider the wants of the children, they would interest themselves. The articles given by Misses Looby have enabled three clever little girls to attend for the first time last Thursday afternoon. We have ten girls learning to write. I ought in course to have observed to you that Mr. Thwaites has for some time past been so concerned about the poor children, that he has begged me, if possible, to get myself taught to make lace or any thing that I could teach the girls; and he has been trying to manufacture the long straw into hats for him to teach them; but he made no hand of it.

We have the happiness to see many bidding fair to be valuable and good women, who would probably by this time have been tending their steps to infamy and woe. But what would have been the use of schools, books, teachers, lectures, &c., had not a few benevolent hands been stretched out to enable the poor little creatures, as well as those who are growing up to womanhood, to come at these good things? Yours, Miss Looby's, and Miss Tait's subscriptions, with the many kind presents, have been very helpful. Our number has so greatly increased this year, I have been obliged to take active steps to obtain more ample assistance for the needy ones. I sent Mr. Brookes a subscription list, with Mr. Gilbert's name and mine. I hear he has twenty subscribers, exclusive of you, Miss Tait, and Miss Looby. I flatter myself that we are at length awakening the feelings of some from whom we might reasonably expect aid. The prospect brightens in every respect, and I hope I shall be able to convey the most pleasing intelligence to you in time to come.

The Rev. Mr. Whitehouse opened the meeting yesterday at Mrs. Gilbert's: he addressed the children with so much feeling and affection, that there was not a dry eye among them, nor have the good impressions of those I have seen to-day in any measure worn off; even Mrs. Gilbert's wild Sarah is deeply affected. Upon the whole, we had a good Sabbath. Mr Whitehouse preached two such sermons, so plain, sound, and energetic, that many of all descriptions were touched. He was a Barnabas in the morning, and a Boanerges in the evening. Some of our family have felt the truths delivered. We had great and attentive congregations. This is indeed our Gospel day. God grant that the little flock may be kept simple and humble, loving and sincere, and that the blessed work may abundantly spread! Sunday after next, when there is to be no Preacher at Lyon's, Mr. Thwaites and I have promised to be there before ten o'clock, on purpose to meet the children, and commence a Sunday-school.

2

Anne Hart Gilbert

(1768–1834)

■

Biographical Narrative

Anne Hart, Elizabeth Hart's elder sister, was also a celebrated Antiguan dissenter. Her texts are also among the first by a black woman in the Caribbean. An abolitionist, educator, and tireless domestic missionary, Anne Hart's conversion to Methodism closely followed upon the death of her mother in 1785. She was baptized in 1786 by Dr. Thomas Coke during his visit to the West Indies.[25]

Her *History of Methodism* (1804) charts the chronological lineage of black women reformists in Antigua. Anne Hart makes a point of praising Mary Alley and Sophia Campbel, hard-working black women in the Methodist cause during the 1770s. She indicts corrupt missionaries and white hypocrites, unconventionally including missionary wives in her forthright condemnation. Both directly and indirectly, she applauds black spirituality while stressing the link between prostitution and the imposition of slavery upon black people by whites. The *History* also doubles as a conversion tale while she explains her transformation from "vilest reptile me." Self-effacingly, she exemplifies black female leadership and rails against racial prejudice (p. 32).

Anne Hart also knew discrimination at first hand. In 1798 despite angry detractors, she agreed to marry John Gilbert, a naval storekeeper and lay preacher who held a commission as a notary public. He was also cousin to the famous Methodist Nathaniel Gilbert, who introduced Methodism to the Caribbean.[26] News of the proposal provoked a clandestine racist backlash, and Glibert's fellow officers in the militia instituted a court-martial to stop him from marrying Anne Hart. The couple returned from their honeymoon to find the door of his notary office painted half white and half yellow, their enemies' reminder of the couple's "unholy union" (p. 73).

In 1803, the Gilberts moved to the town of English Harbour, later joined by her sister, Elizabeth, and brother-in-law, Charles Thwaites. John

Gilbert worked there as a clerk and was later promoted to storekeeper in the naval yard, and was assisted by Anne. Anne Gilbert's philanthropic enterprises continued to expand. As the Reverend William Box reported, the English Harbour Sunday School and the Female Refuge Society were not the only

> charitable institutions which Mrs. Gilbert was engaged in [and co-founded]—there were several others. She kept a weekly school, to teach writing and arithmetic. She superintended, and had the direction of, a large Infant School, supported by the Ladies' Society in London. She was the dispenser of blessings through the poor's fund for many years; visiting the sick, comforting the afflicted, clothing the naked, and feeding the hungry. She devised and organized a Juvenile Association, which has been more useful than could have been imagined in prospect. She presided also over other modes of charity.[27]

Joseph Sturge, a well-known British antislavery activist who traveled to Antigua in 1837 to see how former slaves were being treated after emancipation, made a telling remark about Anne Hart Gilbert's compassion: she held meetings in the dark so that those (often slaves) who had only one set of clothes (often soiled) could attend meetings without shame.[28] Successfully flouting the white Anglican establishment, she and her sister continually generated a vocabulary of rights about slaves that unsettled the colonial order.

Teaching ceased at the Gilberts' house in 1817 at the end of the Napoleonic War, when the Royal Navy reduced its base in English Harbour, thereby eliminating John Gilbert's position. The Gilberts moved their work to St. Johns but returned to English Harbour in 1821 when John was appointed naval storekeeper. By this time the Honorable Lady Grey, patroness of the English Harbour Sunday School Society, had been providing Methodist schoolroom space for four years. In 1817, she appointed Anne Hart Gilbert as superintendent of the girls' department. The Gilberts also took over from Elizabeth Hart Thwaites the responsibility of supervising Sunday schools.

In her endearing memoir of her husband, Anne Hart Gilbert speaks of a holy life that presumes a final redemption, but the biography is more than an account of her husband's life of political and religious struggle. She is also documenting the life of the community and the reaction of its different sectors to the biracial marriage of a couple who promote "God's work."

Moreover, the biography is also, in a sense, her own memoir, an unassuming way of recording her own situation as a black woman.

Anne Hart Gilbert subtly inscribes her own industrious role in their two-person operation: "As the business at English Harbour was pressing, he went there immediately, leaving me to pack up, and follow him, which I did in about ten days."[29] By and large, however, she tends to erase her role as agent in these collective ventures, signifying a conflict she felt between self-recognition and the humility expected of women. Once settled in English Harbour, the family quartet of the Thwaiteses and Gilberts set about to improve the moral tenor (as they saw it) of the free and enslaved communities there. As a consequence, they opened the first Sunday school in the Caribbean. Furthermore, at the end of the Napoleonic War when John Gilbert's job became virtually obsolete, Anne Hart Gilbert became superintendent of the female section of the Methodist school.[30]

Toward the end of the memoir, she explains the effect of their overwork: "Though he was assisted by myself and an active clerk, both his health and my own began to fail under incessant exertion" (p. 85). Speaking of his death, she highlights her own poignant loss in a customarily understated self-reference:

> Many were the mourners made by this event. The poor, the widow, and the fatherless, as well as friends and relative, lament it; but what are all their losses compared with mine? The lapse of almost thirty-five years, with many scenes of sorrow and suffering endured together, had cemented our union, and increased the tenderness of our affection to each other; but he is gone . . . (p. 88).

In other words, Anne Hart Gilbert records her husband's search for a sin-free life and also her own. Silently, she assumes her own claim to redemption as well as the existence of her soul—issues that were frequently debated.[31] In 1834, Anne Hart Gilbert completed *Memoir of John Gilbert* and died of erysipelas; the *Memoir* was published in 1835.

■

Chronology

1768 Born in St. Johns, Antigua, to Barry Conyers Hart and Anne Clarkley Hart.

1785	Anne Clarkley Hart dies.
1785–1798	Instructs her siblings, taking over her mother's role as educator.
1786	Baptized as a Methodist by Dr. Thomas Cole.
1797–1798	John Gilbert proposes. Anne, her father, and Gilbert's colleagues try to dissuade him from entering into a proscribed, biracial marriage. Anne finally accepts.
1798	Marries John Gilbert, cousin of Nathaniel Gilbert, class leader and preacher for the Methodists; endures racist harassment as a result. Gilbert's fellow officers attempt a court-martial; he resigns his commission.
1803	Gilberts move from St. Johns to English Harbour, a few miles south.
1804	Writes *History of Methodism,* particularly mentioning the important role played by African Caribbean women.
1809	Establishes, with Elizabeth, the first Sunday school in the Caribbean for boys and girls, without regard to class or race.
1815	Co-founds, with Elizabeth, the Female Refuge Society.
1817	Appointed by the Honourable Lady Grey, superintendent of the girls' department of English Harbour Sunday school. Later, the Gilberts move back to St. Johns.
1821	Gilberts return to English Harbour.
1833	John Gilbert dies.
1834	Completes *Memoir of John Gilbert.*
1834	Dies of erysipelas.
1835	*Memoir of John Gilbert* is published.

■ ■ ■

FROM *HISTORY OF METHODISM*

Antigua English-Harbor, 1st June 1804

My Dear Sir!

Having seen most of the accounts transmitted to our Brethren in Europe, respecting the rise, progress and present state of Methodism in the

West Indies; and having I think matter of fact, and the concurrent opinions of other impartial persons on my side, for differing with some in many, and with others in a few particulars; I feel some reluctance to giving you the information you require of me, lest the testimony of those that have gone before should render my time so employed, uselessly disposed of. I will however venture; hoping at least to profit my own soul by calling to mind the wonders God has wrought in this benighted Land.

In the Year 1790 One of our Preachers who is now is Europe, requested me to inform him by letter of all that I knew respecting the rise and progress of Methodism in Antigua. I endeavor'd at that time, to collect all the information I could get, and having part of a copy of that letter now in my possession, I will give you the substance of it as far as it goes.

The remotest period to which I can trace the Preaching of the Gospel, in these Islands, is in the year 1671: By William Edmundson a Quaker, who with five other friends visited Bermudas, Jamaica, Barbadoes, Antigua, Barbuda, Nevis, and St. Christophers. He made the attempt at Bermuda also but was not suffered to land, Colonel Stapleton, the Governor, having heard that by means of their preaching seven hundred of the militia had turned Quakers and that Quakers would not fight. They were obliged to return immediately to Antigua from whence they came, and were again graciously received. . . . [Excerpt from Edmundson's journal giving related information.]

This Colonel Windthorpe, was I doubt not ancestor of the person mentioned by W. Nathaniel Gilbert in his letter to Mr. Wesley called "The Dawn of a Gospel Day" and published in the 3rd Volume of the Arminian Magazine. He calls her Miss Molly Windthorpe a first Cousin of his Wife's. In the year 1683 after spending sometime in America, W. Edmundson returned to Ireland, from whence he came. To the best of my knowledge the Islands were destitute of a Gospel ministry till the year 1756 when a Moravian Mission began. The clouds of sin and error began to disperse among the Slaves by their instrumentality; and while they preached the truth, they laboured with their hands to forward the Work in which they were engaged. But yet "darkness covered the Land and gross darkness the hearts of the people." In the Year 1760, the Lord rais'd up Messrs. Nathaniel and Francis Gilbert. . . . [Examples follow of "Witchcraft," "diabolical" work, grave-keeping, thief-finding, superstition—evidence of the need for ministry.] The progress of religion under the ministry of these two blessed men is faithfully transmitted by them in their letters to Mr. Wesley & which are published in the 3d-5th-6th & 9th Vols of the Arminian Magazine. They formed a Small, but lively society of persons who obeyed from their very heart that form of Doctrine delivered unto them; they enforced Mr. Wesley's rules upon every individual & family that received the truth. My Grandmother receiv'd her first Ticket pinn'd in the rules of the Society. Their own families were miniatures of the Primitive Church. Truly it might be said of them.

> —"Their hearts were warm,
> Their hands were pure; Their doctrines and their lives
> Coincident, discover'd lucid proof
> That they were honest in the sacred cause."

But alas! they and their sacred cause were soon in perils from false pretended Brethren: There were two or three white men who came to the Island with a flaming profession of Godliness & soon as they made themselves known as professors, they were patronized & befriended by these two unsuspecting men. "Whose wisdom often woke while their suspicion slept and to simplicity resign'd her charge." The soaring profession and grov'ling practice of these men soon brought much scandal upon the Gospel; And when it pleased the Lord to remove his servants (Messrs. Nath & Francis Gilbert) many who before had been staggered by the Miscarriages of these men, now stumbled over the blocks, some almost imperceptibly declined in spirituality became friends with the world & inwardly enemies to God & his people, others fell into gross scandalous sin. However blessed by God, there were a few who never forsook the Assembling of themselves together. A praying remnant held fast where unto they had attained; and tho' it cannot be said, that they bounded in knowledge, brightness of reason or soundness of speech, yet I say would to God there was the same simplicity, purity & love of the cross in only one half of our greatly increased Society now. The leaders of them were Mrs Alley a Mulatto Woman & Sophia Campbel a black. The former after wading through many trials & temptations is still alive & steady in the good cause. The latter went to her eternal rest in the year 1799. They met together for reading, singing & prayers & with many prayers watered the seed sown by their fathers in the Gospel. The Lord owned & blessed their labors some brought forth fruit to the praise of God and remain to this day. I have witness'd the happy deaths of many that have died gloriously in the faith & left behind them. Finding that their feeble efforts were attended with a divine blessing, they got a friend to write to Mr. Wesley to send them a Preacher; and were fervent in prayer that the Lord would send them one day after his own heart. These remained bright Initials of a Methodist Society 'till the Lord by his providence sent Mr. Baxter. . . . [Need for Mr. Baxter and his successes decried and others mentioned.] Our two dear Sisters Mary Alley & Sophia Campbel mentioned above; ventured in faith to agree for a spot of land to build a Chapel upon: They were greatly discouraged by all to whom they mentioned it, as an undertaking too great & expensive so small a Society to engage in; but being emboldened by faith tho they knew not the way; they struck for the land & had to pay the cash down. Sister S. Campbell went herself with James Watkins (another of our steady old black friends who is now alive & resides in St Christophers) to the Lumber yard & bought materials for building. The most decent, and creditable of the black women did not think it a labour too servile to carry stones and marl, to help with their own hands to clear the Land of the rubbish that lay about it, & to bring ready-dressed victuals for the men that were employed in building the House of God. They now rejoiced to sell their Ear-rings & brace-lets and to buy Lumber & pay Carpenters, to forward this blessed work; and at last they got a comfortable little Chapel, which soon became too small.

Upon Mr Baxter's return, being free from every other employment his labors were more extensive & the Society particularly in the country increased considerably. The events relating to Doctor Coke's arrival you know are circumstantially published in his journals. This I know respecting his labors & the labors of the missionaries that accompanied him, that they were truly blessed so as in every possible way to prove beyond dispute that those winds & waves, which obstinately drove him into St. Johns harbor on the 25th December 1786 were under the peculiar command of an over-ruling providence. . . . [Conflating God's inspiration and intention with Mr. Coke's blessed significance; testimony praising, thanking God.]

But to return to the Chronological account of events from which my full heart upon the recollection of past, & present mercies, had led me to digress. There was at this time a gracious work begun in the hearts of many especially in the Town of St Johns & among the free people of Colour. The ministry of the word by Doctor Coke may be compared to a net which he cast into the Sea, which took in a large draught of fishes, & this net drawn to shore by the faithful labors of Mr Warrener who he left behind & who labor'd among us for two years. The society has continued to increase from that time to this. . . . [Recognizes some preachers.] That blessed servant of

God Bartholomew McDonald arrived here 24th December 1797 and departed this life 4th Dec 1798. . . . [Mr. McDonald's humility and discreet success.]

He lived in our house & all our family felt the influence of his holy conversation. During the time he labor'd among us there was a deep and genuine revival of religion. Our vigilant enemy finding that his Kingdom was shaken, began to work by an instrument which he had prepared to prevent our further success. The immoral conduct of——— who had been received among us as a preacher, stumbled many in the society in the country. He had been a missionary in a Sister Church & for proper reasons was excluded from their communion; unhappy for us he got into our connexion in the capacity of a preacher. His evil deeds being proved, he was also excluded from among us. After his expulsion the redoubled usefulness of Mr McDonald both in Town & Country soon repaired the breaches that had been made, & the word of God ran & was glorified. He had been indisposed, but was in some measure recovered & left us to go into the country, where he relapsed & was brought to Town on a very rainy day as soon as he step'd into the house I perceived he was in a high fever, a fever that seemed like a messenger sent to demand of us, one who we highly, & justly esteemed, & with whom were very reluctant to part. He instantly got to bed, but his disorder with all its dangerous symptoms rapidly increased. . . . [McDonald approaches God and Death with prayer, song, and praise.] He continued to pray & praise . . . to rejoice with Joy unspeakable & full of Glory 'till about 12 O'clock on the fifth night of his illness, his happy spirit freed from mortality took its joyful flight to the thrice blessed abode of Angels & God. The sorrow had filled our hearts at the loss of our dear Brother yet we had precious seasons of joy & love when those newly brought to God and the believers who were vigorously pressing after Holiness met together in our private prayer- & Class-meetings. . . . [An example of "Satan" masked as a preacher; discovered, disgusted the society in fact.] Upon the arrival of Mr & Mrs Birkinhead, She opened a meeting for the religious instruction of children, & also a meeting for teaching the young people to sing, these meetings were the means of drawing many young people of colour, some of which are now steady members of our Society, others in the day of temptation withered away & are no more seen among the people of God. She also established a public prayer-meeting conducted by women and intended for the benefit of young women: The Lord has been pleased greatly to own these meetings, which are still continued: many that were halting between the paths of vice & virtue, have been confirmed to follow the more excellent way; in short they have in general had the effect of enlightening the ignorant & fixing the resolve of wav'ring minds in the side of truth & virtue. . . . [Praising God; scorning immortality.] Allow me Dr Sir to observe that the work in the West-indies should not be entered upon by the sanguine & indeliberate. . . . [Recommending qualities of effective preachers like Dr. Pattison, devotion, selflessness versus sloth, vanity.] It has been very clear to me that the work in Antigua would have been in a more flourishing & advanced State, but from the choice of improper persons as Leaders; especially in the country; many, who if they had been faithfully dealt with would have been happy partakers of a Gospel hope themselves, & useful to their fellow-servants, have been lull'd to sleep in their sins, or led on Hood-winked in the paths of formality and Superstition with a vain hope, that as they were in Society, they were of course in the way to heaven. You well know my dear Sir how difficult you have found it, since you have laboured in Antigua, to drag some of the poor Souls out of this pit; others I know have rejoiced to be freed from the Yoke, tho' the Subordination of their situations made them afraid to complain. You know on the 2 of January last we removed from St Johns to English-Harbor, Mr Gilbert having had the offer of an employment that suited him in his Majesty's Yard. To my great but pleasant surprise I found a small society of black & coloured people, consisting of 28 Members & all but a very few in earnest for Salvation. They have never had one half the advantages of the people of St Johns, having no place of worship to go to on Sundays, & very few of them able to read the word of God. They were also thrown back at different times by the scandal which was brought upon religion in consequence of the Apostasy of a few white people who were members of our Society in England & came out here in the Kings service, & some that removed from other parts of the Island to reside here. My complexion exempted me from those prejudices & that disgust which the instability of their white Brethren had planted in their hearts & they tremblingly ventured to receive us as friends. Mr Baxter desired the women to meet with me; I soon found that they were all desirous to have a little Chapel, & to have service on Sundays; & at the time Mr Lumb laboured here had collected five joes among themselves for that purpose but it was never brought into effect. I told them how our Sisters in St Johns had heartily united together and even labor'd with their hands to forward the building of the Chapel, & they generally agree to do the same. Previous to our coming here they had been in treaty for a house for the purpose of preaching, but the situation is so hot, and so low, that both Preacher, & hearers, run the risk of getting sick as soon as they come into the open air. We have therefore petitioned the Commissioner to give us a Grant of Land to build in a more convenient place & he has readily granted that petition. It was written in the name of "the Negroes belonging to His Majesty & others inhabiting English-Harbor." & it was presented by me of the King's negroes. We intend as our means are very small to build our Chapel of Stone with a ground floor, for the present 'till Providence shall send us help. I am afraid you will not find this account as interesting as you expected; but probably if you had known the wickedness & ignorance, that prevailed even in my time & the thrice blessed effects of the Gospel, not only in civilizing but christianizing, the people of this Island, you would rejoice that ever you were called to perpetuate the glorious sound among us. Some of the blessed influences of a preached Gospel are often over-looked, or ascribed to other causes. But those who view all things as directed, or over-ruled by his wonder-working power rejoice to ascribe all good to the bounteous Author of all our blessings both in time and to all Eternity. I see with heart-felt joy that prostitution is now esteemed abominable & disgraceful by the greater part of the Colour'd Women in St Johns where the great bulk of them reside; and lawful alliances take place as frequently among them as among the whites. This is one happy effect of seeing the Gospel seed sown in the hearts of their Mothers; and many of them seeing themselves, examples corroborating, those truths that recommend, chastity tho' accompanied with labour & self-denial. The great civilization of the Slaves, their gradual emergence, from the depths of ignorance & barbarism, has imperceptibly had an over-awing effect upon the System of tyranny & cruel oppression that was formerly exercised over them with little or no restraint when they differed in so few respects from the Beasts that perish; And as a natural consequence, those that are set over them feel more cautious in dealing with rational creatures than they did with beings imbruted in ev'ry way both body & mind. The Slaves in general that attend a Gospel ministry, whether they are subject themselves to Church discipline or not, become more creditable & decent in their families & manners than those that do not. There is in all a thirst for a knowledge. The greater part of those that can afford it get themselves taught to read & some to write also. There are hundreds of black & coloured children sent to school every year in this little Island; and the great change wrought in the manners & condition of all people of this description is beyond any thing that could have been expected and such as nothing could effect but the wisdom & power of God. Its having been effected by the Un-bloody Sword of truth that has almost unperceivedly cut its way thro' mountainous obstacles;

And not by tumultuous distracting revolution, massacre & bloodshed, is cause of unspeakable thankfulness to God; and has been the means of opening a door free of access to all the preachers of the Gospel. After all that I can say, I only give a faint idea of the blessing brought to our favoured Island by the light of the Gospel. Could our dear friends in Europe conceive only one half of the benefit derived by numbers of our abject & despised fellow-creatures, they would rejoice to contribute all in their power, to carry on the blessed work; nor would they think any self-denial too rigid to impose upon themselves, nor any moments spent in fervent prayer too many to aid or advance the Redeemer's Kingdom among the poor Slaves. I beg leave humbly to observe, That if a preacher is a married man he is doubly useful as a Missionary. provided his Wife is an humble pious Woman. But not else. It is a matter too delicate for a man to tell a whole Society that his Wife is worldly-minded, & not worthy their confidence, or imitation; And often while his soul is cast down, & disquieted within him, because of the Offenses & stumbling-blocks that are laid in the way of God's people, by her that should be his help-mate, & hold up his hands in the good cause, He appears quite neuter, or sides with his wife to the destruction of his usefulness. The Wives of the Moravian Missionaries have no intercourse with the vain Women of the World. Their station in the Church as the Wives of Missionaries furnish them with sufficient employment from morning 'till night, so that they have no time for Tea-parties & feasts, nor can they find leisure to frequent the tables of the Wicked which the scriptures tell us are snares even to themselves. I have at times been grieved to see some of the Wives of our preachers that have been like works for Flatterers and Sycophants to shoot at; Who deceived, by what is falsely called, (and bears a strong resemblance to) Kindness & hospitality; & under the idea of doing good, & winning souls to Christ by familiarity with the World, have lost their simplicity, & deadness, to the world, been shorn of their spiritual strength & had their affections estranged from the real people of God. I am truly sorry to say that some others have appeared in that character in the West-indies, whose conduct has evidently shown that they were destitute of every principle of vital piety, whose pride & extravagance have rendered them as painful & irksome to those who endeavor to adorn the Gospel themselves & promote the interests of religion, as "Smoke to the eyes & vinegar to the teeth." Proverbs 10th Chapt 26th verse. Thank God Antigua does not labour under such burdens at present; But it is from the piety and usefulness of those that are with us now, that we are more than ever convinced of the great Utility of a Preacher's being a married man. I think from what we have seen within the last 16 Months I may safely add that a missionary who is zealous and active himself & has a Wife like-minded, who will meet the Women & deal faithfully with them & visit the sick etc, etc, makes his way quite easily with respect to temporals as a single man who is not equally devoted to God & the good of his fellow-mortals.

After all we may with great propriety ask with the Apostle "Who is sufficient for these things?" "The Harvest truly is plenteous but the labourers are few. Pray ye therefore the Lord of the Harvest that he would thrust forth more labourers into the Harvest." Let us in faith come boldly to the throne of Grace, and pray. "Thy Kingdom Come."

I am My Dear Sir

Your sister & servant in Christ, Anne Gilbert

■

FROM *MEMOIR OF JOHN GILBERT*

[At this point, Mr. Gilbert's part of the narrative breaks off, and Mrs. Gilbert takes it up. Internal references suggest she wrote it not long before she died.]

My beloved husband, though born with very different expectations, gladly set about baking, as an occupation in which I could assist him, and which, with such assistance, would enable him to employ himself in the use of his pen. A strong temptation had been set before him; but he resisted it, in the power of the Holy Spirit, with his usual decision of character. While he was in partnership with his friends Playfair and Crichton, and, as he thought, growing rich, he had been very liberal to the French emigrants who fled from Guadaloupe and Martinique, during the revolution in France. Some of them, though men of high rank in their native country, were constrained to seek a subsistence for themselves and families by various employments opposed to their former habits and education; while their wives, who were women of fashion and refinement, aided the design by the use of their needles, in which they were remarkably well skilled, and produced most beautiful specimens of ornamental work. Nor was the benefit of the laudable efforts of these ladies confined to themselves; for, from their example, many of the young females of Antigua learnt the importance of exertion in the feebler sex. These interesting individuals were much attached to my dear husband: he could speak their own language, and they felt great sympathy towards us both, regarding us as oppressed strangers in our native land. . . .

[Generosity of admirers; determination for self-sustenance.] My dear husband fell sick, and was brought nigh to the grave: soon after his recovery, I had an illness, which confined me to my bed for six months. As he was at this time (after being up from three o'clock in the morning to bake) engaged through the day in settling some intricate accounts of an extensive firm, it may be easily conceived his labour, both of body and mind, was great. He settled one account in particular, for which the sum of eight hundred dollars was awarded him by arbitration, and which would not have been put into his hands if any other person in the Island could have been found equal to it. The greater part of this money was appropriated to purchasing the freedom of a young person who had some claims upon him, and who was saved from vice and wretchedness by being rescued from slavery. His being obliged to spend some hours every day at the merchant's counting-house where the books were deposited, and my inability to attend to business at home, rendered our circumstances very trying; we therefore determined upon giving up baking, and opening a school, in which we could have the assistance of my late dear sister, Mrs. Thwaites. We accordingly hired a house, and every arrangement was made for our removal, as soon as I should recover my strength sufficiently to attend to it. My heart sunk at the prospect of his engaging in a school: I knew that he would find it impossible to obtain regular payments for the children, some of whom were to board with us; and that his punctual and upright mind would be continually upon the rack to obtain the means of defraying the daily expenses of the establishment; while, after all, his income would be fluctuating and precarious. . . . [Imploring God's help.] With his accustomed tenderness, he soothed my fears, and strove to dissipate my alarm, but did not know what opinion to give on the proposal which had been made to him. Mr. M——h, the then Naval Storekeeper, had written to Mr. D. to request him to ask Mr. Gilbert to take the situation of second clerk in the Storekeeper's Office, as the first clerk appeared to be dying. Mr. G. requested Mr. D. to give him his advice, as he had already obtained a license as a schoolmaster, and was promised a good number of scholars. Mr. D. told him, though he should be very sorry to lose him as a neighbour, and should not be able to procure any body to fill his place in settling the accounts in Mr. K.'s office, he thought employment in the Naval yard more congenial to his habits, as it was the place in which he had already spent many years of his life; but that he must at the same time warn him he would find the business of the Storekeeper's Office oppressive, as the clerks were negligent, and he understood the writing department to be in a very backward state; that as, in consequence of a French fleet being in these seas, there were constantly from six to eight ships of war in the harbour, he would probably be under the necessity of writing almost all night, and, he was afraid, would sink under it. Mr. D. concluded by advising Mr. G. to go to English Harbour, and speak to Mr. M——h himself, and kindly offered him his gig for the purpose. My dear husband told me his heart shrunk from the idea of taking me to live in a place where vice of every kind held its undisturbed dominion, and where there was scarcely a single female with whom I could associate. I told him I was willing to go with him under any circumstances, provided we were convinced that divine Providence pointed the way. He accordingly went to English Harbour, and waited upon the Store-keeper, who told him the office was much in want of an efficient clerk; that the second would of course expect to succeed the first, in the event of his death; and that then there would be a vacancy for the second clerk's place, which he would be very glad to see filled by my dear Mr. G. He, however, declined accepting the situation, as the income would be insufficient for the support of his family, and he had the prospect of more ample maintenance as schoolmaster. The Storekeeper replied that the second clerk was not willing to give up his promotion nominally; but that he would let Mr. G. receive the first clerk's salary, and be content with that of the second. My dear Mr. G. objected to this, and preferred entering upon the school. Accordingly he concluded the lease of the house, and we removed into it. The week before the school was to be opened, an order from Commissioner Lane was handed him, appointing him first clerk in the Store-keeper's Office. He, with his usual consideration for my comfort in all things, referred it to me, and I had no hesitation in preferring English Harbour, though attended with many privations and new trials, considering it an answer to prayers which I had put up, in great anguish of spirit, at the prospect of his wearing out his valuable life without even suitable remuneration for his toils. He had to pay a sum of money to be released from the contract about the house. As the business at English Harbour was pressing, he went there immediately, leaving me to pack up, and follow him, which I did in about ten days.

We had not long taken up our residence there, when the integrity of my husband's principles began to give offence, and to occasion gross misrepresentations of his character. . . . [Despite slander, she remains determined to work there.] My beloved husband, then filling a situation which all around us thought incompatible with such an employment, preached in a small thatched house, in what was at that time a most wretched place, called Spring Gardens. None other could be obtained for such a sacred purpose, and, oh! for ever blessed be the name of that God who made him instrumental to the conversion of many precious souls, some of whom not only hold fast the beginning of their confidence to this day (though they had to endure bitter persecution, and even corporal suffering, for the truth's sake), but have been eminently useful to others. . . . [Converted friends' fondness, generosity.]

About this time, my late dear sister, Mrs. Thwaites, was united to Mr. Thwaites, who was also employed in the Naval Yard. The congregations became too large for the little thatched house in Spring Gardens, and Mr. T. opened his house for the purpose.

We became acquainted with a Mr. A——r, Ordnance Store-keeper, who had been religiously brought up, by a pious father. Mr. A. sought the acquaintance of my dear Mr. G., and was very desirous of having him in the same department with himself . . . [through various connections and recommendations]. Mr. M——n, who resided at Southampton, went up to London,—and if Mr. G. had been his own son, he could not have exerted himself more on his behalf,—and finally succeeded in obtaining for him the appointment, in the year 1807. . . . [Account of obstacles and tricks of those opposed to Mr. Gilbert's appointment.]

It was now generally reported, that Mr. G. did not intend to preach any more; in short, that we were going to lay religion aside. Some of the poor were much grieved at this, and one woman actually returned to her house on Sunday morning, weeping bitterly. But, for ever blessed be that God, who kept us be his grace, my beloved husband waxed stronger and stronger in confessing Christ, and as Mr. Thwaites' house became too contracted for the increased congregations, our own was opened for that purpose, and Mr. G. preached or expounded the scriptures every Sabbath, the Wesleyan missionaries preaching once a fortnight, on a night in the week. We had soon all our rooms, the bed chambers excepted, quite full, when the weather was good. . . . [Notes those influenced by religion.]

In 1809, the first Sunday School known in the West Indies was commenced in Mr. G.'s house, and he became a teacher in it himself. Any attempt to detail the benefits which have resulted from this institution would swell this memoir, intended only as a sketch, beyond its proper limits; suffice it to say, "many arise and call it blessed." After the arrival in this Island of his brother-in-law, Mr. D[awes], at his suggestion to Mr. G., they united informing an Auxiliary Bible Society, which was organized in our house, and many of its committee meetings held there. The Female Refuge Society was formed in the same year, 1815, and all its meetings carried on in the same place, until, in consequence of Lady D'Urban's kind patronage, a general meeting was held at the Honourable Lady Grey's school room, and the children, who before that period had been placed out in different families for instruction, were collected together, and a regular establishment was formed. From their vicinity to us, and the circumscribed limits of the house they inhabited, several of the children were constant residents at Clarence house, except when, in seasons of ill health, or other peculiarities of circumstance, others by turns took their places; but on some occasions they were all collected there, and at such times assembled round Mr. G. as their common parent, and now bewail his loss as such. Of this institution it may be truly said, the blessed effects are evident to all who know anything of it.

The congregations usually assembling for preaching increased so much, that they could no longer be accommodated in our house; subscriptions were therefore set on foot for building a Methodist chapel. Mr. G. gave all the assistance in his power, and when Mr. Thwaites, upon whom the responsibility of erecting the building rested, found himself deficient in the means of making up one of the installments, my dear husband, having already given all that he could spare consistently with other demands of a similar nature, sent him his gold watch-chain, and ever after wore a bit of black ribbon. A communication was made to him, from a superior officer, though not in the form of a direct message, that he had better desist from preaching. "I will die first," was his laconic reply. It was sarcastically enquired of him, how the chapel was built, and whether the land was public or private property. He replied, the land had been purchased and was private property; and the chapel was built by subscription; adding, that he was trustee for it. Thus, on many occasions, did he silence malice and opposition, by a firm and calm acknowledgment of the truth.

Soon after we became resident at English Harbour, Mr. G. formed a fund for relieving the poor, to which he liberally contributed. He was the treasurer, and, from the period of its formation until a few months before his death, though the number of subscribers was few, had distributed nine hundred and sixty-one pounds, three shillings, and three half-pence. . . . [Mr. Gilbert's concern and self-sacrifice praised.] At the time of his death, Mr. G. was secretary and treasurer to four charitable institutions in this neighbourhood, and the friend, director, and upholder of three others.

At the conclusion of the peace, 1815, the naval establishment at English Harbour was reduced, and the department left in charge of the Master Shipwright. My dear husband settled his accounts honourably with Government, and we removed to St. John's, never expecting to reside again at English Harbour. He engaged in selling goods on commission, and soon obtained so much business, that, though he was assisted by myself and an active clerk, both his health and my own began to fail under incessant exertion. The Master Shipwright being advanced in years, and wishing to retire, recommended to my dear Mr. G. to apply to be re-entered as Store-keeper. It seemed a hopeless attempt, as there were many applicants on the spot; he yielded, however, without reluctance, to the solicitations of his friends, and wrote to the Board. He was in consequence appointed, and, after an absence of twenty months, we returned to English Harbour. Many were astonished at his reinstatement; but most persons saw the divine hand in it, and were convinced that God was with him. During my life, I have had frequent occasion to notice, with gratitude to our Almighty Benefactor, not only His goodness in delivering us *unexpectedly* from painful and embarrassing circumstances, but in providing at the same time a comfortable situation for us in future; and thus conferring a *double* benefit at once. So it was in this instance.

It pleased God, after our return, to pour out His blessing on the Sunday School particularly; its numbers greatly increased, and some young persons, who were the first objects of its care, were brought to a saving acquaintance with the truth as it is in Jesus; and, I am happy to add, continue to this day, and are among its most valuable teachers. He re-commenced preaching in the chapel, and some of those who appeared dissatisfied with his return became steady hearers of the word, and doers of it also. He had occasionally to contend with unreasonable men; but the result, blessed be God, was invariably such as proved favourable to the cause of religion, and creditable to his own character: insomuch that a certain individual, who had shown more enmity to him on account of his religious principles than any one else, upon his retiring from office in April, 1832, wrote of him to the Admiralty in strong terms of recommendation and approbation. But it is not to public testimonies that I need appeal, for the most important fruits of that grace, which wrought effectually by the Holy Spirit upon his heart to make him a Christian in word and deed. If there was one *trait* more conspicuous than the rest, amidst the lovely harmony of graces visible in his character, it was his *total renunciation of self,* and *entire dependence on the atonement of our blessed Saviour:* and that which made him so remarkable as a man, and a man filling an important station in society, was his scrupulous integrity, and an openness and candor in all his intercourse with others, which even persons not devoid of piety and wisdom thought sometimes carried too far, in a disingenuous and unfriendly world. Upon his retirement from office he presented a memorial to the Navy Board, the reply to which, through mistake, went so circuitous a route, that he was kept in a state of suspense for some months. He thought it necessary, therefore, to forward another to the Board of Admiralty, a copy of which may be seen at the end of this statement; and in consequence, a pension of 350 sterling was granted.

For the last three or four years of his residence in this vale of tears, he was a considerable sufferer from local complaints, of a nature seldom removed at an advanced period of life; but his active habits and astonishing patience kept him to the steady performance of all his duties till within a few months before his death. Then indeed the cup of bodily suffering was greatly augmented in bitterness. In January, 1833, a severe bowel complaint as succeeded by a degree of nervous excitement which occasioned incessant restlessness, exhausting to the animal frame; and a frequent rush of blood to the head and lungs produced sensations of suffocation, and other feelings, the effects of which it was distressing in no small degree even to witness. In the midst of his severest sufferings, no impatient expression escaped his lips; sometimes he would cast an imploring look upward, and exclaim, in the most affecting manner, "Pity me, my Savior!" As far as related to spiritual concerns, his mind was calm and undisturbed, though his superior understanding was clouded and impaired by disease. He had often declared to me, when in his best health, that the subject of death was more familiar to him than any other, and he experienced no dismay at any time when it seemed to approach. He said to his kind medical friends, "I am not afraid to die. I love my Saviour, and my Saviour loves me too well to dispose of me in any way that will not be for my everlasting benefit; but I should be glad if any thing could be done to mitigate my bodily sufferings. This want of breath is very distressing." His heart glowed with the tenderest affection towards me, and with almost parental kindness to all around him, particularly to a dear, amiable niece of mine, and an interesting and affectionate young person in the family, who read to him daily; both of whom attended upon him with the most assiduous and reverential regard.

The day of his death, July 16, 1833, (ever memorable to me!) he took his usual drive out, and, when he returned, his accustomed refreshment, and did not appear worse than he had been lately. He dined at table, carved a chicken, and ate a small bit; he then called my attention to the large drops of perspiration which fell from his eyelids and under his eyes. Alas! it was the dew of death, though I knew it not. I begged him to lie down a little. He rose, and I accompanied him into the chamber. Being much fatigued and indisposed myself, I was preparing to take a little rest, and one of the young friends already mentioned assisted him into the sitting-room. Almost immediately one of them came in, and, not wishing to alarm me, said he appeared poorly. I went instantly to him, and found him lying in a posture of ease on the sofa, but his complexion darker than usual. With a sensation of anguish not to be described, I took hold of his hand, and fancied I felt his pulse beat; but it was a delusion—the medical men came, and found the happy spirit had fled to the paradise of God! Oh! what tongue or pen can express the agonies of that moment.—I could only fall upon my knees, and afresh commend myself and the orphans around me into the hands of God. I afterwards learned that when his young guide was leading him into the sitting-room, he asked with a smile, "Where are we going to now?" to which she replied, "I will go wherever you please, sir," "I am going to a good place," he said, (meaning heaven,) "where I hope you will meet me." His other young attendant asked, as he reclined upon the sofa, "Shall I fan you, Sir?" He smiled at her, and playfully repeating her words, "Shall I fan you, Sir?" added "Yes, very gently." She had scarcely begun to do so, when he threw his head back, shuddered, groaned, and died! The whole was almost instantaneous.

Many were the mourners made by this event. The poor, the widow, and the fatherless, as well as friends and relative, lament it; but what are all their losses compared with mine? The lapse of almost thirty-five years, with many scenes of sorrow and suffering endured together, had cemented our union, and increased the tenderness of our affection to each other; but he is gone; and to me:

> "The disenchanted earth has lost its lustre,
> The great Magician's dead!
> No, not dead!
> He lives! he greatly lives! a life on earth
> Unkindled, unconceived; and from an eye
> Of tenderness lets heavenly pity fall
> On me, more justly numbered with the dead."

3

Mary Prince
(ca. 1788–after 1833)

■

Introduction

Like the Hart sisters' lives, Mary Prince's life was inevitably affected by the struggle for abolition being waged in Britain because passage of the emancipation bill would have affected all of them substantially. England's role in the slave trade was deep and long-standing.[32] In 1772, a celebrated court case had been initiated by the abolitionist Granville Sharp on behalf of a slave named James Somerset, whose owner had brought him to Britain. Lord Chief Justice Mansfield decreed that slaves could not be forced by owners to leave England.[33] By the year Mary Prince was born in Bermuda, anti-slavery forces in England were waging a campaign against slavery in full force: "Between 1826 and 1832 more than 3,500 [anti-slavery] petitions were submitted to the House of Lords alone."[34] In fact, both houses of Parliament discussed parliamentary reform and emancipation in every session the year that Mary Prince's *History* was published, and in the previous session (1830–1831) a motion had been introduced "for measures to promote its [slavery's] abolition . . . and for compensation should it be abolished."[35]

Bermuda itself was in serious flux during Prince's childhood. In 1788, fewer than two hundred acres of land were being cultivated and the population numbered between ten and eleven thousand, of whom five thousand were slaves.[36] The first black people arrived in 1616, sought after for skills much needed in territory that was little more than a haven of "seabirds and swine." They were "the expert divers and sugar cane growers. . . . Most of these men came from West Indian islands or were seized on board Spanish and Portuguese ships. And early success in agricultural pursuits was due in large measure to skilled blacks."[37] By 1618 it was well known in London colonial circles that there was a sizeable black Bermudian population and according to Craven, "though the term slave is used as early as 1617, it does not seem to have come into general use for two or three years after" (p. 361).

Later in the seventeenth century and in the eighteenth century, descendants of these early black inhabitants organized plots and led revolts that Prince might well have heard about from family members.[38] Her desire to accompany Bermudian owners Mr. and Mrs. John Wood to Antigua probably stemmed from a sense of resistance to slavery, together with her knowledge of the less stringent laws about slavery on that island. Free black men were permitted to vote there and, although this law did not apply to Prince, its relative liberality in terms of old Caribbean islands was symbolically significant.[39] More than an expansion of the franchise, the law implicitly recognized that all slaves were potentially entitled to civil rights. The franchise weakened owner control. Mary Prince's self-emancipatory act in walking away from the Woods' household in London marked a cumulative opposition to human enslavement, both historical and personal.

■

Biographical Narrative

Mary Prince was born a slave about 1788 in Brackish Pond, in Devonshire Parish, Bermuda, then a self-governing British colony. The date of her death is unknown. Slaves constituted half of Bermuda's population at the time. Mary Prince was the daughter of slaves, a house servant and sawyer, and had at least ten siblings. Prince was apparently her father's given first name (or nickname), and Mary Prince used it, rather than her owners' surname, as her surname. The first black British woman to "walk away" from slavery and claim her freedom, she dictated her experiences to a white abolitionist after she came to London from Antigua and voluntarily left the household.[40] Her narrative entitled *The History of Mary Prince, a West Indian Slave, Related by Herself,* was published in London in 1831 and sponsored by the Anti-Slavery Society, which won public support by detailing atrocities and portraying female slaves as pure and Christian-like individuals. It went into a third edition that same year.[41]

Mary Prince's is the first known recorded autobiography by a freed West Indian slave. In it, she documents her intrepid struggle to survive in Bermuda, Turks Island, Antigua, and then England. Her inimitable diction offsets the inevitable challenges to the text's authenticity. By the time that she left her owners' home in London, petitions for Prince's freedom were being presented in the House of Commons.[42] Thus she directly contributed to the parliamentary debate on abolition.

Mary Prince's earliest years were spent in a succession of households in Bermuda, including those of Captain and Mrs. Darrel and Captian and Mrs. Williams.[43] Then she was sold again at the age of twelve. While with the impoverished Williams family, she was hired out to Mrs. Pruden, who lived in the adjoining parish; there she worked as nursemaid and general servant. The young daughter, Fanny Pruden, taught Prince to read and spell. The new owners of the twelve-year-old, Captain and Mrs. I——, who lived at Spanish Point, treated Prince harshly, and she witnessed gruesome events, including the brutal murder of the French slave Hetty. During this five years or more of servitude, Prince ran away and was returned by her father. Perhaps emboldened by her father's presence and her own dire situation, she protested the conditions of her life. The sadistic treatment she endured induced her to wish "more than ever to die" (p. 59).

Prince's subsequent situation was not a qualitative improvement. A new owner, Mr. D——, brought her to work in his salt ponds near Grand Quay, Turks Island. On a daily basis, Sunday excepted, she stood knee-deep in water from four A.M. until dark, with two brief breaks: one for Indian corn boiled in water; and one at noon for corn soup. The sun blistered all her uncovered skin and constant boils resulted. In the *History*, Prince notes a particular difference between Captain I——, and Mr. D——. The former frequently beat her while "raging and foaming with passion"; Mr. D——, "with the greatest composure . . . stripped me naked, hung me up by the wrists, and beat me with the cow-skin . . . till my body was raw with gashes. Yet there was nothing very remarkable in this." At the end of each day, Prince and other workers slept on wooden planks in a shack.

Mary Prince characterizes her ten years on Turks Island as "work, work, work." Once again, she witnessed the torture and murder of slaves. Her mother and some of her siblings also worked on Turks Island for a while before being retransported to Bermuda. Prince only hazily remembers the deaths of her parents and the fate of two of her ten siblings.

Prince's return to Bermuda about 1810 marked the beginning of another stage in her life. She cared for D——'s family but also had to work "on the grounds." The latter substantially influenced her future because the cultivation and sale of crops were the means by which many slaves earned an income and achieved a modicum of self-sufficiency.

A heightened sense of self-worth may have given Prince the courage to defend D——'s daughter during one of his habitual drunken beatings. When he savagely sought vengeance against her, she reminded him: "Sir, this is not Turks Island." The action earned her community praise and further fortified her. Prince's self-selected role as activist and spokeswoman put her on and beyond the margins of acceptable slave behavior and discourse. The fact that she conducted herself in such fashion "back home" and not on Turks Island suggests a woman of sense and patience. She had bided her time, anticipating a more propitious moment. The Turks Island black inhabitants undoubtedly encouraged her posture of resistance, for she mentions some who came to Bermuda after her return and told her of a makeshift prayershed's having been destroyed. She intimates that the slaves had been trying to create a separate space for themselves. Even more important, talk of freedom was rife, for Turks Island lay only two hundred miles from San Domingo, where a successful revolution in 1791 by slaves led by Toussaint L'Ouverture and his allies had brought into being a free republic. Slaves from Turks Island frequently escaped to San Domingo.[44]

Eventually, Prince decided to resist D——'s sexual advances and attempted to salt away money by being hired as a washerwoman. She proudly asserts that she refused to wash him naked. Most likely, she was obliged to speak discreetly about sexuality in print because of the evangelical editor's dictates. Slave narratives were presented as moral testimony for consumption in British family homes.

Prince was ultimately sold at her own request to Mr. and Mrs. John Wood and accompanied them to Antigua around 1818. In the *History*, she records aspects of a severe daily life on that eastern Caribbean island, removed from her natal land and family and working mainly as a washerwoman. Prince's health deteriorated still further during this period; severe rheumatism was probably produced and exacerbated by constant laundering labor. In the Antiguan section of her narrative, Prince particularly addresses illness, religion, marriage, and her relationship with the Woods, complicated by her efforts to be free. In 1817, she was baptized by the Reverend James Curtin of the Anglican Church. Later she began to attend the Moravian Church, where she met a widower, Daniel James, a free carpenter and cooper. They married in 1820 in the Moravian Chapel in Spring Garden because slaves could not marry in the Anglican Church. Prince's new self-consciousness about her right to freedom dictated new alliances. Her conversion to Moravianism allied her with other slaves, with free blacks, and with the minority of whites who believed in spiritual equality. Because she had been separated from her family, we could surmise that being a part of another "family" considerably attracted her.

Religion combined resistance, escape, relief, spiritual satisfaction, and an opportunity for wider human connection. For Prince, religion built a bridge to freedom and social acceptance. Cruelty and injustice had induced incurable restlessness in her; whenever and however she could, she was fracturing old oppressive bonds. The fact that she married soon after conversion further affirms her heightened consciousness, her refusal of the role of slave, her insistence on looking as attractive as she could, despite attempts to render her abject. She resists with the means at her disposal. As a motif, religion was favored by white abolitionists to attract a white Christian audience to the anti-slavery cause. A slave's conversion affirmed for a white audience the "validity" of their values, false perceptions about the inferiority of African values, and the moral bankruptcy of Christian slave owners. With conversion a critical propaganda motif, Prince must have been encouraged to display religion as the apex in her life as a slave.

Around 1827 and 1828, Prince's life took a different turn when she accompanied Mrs. and Mrs. Wood to London. During the voyage her limbs had swelled considerably and she felt unable to wash the dirty clothes that had accumulated. The Woods nevertheless pressed her to work. The cold weather, her arthritis, and the physical wear and tear of years of toil left her inervated but not without spirit. After the Woods' fourth threat to turn her out on the street, she decided she had endured enough and voluntarily departed. The Woods' shoe blackener, Mr. Mash, and his wife directed Prince to Moravian missionaries, and then she made her way to the Anti-Slavery Society in Aldermanbury in November 1828. After receiving assistance from Quaker women and temporary work as a charwoman, she joined the domestic service of Mr. and Mrs. Thomas Pringle in December 1829. Thomas Pringle was then secretary of the Anti-Slavery Society.

Pringle asked solicitor George Stephen about the possibility of Prince's emancipation. Her owners refused to consider the possibility, whereupon the Anti-Slavery Society brought the case under the notice of Parliament. The Woods left for Antigua before the petition was resolved. At some point between 1829 and 1831, Mary Prince suggested to the Pringles that she tell her own story; she wanted the British public to hear about the life of a slave from a slave's own lips. Susanna Strickland, a guest of the Pringles, was Mary Prince's amanuensis.[45] According to Thomas Pringle, no important facts of Prince's life were omitted from the narrative, nor a "single circumstance or sentiment" added.

On the last page, Prince thanks Martha Pringle for teaching her "daily to read the word of God . . . [and] the great privilege of being enabled to attend church three times on the Sunday." She ends by praising the Reverend

Mr. Young, who had "taken much pains to instruct me," and the Reverend Mr. Mortimer, "under whose ministry I have now sat for upwards of twelve months."[46] Through this probably editor-mandated discussion of religion and past "sins," Prince can offer us one of the few glimpses of her sexual reality, all but suppressed throughout the narrative.

The History of Mary Prince generated a rancorous controversy in the press, so stimulating sales that the book went into a third edition the same year. In the preface, Thomas Pringle relates that Prince's health was deteriorating and she was going blind. There were two last glimpses of her, however, as a result of two court cases.[47] Clearly, Prince had touched a raw public nerve with her unalloyed presentation. The furor that it raised marks how persuasively she expressed the popular ideology of freedom—anathema to pro-slavery editor James Macqueen and his allies[48]—and also signifies that her implied message had worked its way under the skin of the pro-slavery advocates, sensitive to every nuance of expressed black will.

Ironically, both court cases were settled the same year that the Emancipation Bill finally passed the House of Lords, 1833. In the first, Pringle sued Thomas Cadell, the publisher of *Blackwood's Magazine,* which had published Macqueen's savage diatribe against Prince, Pringle, and emancipation. The transcript affords us one of the few images we have of Mary Prince outside her narrative:

> At the London court of Common Pleas, Thursday, February 21st, 1833, before Lord Chief Justice Tindal and a special jury . . . there was an action brought by Thomas Pringle . . . against [the publisher Thomas Cadell]. Mary Prince was then called in and sworn. She is a negress of very ordinary features and appears to be about thirty-five years of age. She stated that she gave an account of her life to Mr. Pringle. No other question was put to her by the plaintiff's counsel, and the other side declined to cross-examine her.

John Wood (Prince's owner), his legal team, and their plantocratic allies seem to have realized that Prince's discourse and her ability to improvise constituted abolitionist intervention; the trial itself was free publicity against slavery in the presence of reporters. Five days later at the King's Bench, Guildhall, Wood brought an act for libel against Pringle and won by default because Pringle could not produce witnesses from the West Indies to prove his allegations.[49]

The second case is the last-noted appearance of Mary Prince, who testified at some length and reaffirmed several of the brutalizing incidents described in the *History*.[50] Her testimony also confirms that the evangelical editors had censored several accounts of sexual activity from her narrative; past brush-ins with the law that she recounts were clearly related to her vulnerability as a slave to sexual predation.

With *The History* Mary Prince, a remarkable woman who contributed a groundbreaking oral narrative to world history, inaugurated a black female counteroffensive against a reductive conception of black women as flogged, half-naked victims. Through Prince, we learn how slaves struggled to overcome psychological trauma, physical torture, and hardship; how legal, economic, and social shackles affected their lives; and how they used and shaped their environment to exercise some control over those lives. Hers is a tale of suffering endured, but a tale as well of the human spirit triumphant.

■

Chronology[51]

ca. 1788	Born in Bermuda to a father named Prince, a sawyer in the Trimmingham household, and an unnamed mother, a household slave. Lives with Captain and Mrs. Darrel, then Mrs. Williams. Sent out to work at Mrs. Pruden's as a nursemaid and general servant.
ca. 1800	Sold to Captain and Mrs. I—— at Spanish Point.
ca. 1805	Sold to Mr. D——. Works on Grand Quay, Turks Island, in salt ponds; endures constant painful sun blistering. Parents die. Siblings are dispersed and she loses touch with them.
1810	Returns to Bermuda; defends D——'s daughter against father's abuse; works on the grounds and sells crops; attempts to save for manumission and some economic independence.
1817	Baptized by the Reverend James Curtin of the Anglican Church.
ca. 1818	Sold to Mr. and Mrs. John Wood; goes to Antigua, where she works as a washerwoman; rheumatism worsens.
1820?	Marries Daniel James, a free carpenter and cooper, in Moravian Church; converts to Moravianism around this time.
1827–1828	Severely rheumatoid, sails to London with the Woods, who demand that she carry on with her work.

November 1828	Leaves the Woods, after they threaten several times to put her out in the street. Goes to the Anti-Slavery Society in Aldermanbury, London.
1829	Enters domestic service of Martha and Thomas Pringle; he is secretary of the Anti-Slavery Society.
1829–1831	Dictates her life experiences to Methodist Susanna Strickland.
February 21 1833	Testifies in Pringle's lawsuit against Thomas Cadell, publisher of *Blackwood's* Magazine, for slander.
February 26 1833	Testifies in John Wood's lawsuit against Thomas Pringle for libel.
	Date of death is unknown.

■ ■ ■

From *The History of Mary Prince, A West Indian Slave, Related by Herself*

I was born at Brackish-Pond, in Bermuda, on a farm belonging to Mr. Charles Myners. My mother was a household slave; and my father, whose name was Prince, was a sawyer belonging to Mr. Trimmingham, a ship-builder at Crow-Lane. When I was an infant, old Mr. Myners died, and there was a division of the slaves and other property among the family. I was bought along with my mother by old Captain Darrel, and given to his grandchild, little Miss Betsey Williams. Captain Williams, Mr. Darrel's son-in-law, was master of a vessel which traded to several places in America and the West Indies, and he was seldom at home long together. . . . [When Mrs. Williams becomes ill, Prince is hired out to Mrs. Pruden.]

At this time Mrs. Williams died. I was told suddenly of her death, and my grief was so great that, forgetting I had the baby in my arms, I ran away directly to my poor mistress's house; but reached it only in time to see the corpse carried out. . . . [She returns to Mr. Williams to be sold.]

The black morning at length came; it came too soon for my poor mother and us. Whilst she was putting on us the new osnaburgs in which we were to be sold, she said in a sorrowful voice, (I shall never forget it!) "See, I am *shrouding* my poor children; what a task for a mother!"—She then called Miss Betsey to take leave of us. "I am going to carry my little chickens to market," (these were her very words) "take your last look of them; may be you will see them no more.". . . When I left my dear little brothers and the house in which I had been brought up, I thought my heart would burst.

Our mother, weeping as she went, called me away with the children Hannah and Dinah, and we took the road that led to Hamble Town, which we reached about four o'clock in the afternoon. We followed my mother to the market-place, where she placed us in a row against a large house, with our backs to the wall and our arms folded across our breasts. I, as the eldest, stood first, Hannah next to me, then Dinah; and our mother stood beside, crying over us. My heart throbbed with grief and terror so violently, that I pressed my hands quite tightly across my breast, but I could not keep it still, and it continued to leap as though it would burst out of my body. But who cared for that? Did one of the many bystanders, who were looking at us so carelessly, think of the pain that wrung the hearts of the negro woman and her young ones? No, no! They were not all bad, I dare say, but slavery hardens white people's hearts towards the blacks; and many of them were not slow to make their remarks upon us aloud, without regard to our grief—though their light words fell like cayenne on the fresh wounds of our hearts. Oh those white people have small hearts who can only feel for themselves. . . . [She is exhibited and sold.]

I then saw my sisters led forth, and sold to different owners; so that we had not the sad satisfaction of being partners in bondage. When the sale was over, my mother hugged and kissed us, and mourned over us, begging of us to keep up a good heart, and do our duty to our new masters. It was a sad parting; one went one way, one another, and our poor mammy went home with nothing.*

---

*Let the reader compare the above affecting account, taken down from the mouth of this negro woman, with the following description of a vendue of slaves at the Cape of Good Hope, published by me in 1826, from the letter of a friend,—and mark their similarity in several characteristic circumstances. The resemblance is easily accounted for: slavery wherever it prevails produces similar effects.—"Having heard there was to be a sale of cattle, farm stock, &c. by auction, at a Veld-Cornet's in the vicinity, we halted our waggon one day for the purpose of procuring a fresh spann of oxen. Among the stock of the farm sold, was a female slave and her three children. The two oldest children were girls, the one about thirteen years of age, and the other about eleven; the youngest was a boy. The whole family were exhibited together, but they were sold separately, and to different purchasers. The farmers examined them as if they had been so many head of cattle. While the sale was going

My new owners were a Captain and Mrs. I——, who lived at Spanish Point. After parting with my mother and sisters, I followed him to his store, and he gave me into the charge of his son, a lad about my own age, Master Benjy, who took me to my new home. I did not know where I was going, or what my new master would do with me. My heart was quite broken with grief, and my thoughts went back continually to those from whom I had been so suddenly parted. "Oh, my mother! my mother!" I kept saying to myself, "Oh, my mammy and my sisters and my brothers, shall I never see you again!"

Oh, the trials! the trials! they make the salt water come into my eyes when I think of the days in which I was afflicted—the times that are gone; when I mourned and grieved with a young heart for those whom I loved.

It was night when I reached my new home. The house was large, and built at the bottom of a very high hill; but I could not see much of it that night. I saw too much of it afterwards. The stones and the timber were the best things in it; they were not so hard as the hearts of the owners.*

Before I entered the house, two slave women, hired from another owner, who were at work in the yard, spoke to me, and asked who I belonged to? I replied, "I am come to live here." "Poor child, poor child!" they both said; "you must keep a good heart, if you are to live here.". . . [Prince witnesses and suffers severe beatings.]

---

on, the mother and her children were exhibited on a table, that they might be seen by the company, which was very large. There could not have been a finer subject for an able painter than this unhappy group. The tears, the anxiety, the anguish of the mother, while she met the gaze of the multitude, eyed the different countenances of the bidders, or cast a heart-rending look upon the children; and the simplicity and touching sorrow of the young ones, while they clung to their distracted parent, wiping their eyes, and half concealing their faces,—contrasted with the marked insensibility and jocular countenances of the spectators and purchasers,—furnished a striking commentary on the miseries of slavery, and its debasing effects upon the hearts of its abettors. While the woman was in this distressed situation she was asked, 'Can you feed sheep?' Her reply was so indistinct that it escaped me; but it was probably in the negative, for her purchaser rejoined, in a loud and harsh voice, 'Then I will teach you with the sjamboc,' (a whip made of the rhinoceros' hide.) The mother and her three children were sold to three separate purchasers; and they were literally torn from each other."—Ed.

*These strong expressions, and all of a similar character in this little narrative, are given verbatim as uttered by Mary Prince.—Ed.

Poor Hetty, my fellow slave, was very kind to me, and I used to call her my Aunt; but she led a most miserable life, and her death was hastened (at least the slaves all believed and said so,) by the dreadful chastisement she received from my master during her pregnancy. It happened as follows. One of the cows had dragged the rope away from the stake to which Hetty had fastened it, and got loose. My master flew into a terrible passion, and ordered the poor creature to be stripped quite naked, notwithstanding her pregnancy, and to be tied up to a tree in the yard. He then flogged her as hard as he could lick, both with the whip and cow-skin, till she was all over streaming with blood. He rested, and then beat her again and again. Her shrieks were terrible. The consequence was that poor Hetty was brought to bed before her time, and was delivered after severe labour of a dead child. She appeared to recover after her confinement, so far that she was repeatedly flogged by both master and mistress afterwards; but her former strength never returned to her. Ere long her body and limbs swelled to a great size; and she lay on a mat in the kitchen, till the water burst out of her body and she died. All the slaves said that death was a good thing for poor Hetty; but I cried very much for her death. The manner of it filled me with horror. I could not hear to think about it; yet it was always present to my mind for many a day.

After Hetty died all her labours fell upon me, in addition to my own. I had now to milk eleven cows every morning before sunrise, sitting among the damp weeds; to take care of the cattle as well as the children; and to do the work of the house. There was no end to my toils—no end to my blows. I lay down at night and rose up in the morning in fear and sorrow; and often wished that like poor Hetty I could escape from this cruel bondage and be at rest in the grave. But the hand of that God whom then I knew not, was stretched over me; and I was mercifully preserved for better things. It was then, however, my heavy lot to weep, weep, weep, and that for years; to pass from one misery to another, and from one cruel master to a worse. But I must go on with the thread of my story.

One day a heavy squall of wind and rain came on suddenly, and my mistress sent me round the corner of the house to empty a large earthen jar. The jar was already cracked with an old deep crack that divided it in the middle, and in turning it upside down to empty it, it parted in my hand. I could not help the accident, but I was dreadfully frightened, looking forward to a severe punishment. I ran crying to my mistress, "O mistress, the jar has come in two." "You have broken it, have you?" she replied; "come directly here to me." I came trembling: she stripped and flogged me long and severely with the cow-skin; as long as she had strength to use the lash, for she did not give over till she was quite tired.—When my master came home at night, she told him of my fault; and oh, frightful! how he fell a swearing. After abusing me with every ill name he could think of, (too, too bad to speak in England,) and giving me several heavy blows with his hand, he said, "I shall come home to-morrow morning at twelve, on purpose to give you a round hundred." He kept his word—Oh sad for me! I cannot easily forget it . He tied me up upon a ladder, and gave me a hundred lashes with his own hand, and master Benjy stood by to count them for him. When he had licked me for some time he sat down to take breath; then after resting, he beat me again and again, until he was quite wearied, and so hot (for the weather was very sultry), that he sank back in his chair, almost like to faint. While my mistress went to bring him drink, there was a dreadful earthquake. Part of the roof fell down, and every thing in the house went—clatter, clatter, clatter. Oh I thought the end of all things near at hand; and I was so sore with the flogging, that I scarcely cared whether I lived or died. The earth was groaning and shaking; every thing tumbling about; and my mistress and the slaves were shrieking and crying out, "The earthquake! the earthquake!" It was an awful day for us all.

During the confusion I crawled away on my hands and knees, and laid myself down under the steps of the piazza, in front of the house. I was in a dreadful state—my body all blood and bruises, and I could not help moaning piteously. The other slaves, when they saw me, shook their heads and said, "Poor child! poor child"—I lay there till the morning, careless of what might happen, for life was very weak in me, and I wished more than ever to die. But when we are very young, death always seems a great way off, and it would not come that night to me. The next morning I was forced by my master to rise and go about my usual work, though my body and limbs were so stiff and sore, that I could not move without the greatest pain.—Nevertheless, even after all this severe punishment, I never heard the last of that jar; my mistress was always throwing it in my face.

Some little time after this, one of the cows got loose from the stake, and eat one of the sweet-potatoe slips. I was milking when my master found it out. He came to me, and without any more ado, stooped down, and taking off his heavy boot, he struck me such a severe blow in the small of my back, that I shrieked with agony, and thought I was killed; and I feel a weakness in that part to this day. The cow was frightened by his violence, and kicked down the pail and spilt the milk all about. My master knew that this accident was his own fault, but he was so enraged that he seemed glad of an excuse to go on with his ill usage. I cannot remember how many licks he gave me then, but he beat me till I was unable to stand, and till he himself was weary.

After this I ran away and went to my mother, who was living with Mr. Richard Darrell. My poor mother was both grieved and glad to see me; grieved because I had been so ill used, and glad because she had not seen me for a long, long while. She dared not receive me into the house, but she hid me up in a hole in the rocks near, and brought me food at night, after every body was asleep. My father, who lived at Crow-Lane, over the salt-water channel, at last heard of my being hid up in the cavern, and he came and took me back to my master. Oh I was loth, loth to go back; but as there was no remedy, I was obliged to submit.

When we got home, my poor father said to Capt. I——, "Sir, I am sorry that my child should be forced to run away from her owner; but the treatment she has received is enough to break her heart. The sight of her wounds has nearly broke mine.—I entreat you, for the love of God, to forgive her for running away, and that you will be a kind master to her in future." Capt. I—— said I was used as well as I deserved, and that I ought to be punished for running away. I then took courage and said that I could stand the floggings no longer; that I was weary of my life, and therefore I had run away to my mother; but mothers could only weep and mourn over their children, they could not save them from cruel masters—from the whip, the rope, and the cow-skin. He told me to hold my tongue and go about my work, or he would find a way to settle me. He did not, however, flog me that day.

For five years after this I remained in his house, and almost daily received the same harsh treatment. . . . [She is sold by the I——s and sent to Turks Island; meets new owner Mr. D——, and has her "value" assessed.]

My new master was one of the owners or holders of the salt ponds, and he received a certain sum for every slave that worked upon his premises, whether they were young or old. This sum was allowed him out of the profits arising from the salt works. I was immediately sent to work in the salt water with the rest of the slaves. This work was perfectly new to me. I was given a half barrel and a shovel, and had to stand up to my knees in the water, from four o'clock in the morning till nine, when we were given some Indian corn boiled in water, which we were obliged to swallow as fast as we could for fear the rain should come on and melt the salt. We were then called again to our tasks, and worked through the heat of the day; the sun flaming upon our heads like fire, and raising salt blisters in those parts which were not completely covered. Our feet and legs, from standing in the salt water for so many hours, soon became full of dreadful boils, which eat down in some cases to the very bone, afflicting the sufferers with great torment. We came home at twelve; ate our corn soup, called *blawly* . . . and went back to our employment till dark at night. . . . [She describes inhuman work conditions, including atrocities inflicted.]

I think it was about ten years I had worked in the salt ponds at Turk's Island, when my master left off business, and retired to a house he had in Bermuda, leaving his son to succeed him in the island. He took me with him to wait upon his daughters; and I was joyful, for I was sick, sick of Turk's Island, and my heart yearned to see my native place again, my mother, and my kindred. . . . [Prince's mother arrives on sloop with daughter Rebecca.]

After I left Turk's Island, I was told by some negroes that came over from it, that the poor slaves had built up a place with boughs and leaves, where they might meet for prayers, but the white people pulled it down twice, and would not allow them even a shed for prayers. A flood came down soon after and washed away many houses, filled the place with sand, and overflowed the ponds; and I do think that this was for their wickedness; for the Buckra* men there were very wicked. I saw and heard much that was very very bad at that place.

I was several years the slave of Mr. D—— after I returned to my native place. Here I worked in the grounds. My work was planting and hoeing sweet-potatoes, Indian corn, plantains, bananas, cabbages, pumpkins, onions &c. I did all the household work, and attended upon a horse and cow besides,—going also upon all errands. I had to curry the horse—to clean and feed him—and sometimes to ride him a little. I had more than enough to do—but still it was not so very bad as Turk's Island.

My old master often got drunk, and then he would get in a fury with his daughter, and beat her till she was not fit to be seen. I remember on one occasion, I had gone to fetch water, and when I was coming up the hill I heard a great screaming; I ran as fast as I could to the house, put down the water, and went into the chamber, where I found my master beating Miss D—— dreadfully. I strove with all my strength to get her away from him; for she was all black and blue with bruises. He had beat her with his fist, and almost killed her. The people gave me credit for getting her away. He turned round and began to lick me. Then I said, "Sir, this is not Turk's Island." I

*Negro term for white people.—Ed.

can't repeat his answer, the words were too wicked—too bad to say. He wanted to treat me the same in Bermuda as he had done in Turk's Island.

He had an ugly fashion of stripping himself quite naked and ordering me then to wash him in a tub of water. This was worse to me than all the licks. Sometimes when he called me to wash him I would not come, my eyes were so full of shame. He would then come to beat me. One time I had plates and knives in my hand, and I dropped both plates and knives, and some of the plates were broken. He struck me so severely for this, that at last I defended myself, for I thought it was high time to do so. I then told him I would not live longer with him, for he was a very indecent man—very spiteful, and too indecent; with no shame for his servants, no shame for his own flesh. So I went away to a neighbouring house and sat down and cried till the next morning, when I went home again, not knowing what else to do.

After that I was hired to work at Cedar Hills, and every Saturday night I paid the money to my master. I had plenty of work to do there—plenty of washing; but yet I made myself pretty comfortable. I earned two dollars and a quarter a week, which is twenty pence a day.

During the time I worked there, I heard that Mr. John Wood was going to Antigua. I felt a great wish to go there, and I went to Mr. D——, and asked him to let me go in Mr. Wood's service. Mr. Wood did not then want to purchase me; it was my own fault that I came under him, I was so anxious to go. It was ordained to be, I suppose; God led me there. The truth is, I did not wish to be any longer the slave of my indecent master.

Mr. Wood took me with him to Antigua, to the town of St. John's, where he lived. This was about fifteen years ago. . . . [Mary Prince is then bought by Mr. and Mrs. Wood.]

My work there was to attend the chambers and nurse the child, and to go down to the pond and wash clothes. But I soon fell ill of the rheumatism, and grew so very lame that I was forced to walk with a stick. I got the Saint Anthony's fire, also, in my left leg, and became quite a cripple. No one cared much to come near me, and I was ill a long long time; for several months I could not lift the limb. I had to lie in a little old out-house, that was swarming with bugs and other vermin, which tormented me greatly; but I had no other place to lie in. I got the rheumatism by catching cold at the pond side, from washing in the fresh water; in the salt water I never got cold. The person who lived in the next yard, (a Mrs. Greene,) could not bear to hear my cries and groans. She was kind, and used to send an old slave woman to help me, who sometimes brought me a little soup. When the doctor found I was so ill, he said I must be put into a bath of hot water. The old slave got the bark of some bush that was good for pains, which she boiled in the hot water, and every night she came and put me into the bath, and did what she could for me; I don't know what I should have done, or what would have become of me, had it not been for her.—My mistress, it is true, did send me a little food; but no one from our family came near me but the cook, who used to shove my food in at the door, and say, "Molly, Molly, there's your dinner." My mistress did not care to take any trouble about me; and if the Lord had not put it into the hearts of the neighbours to be kind to me, I must, I really think, have lain and died. . . . [Mrs. Wood's deliberate cruelty; Prince appeals to Adam White to buy her with her own money. The Woods foil her plan and refuse.]

The way in which I made my money was this.—When my master and mistress went from home, as they sometimes did, and left me to take care of the house and premises, I had a good deal of time to myself and made the most of it. I took in washing, and sold coffee and yams and other provisions to the captains of ships. I did not sit still idling during the absence of my owners; for I wanted, by all honest means, to earn money to buy my freedom. Sometimes I bought a hog cheap on board ship, and sold it for double the money on shore; and I also earned a good deal by selling coffee. By this means I by degrees acquired a little cash. A gentleman also lent me some to help to buy my freedom—but when I could not get free he got it back again. His name was Captain Abbot. . . . [The Woods take Mary Prince to Date Hill as a trusted servant.]

The slave woman who had the care of the place (which then belonged to Mr. Roberts the marshal), asked me to go with her to her husband's house, to a Methodist meeting for prayer, at a plantation called Winthorps. . . .

I felt sorry for my sins also. I cried the whole night, but I was too much ashamed to speak. I prayed God to forgive me. This meeting had a great impression on my mind, and led my spirit to the Moravian church; so that when I got back to town, I went and prayed to have my name put down in the Missionaries' book; and I followed the church earnestly every opportunity. I did not then tell my mistress about it; for I knew that she would not give me leave to go. But I felt I *must* go. Whenever I carried the children their lunch at school, I ran round and went to hear the teachers. . . . [Mary Prince learns to read and continues church attendance.]

Some time after I began to attend the Moravian Church, I met with Daniel James, afterwards my dear husband. He was a carpenter and cooper to his trade; an honest, hard-working, decent black man, and a widower. He had purchased his freedom of his mistress, old Mrs. Baker, with money he had earned whilst a slave. When he asked me to marry him, I took time to consider the matter over with myself, and would not say yes till he went to church with me and joined the Moravians. He was very industrious after he bought his freedom; and he had hired a comfortable house, and had convenient things about him. We were joined in marriage, about Christmas 1826, in the Moravian Chapel at Spring Gardens. . . . [Still a slave, she copes with the Woods' anger at her spirit.]

I had not much happiness in my marriage, owing to my being a slave. It made my husband sad to see me so ill-treated. Mrs. Wood was always abusing me about him. She did not lick me herself, but she got her husband to do it for her, whilst she fretted the flesh off my bones. Yet for all this she would not sell me. She sold five slaves whilst I was with her; but though she was always finding fault with me, she would not part with me. However, Mr. Wood afterwards allowed Daniel to have a place to live in our yard, which we were very thankful for.

After this, I fell ill again with the rheumatism, and was sick a long time; but whether sick or well, I had my work to do. About this time I asked my master and mistress to let me buy my own freedom. With the help of Mr. Burchell, I could have found the means to pay Mr. Wood; for it was agreed that I should afterwards serve Mr. Burchell a while, for the cash he was to advance for me. I was earnest in the request to my owners; but their hearts were hard—too hard to consent. Mrs. Wood was very angry — she grew quite outrageous—she called me a black devil, and asked me who had put freedom into my head. "To be free is very sweet," I said: but she took good care to keep me a slave. I saw her change colour, and I left the room.

About this time my master and mistress were going to England to put their son in school, and bring their daughters home; and they took me with them to take care of the child. I was willing to come to England: I thought that by going there I should probably get cured of my rheumatism, and should return with my master and mistress, quite well, to my husband. . . .

After that, when we came up to live in Leigh Street, Mrs. Wood sorted out five bags of clothes which we had used at sea, and also such as had been worn since we came on shore, for me and the cook to wash. Elizabeth the cook told her, that she did not think that I was able to stand to the tub, and that she had better hire a woman. . . . [Mary Prince's rheumatism worsens considerably; Woods are pitiless in making her launder vast quantities.]

Shortly after, the cook left them, and then matters went on ten times worse. I always washed the child's clothes without being commanded to do it, and any thing else that was wanted in the family; though still I was very sick—very sick indeed. When the great washing came round, which was every two months, my mistress got together again a great many heavy things, such as bed-ticks, bed-coverlets, &c. for me to wash. I told her I was too ill to wash such heavy things that day. She said, she supposed I thought myself a free woman, but I was not; and if I did not do it directly I should be instantly turned out of doors. I stood a long time before I could answer, for I did not know well what to do. I knew that I was free in England, but I did not know where to go, or how to get my living; and therefore, I did not like to leave the house. But Mr. Wood said he would send for a constable to thrust me out; and at last I took courage and resolved that I would not be longer thus treated, but would go and trust to Providence. This was the fourth time they had threatened to turn me out, and, go where I might, I was determined now to take them at their word; though I thought it very hard, after I had lived with them for thirteen years, and worked for them like a horse, to be driven out this way, like a beggar. My only fault was being sick, and therefore unable to please my mistress, who thought she never could get work enough out of her slaves; and I told them so: but they only abused me and drove me out. This took place from two to three months, I think, after we came to England.

When I came away, I went to the man (one Mash) who used to black the shoes of the family, and asked his wife to get somebody to go with me to the Moravian Missionaries: these were the only persons I knew in England. The woman sent a young girl with me to the mission house, and I saw there a gentleman called Mr. Moore. I told him my whole story. . . . [Prince is taken in and nursed by Mash and his compassionate wife.]

About this time, a woman of the name of Hill told me of the Anti-Slavery Society, and went with me to their office, to inquire if they could do any thing to get me my freedom, and send me back to the West Indies. The gentlemen of the Society took me to a lawyer, who examined very strictly into my case; but told me that the laws of England could do nothing to make me free in Antigua.* However they did all they could for me: they gave me a little money from time to time to keep me from want; and some of them went to Mr. Wood to try to persuade him to let me return a free woman to my husband; but though they offered him, as I have heard, a large sum for my freedom, he was sulky and obstinate, and would not consent to let me go free.

---

*She came first to the Anti-Slavery Office in Aldermanbury, about the latter end of November 1828; and her case was referred to Mr. George Stephen to be investigated. More of this hereafter.—Ed.

This was the first winter I spent in England, and I suffered much from the severe cold, and from the rheumatic pains, which still at times torment me. . . . [Kindness of Quaker women; employed as charwoman.]

In the spring, I got into service with a lady, who saw me at the house where I sometimes worked as a charwoman. This lady's name was Mrs. Forsyth. She had been in the West Indies, and was accustomed to Blacks, and liked them. I was with her six months, and went with her to Margate. She treated me well, and gave me a good character when she left London.* . . . [Homeless, then destitute, she appeals to the Anti-Slavery Society and obtains relief.]

At last I went into the service of Mr. and Mrs. Pringle, where I have been ever since, and am as comfortable as I can be while separated from my dear husband, and away from my own country and all old friends and connections. . . . [Reads Bible and is treated respectfully.]

I still live in the hope that God will find a way to give me my liberty, and give me back to my husband. I endeavour to keep down my fretting, and to leave all to Him, for He knows what is good for me better than I know myself. Yet, I must confess, I find it a hard and heavy task to do so.

I am often much vexed, and I feel great sorrow when I hear some people in this country say, that the slaves do not need better usage, and do not want to be free.† They believe the foreign people,‡ who deceive them, and say slaves are happy. I say, Not so. How can slaves be happy when they have the halter round their neck and the whip upon their back? and are disgraced and thought no more of than beasts?—and are separated from their mothers, and husbands, and children, and sisters, just as cattle are sold and separated? Is it happiness for a driver in the field to take down his wife or sister or child, and strip them, and whip them in such a disgraceful manner?—women that have had children exposed in the open field to shame! There is no modesty or decency shown by the owner to his slaves; men, women, and children are exposed alike. Since I have been here I have often wondered how English people can go out into the West Indies and act in such a beastly manner. But when they go to the West Indies, they forget God and all feeling of shame, I think, since they can see and do such things. They tie up slaves like hogs—moor* them up like cattle, and they lick them, so as hogs, or cattle, or horses

---

*She refers to a written certificate which will be inserted afterwards.—Ed.

†The whole of this paragraph especially, is given as nearly as was possible in Mary's precise words.—Ed.

‡She means West Indians.—Ed.

never were flogged;—and yet they come home and say, and make some good people believe, that slaves don't want to get out of slavery. But they put a cloak about the truth. It is not so. All slaves want to be free—to be free is very sweet. I will say the truth to English people who may read this history that my good friend, Miss S——, is now writing down for me. I have been a slave myself—I know what slaves feel—I can tell by myself what other slaves feel, and by what they have told me. The man that says slaves be quite happy in slavery—that they don't want to be free—that man is either ignorant or a lying person. I never heard a slave say so. I never heard a Buckra man say so, till I heard tell of it in England. Such people ought to be ashamed of themselves. They can't do without slaves, they say. What's the reason they can't do without slaves as well as in England? No slaves here—no whips—no stocks—no punishment, except for wicked people. They hire servants in England; and if they don't like them, they send them away: they can't lick them. Let them work ever so hard in England, they are far better off than slaves. If they get a bad master, they give warning and go hire to another. They have their liberty. That's just what *we* want. We don't mind hard work, if we had proper treatment, and proper wages like English servants, and proper time given in the week to keep us from breaking the Sabbath. But they won't give it; they will have work—work—work, night and day, sick or well, till we are quite done up; and we must not speak up nor look amiss, however much we be abused. And then when we are quite done up, who cares for us, more than for a lame horse? This is slavery. I tell it to let English people know the truth; and I hope they will never leave off to pray God, and call loud to the great King of England, till all the poor blacks be given free, and slavery done up for evermore.

*A West Indian phrase: to fasten or tie up.—Ed.

4

Mary Jane Grant Seacole (1805–1881)

■

Introduction

A quarter of a century separates the birth date of Mary Jane Grant Seacole from the birth dates of the Antiguan Hart sisters. Most surprisingly, because she lived on the island of Jamaica where the majority of slave uprisings took place, she scarcely commented on slavery and emancipation.[52] Like Mary Prince, Mary Seacole used mobility, although in a rather different way.

Jamaica had always been a hotbed of slave resistance. From the earliest attempts by Europeans to colonize, indigenous people resisted, usually by guerilla warfare. Termed "maroons," the insurgents often came from the West African community of Akan-speaking "Coromantees."[53]

Having chosen not to enter the abolitionist debate as a polemicist, Seacole became instead a crucial presence in the "Black Atlantic" world, in Paul Gilroy's phrase.[54] That world was "a hybrid sphere of black culture in which ideas and activities, thinkers and activists, circulate among Africa, America, the Caribbean and Europe."[55] As part of this black diaspora, Seacole transported ideas and talents around the world. She modeled vision and independence at a time when black equality was continually questioned and debated. Seacole's itinerancy, her constant movement, moreover, was voluntary. Mary Prince's, by contrast, was often forced upon her, for she usually had no say about her whereabouts.

Thus Seacole, consciously or not, distanced herself from the intense, deeply contested agitation over slavery in Jamaica, preferring to seek peace and freedom in new ways. She seems to have rejected any self-identification as an abolitionist. Frequently, she mentions her white Scottish father, and seems proud to follow in her doctress mother's professional footsteps. She forged an independent identity based on ancestry, profession, travel, and personal courage.

■

Biographical Narrative

Caribbean autobiographer, adventurer, doctor, and free woman, Mary Jane Grant Seacole was born in 1805 in Kingston, Jamaica. Her father was a Scottish army officer; her mother, a free black woman who ran a boardinghouse for military personnel. Well-educated, she became a skilled, peripatetic nurse and doctor for the soldiers staying in the boardinghouse who were afflicted with cholera and yellow fever. Seacole grew up and lived until she was almost thirty in a slave society, after the British government encouraged black Jamaicans to assume British citizenship. She witnessed the island's transition to a slave-free society,[56] and on and off throughout most of her life, seemingly remained patriotic to the British.

Mrs. Grant, Seacole's mother, was also a notable, hardworking, homeopathic doctress, a profession and dedication inherited by her daughter. Her dual career was a result of the economic restrictions imposed on mulattoes. The maternal side of the family was legally classified as mulatto, in Seacole's words, a mulatto or mulatta being a person "of mixed race."[57] About thirty-five thousand free mulattoes lived in Jamaica's leading towns—a well-educated community despite disbarment from public and professional life and disenfranchisement, its alleged superiority over black members of the community an assumed phenomenon. Tending the sick was one way to transcend the severe economic restrictions imposed on the community.

A Jamaican doctress was conversant with folk medicine, knew about tropical diseases, and had a general practitioner's skill in treating ailments and injuries. "Creole medical art" was the accumulated expertise consequent to blacks' having to look after one another on plantations. Originally, the knowledge derived from African herbal medicine. Over the years, Jamaican doctresses attended to such celebrated patients as Horatio Nelson. Seacole's mother passed on an accumulated personal and professional wisdom to her daughter.

In her twenties, Seacole visited England twice, then the Bahamas, Haiti, and Cuba. Her short marriage in 1836 to Edwin Horatio Seacole, whose godfather was Horatio Nelson, ended with his death not long after. Following her mother's death, Seacole ran the boardinghouse, which after a fire in 1843, she had rebuilt. During the Kingston cholera epidemic of 1850, Seacole treated many patients.

Seacole then traveled extensively with her brother Edward in North America, later spending three years in the gold-prospecting town of Cruces in New Granada, present day Columbia and Panama. Her flouting of convention was occasioned by unshakable self-possession. Accounts of her elaborate outfits mark a pride in appearance, an insistence perhaps on class status. Like Mary Prince, Seacole used vanity as a subversive tool of sorts. During the second cholera epidemic in Cruces and subsequently in Gorgona and Escribanos, she developed considerable skill in fighting disease and in general surgery. Back in Jamaica in 1853, she was asked by official medical personnel to assist them during an epidemic of yellow fever. Seacole's next role of that nature was played half a world away, in the Crimean War.

In March 1854 Turkey, France, and Britain went to war against Russia in the Crimean region.[58] Twenty-seven thousand British troops were engaged in the peninsula, and one thousand lay stricken with cholera in the medical unit at Scutari, Turkey. After Britain's battle with the Russian forces at Sebastopol, in addition to the soldiers injured, another seven thousand men contracted cholera and malaria. The skyrocketing death rate brought on a general outcry from the British press. The traditionally male arena of war was being stretched beyond capacity.

A party of nurses headed by Florence Nightingale and the Sisters of Mercy hastened to the battlefields and medical units. Seacole asked to join the effort. Here, she was surely following in the footsteps of the Scottish army officer father she mentioned and admired so much. British administrators rejected her request—presumably for racist reasons. A form of black motherhood on the battlefield did not mesh with the colonial image of Anglo-Saxon fighting men. Piers Compton, moreover, suggests that Nightingale was insecure about Seacole, who was the daughter of a black doctress and a white army officer.[59] Seacole decided to finance her own mission and set out alone. She is at pains to make readers aware of her unconventionality while appearing to conform.

Emulating her mother, Seacole made arrangements to be a sutler—a person who follows an army and sells provisions to the soldiers. She established the *British Hotel*, about two miles from Balaclava, which became a celebrated headquarters among foot soldiers and high-ranking personnel alike. With medical supplies on one mule, and ham and wine on another, she tended the war wounded: "'the first woman to enter Sebastopol from the English lines' and also 'the first to carry refreshments into the fallen city'" (p. 25).

Unlike Nightingale's nurses, who were permitted only to undo bandages, wash wounds, and spoon-feed patients in the hospital wards at Scutari,

Seacole was busy on the battlefields and in makeshift hospitals. In Ziggi Alexander's and Audrey Dewjee's words: "There were times when she refused to wait for the cease-fire or retreat, but carefully picked her way through the mutilated bodies of men hit by round shot and shell, seeking out the wounded and dying, whether enemy or ally" (p. 28).

When the war suddenly ended in March 1856, Seacole was left with large amounts of mostly unusable supplies. Later in London she had trouble making ends meet. The *Times,* whose famous war correspondent William H. Russell was an admirer of hers, established a fund in her behalf. Although she was the guest of honor at several splendid functions and was warmly welcomed everywhere by military men high and low, she ended up in bankruptcy court. By 1857, British supporters had cleared her debts.

Seacole's autobiography, *Wonderful Adventures of Mrs. Seacole in Many Lands,* became an overnight bestseller in 1857. Russell wrote in the preface to the first edition:

> "I trust that England will not forget one [in the Crimean War] who nursed her sick, who sought out her wounded to aid and succor them, and who performed the last offices for some of her illustrious dead."[60]

The London weekly *Punch* featured a drawing of Seacole caring for the wounded in a battlefield hospital; the caption: "Our Own Vivandière."[61] Other publications dubbed her "The Crimean Heroine" and "The Mother of the Regiment" ("La Madre del Reggimento") (p. 30). To Lord Palmerston, she was "a treasure to the army" (p. 34).

In 1857, Seacole was honored at a four-night-long benefit at the Royal Surrey Gardens; more than forty thousand people joined in the festivities. She received four government medals "for her kindness to the British soldiers" (p. 56); among them the French Legion of Honour and the Turkish Order of the Mejidie (p. 36). Queen Victoria's nephew Count Gleichen carved a bust in her likeness.

Seacole speaks positively of her involvement, despite the "pecuniarily disastrous" misadventures and her shattered health —"a little labour fatigues me now" (pp. 231–232). Had she become rich, she asserts, she would have forfeited what matters to her now: the "tender love of relatives and sympathy of friends . . . in omnibuses, in river steamboats, in places of public amusement, on quiet streets and courts" (p. 233).

Seacole's optimism hides a certain erasure of the difficulties that she confronted as a dauntless doctress and black Atlantic traveler in the heart of empire. A telling aspect of her autobiography emerges from the conflicts she experiences as a woman of color seeking acceptability in British imperial communities.[62] In her final years, she divided her time between Jamaica and London. She died from apoplexy on May 14, 1881.

■

Chronology

1805	Born in Kingston, Jamaica, to a white Scottish army officer father and a free black mother, a well-known doctress and caterer.
1820s	Visits England, Bahamas, Haiti, and Cuba.
1836	Marries Edwin Horatio Seacole (a godson of Horatio Nelson), who dies soon after.
1838–1842	Mother dies; Seacole runs the boardinghouse.
1843	Boarding house burns down; Seacole has it rebuilt.
1850	Travels in North and Central America.
1853	Returns to Jamaica and nurses yellow fever victims during epidemic.
1854	Travels to London to volunteer as nurse/doctress in the Crimean War; British government declines her offer.
1855–1856	Arranges to be a sutler in the British army; establishes the British Hotel in the Crimea; assists the wounded on battlefield and displays enormous courage.
1856	Returns to London destitute after the war.
1857	Autobiography, *Wonderful Adventures of Mary Seacole in Many Lands,* published to glowing reviews; Seacole honored at Royal Surrey Gardens; Queen Victoria's nephew carves a bust of her; many news accounts of her activites appear in the press.
1857–1881	Divides time between Jamaica and London.
1881	Dies.

■ ■ ■

From *Wonderful Adventures of Mrs. Seacole in Many Lands*

I was born in the town of Kingston, in the island of Jamaica, some time in the present century. As a female, and a widow, I may be well excused giving the precise date of this important event. But I do not mind confessing that the century and myself were both young together and that we have grown side by side into age and consequence. I am a Creole, and have good Scotch blood coursing in my veins. My father was a soldier, of an old Scotch family; and to him I often trace my affection for a camp-life, and my sympathy with what I have heard my friends call "the pomp, pride, and circumstance of glorious war." Many people have also traced to my Scotch blood that energy and activity which are not always found in the Creole race, and which have carried me to so many varied scenes: and perhaps they are right. I have often heard the term "lazy Creole" applied to my country people; but I am sure I do not know what it is to be indolent. All my life long I have followed the impulse which led me to be up and doing; and so far from resting idle anywhere, I have never wanted inclination to rove, nor will powerful enough to find a way to carry out my wishes. That these qualities have led me into many countries, and brought me into some strange and amusing adventures, the reader, if he or she has the patience to get through this book, will see. Some people, indeed, have called me quite a female Ulysses. I believe that they intended it as a compliment; but from my experience of the Greeks, I do not consider it a very flattering one.

It is not my intention to dwell at any length upon the recollections of my childhood. My mother kept a boarding-house in Kingston, and was, like many of the Creole women, an admirable doctress; in high repute with the officers of both services, and their wives, who were from time to time stationed at Kingston. It was very natural that I should inherit her tastes. . . . [Taken in by patroness, ambitious to become doctress; at twelve years old, she helps nurse at mother's boardinghouse.]

As I grew into womanhood, I began to indulge that longing to travel which will never leave me while I have health and vigour. I was never weary of tracing upon an old map the route to England; and never followed with my gaze the stately ships homeward bound without longing to be in them, and see the blue hills of Jamaica fade into the distance. At that time it seemed most improbable that these girlish wishes should be gratified; but circumstances, which I need to explain, enabled me to accompany some relatives to England while I was yet a very young woman.

I shall never forget my first impressions of London. . . . [Will not disclose year of London visit or her age.] Strangely enough, some of the most vivid of my recollections are the efforts of the London street-boys to poke fun at my and my companion's complexion. I am only a little brown—a few shades duskier than the brunettes whom you all admire so much; but my companion was very dark, and a fair (if I can apply the term to her) subject to their rude wit. She was hot-tempered, poor thing! and as there were no policemen to awe the boys and turn our servants' heads in those days, our progress through the London streets was sometimes a rather chequered one.

I remained in England, upon the occasion of my first visit, about a year; and then returned to Kingston. Before long I again started for London, bringing with me this time a large stock of West Indian preserves and pickles for sale. After remaining two years here, I again started home; and on the way my life and adventures were very nearly brought to a premature conclusion. Christmas-day had been kept very merrily on board our ship the "Velusia"; and on the following day a fire broke out in the hold. I dare say it would have resisted all the crew's efforts to put it out, had not another ship appeared in sight; upon which the fire quietly allowed itself to be extinguished. Although considerably alarmed, I did not lose my senses; but during the time when the contest between fire and water was doubtful, I entered into an amicable arrangement with the ship's cook, whereby, in consideration of two pounds—which I was not, however, to pay until the crisis arrived—he agreed to lash me on to a large hen-coop.

Before I had long been in Jamaica I started upon other trips, many of them undertaken with a view to gain. Thus I spent some time in New Providence, bringing home with me a large collection of handsome shells and rare shell-work, which created quite a sensation in Kingston, and had a rapid sale; I visited also Hayti and Cuba. But I hasten onward in my narrative.

Returned to Kingston, I nursed my old indulgent patroness in her last long illness. After she died, in my arms, I went to my mother's house, where I stayed, making myself useful in a variety of ways, and learning a great deal of Creole medical art, until I couldn't find courage to say "no" to a certain arrangement timidly proposed by Mr. Seacole, but married him, and took him down to Black River, where we established a store. Poor man! he was very delicate; and before I undertook the charge of him, several doctors had expressed most unfavourable opinions of his health. I kept him alive by kind nursing and attention as long as I could; but at last he grew so ill that we left Black River, and returned to my mother's house at Kingston. Within a month of our arrival there he died. . . . [Despairs.]

I had one other great grief to master—the loss of my mother, and then I was left alone to battle with the world as best I might. The struggles which it cost me to succeed in life were sometimes very trying. . . . [Sustains herself financially.] The great fire of 1843, which devastated Kingston, burnt down my poor home. As it was, I very nearly lost my life, for I would not leave my house until every chance of saving it had gone, and it was wrapped in flames. But, of course, I set to work again in a humbler way, and rebuilt my house by degrees, and restocked it, succeeding better than before; for I had gained a reputation as a skilful nurse and doctress, and my house was always full of invalid officers and their wives from Newcastle, or the adjacent Up-Park Camp. . . . [Acknowledges friends, surgeons from whom she learned.]

And here I may take the opportunity of explaining that it was from a confidence in my own powers, and not at all from necessity, that I remained an unprotected female. Indeed, I do not mind confessing to my reader, in a friendly confidential way, that one of the hardest struggles of my life in Kingston was to resist the pressing candidates for the late Mr. Seacole's shoes. . . . [Again she acknowledges friends who, since living in her house, have gained fame.]

In the year 1850, the cholera swept over the island of Jamaica with terrible force. . . . [Witnesses and learns the nature of cholera for future use.]

Early in the same year my brother had left Kingston for the Isthmus of Panama, then the great high-road to and from golden California, where he had established a considerable store and hotel. Ever since he had done so, I had found some difficulty in checking my reviving disposition to roam, and at last persuading myself that I might be of use to him (he was far from strong), I resigned my house into the hands of a cousin, and made arrangements to journey to Chagres [in Panama]. . . . [Prepares for and arrives at Navy Bay; witnesses disease and general dreariness; preyed upon by greedy porters. Resumes journey by boat from Gatua to Gorgona, then to Cruces, with little food.]

I was looking forward with no little pleasurable anticipation to reaching my brother's cheerful home at Cruces. After the long night spent on board the wretched boat in my stiff, clayey dress, and the hours of fasting, the warmth and good cheer of the Independent Hotel could not fail to be acceptable. My brother met me on the rickety wharf with the kindest welcome in his face, although he did not attempt to conceal a smile at my forlorn appearance, and giving the necessary instructions about my luggage, led the way at once to his house, which was situated at the upper end of the street. A capital site, he said, when the rest of the town was under water—

which agreeable variety occurred twice or thrice a year unexpectedly. On our way, he rather damped my hopes by expressing his fears that he should be unable to provide his sister with the accommodation he could wish. "For you see," he said, "the crowd from Panama has just come in, meeting your crowd from Navy Bay; and I shouldn't be at all surprised if very many of them have no better bed than the store floors." But, despite this warning, I was miserably unprepared for the reception that awaited me. To be sure, I found Cruces as like Gorgona, in its dampness, dirt, and confusion, as it well could be; but the crowd from the goldfields of California had just arrived, having made the journey from Panama on mules, and the street was filled with motley groups in picturesque variety of attire. The hotels were also full of them, while many lounged in the verandas after their day's journey. Rude, coarse gold-diggers, in gay-coloured shirts, and long, serviceable boots, elbowed, in perfect equality, keen Yankee speculators, as close-shaven, neat, and clean on the Isthmus of Panama as in the streets of New York or New Orleans. The women alone kept aloof from each other, and well they might; for, while a very few seemed not ashamed of their sex, it was somewhat difficult to distinguish the majority from their male companions, save by their bolder and more reckless voice and manner. I must say, however, that many of them adopted male attire for the journey across the isthmus only, as it spared them many compliments which their husbands were often disposed to resent, however flattering they might be to their choice.

Through all these I pressed on, stiff, cold, and hungry, to the Independent Hotel, eagerly anticipating the comforts which awaited me there. At length we reached it. But, rest! warmth! comfort!—miserable delusions! Picture to yourself, sympathizing reader, a long, low hut, built of rough, unhewn, unplaned logs, filled up with mud and split bamboo; a long, sloping roof and a large veranda, already full of visitors. And the interior: a long room, gaily hung with dirty calico, in stripes of red and white; above it another room, in which the guests slept, having the benefit of sharing in any orgies which might be going on below them, through the broad chinks between the rough, irregular planks which formed its floor. At the further end, a small corner, partitioned roughly off, formed a bar, and around it were shelves laden with stores for the travelers, while behind it was a little room used by my brother as his private apartment; but three female travelers had hired it for their own especial use for the night, paying the enormous sum of £10 for so exclusive a luxury. At the entrance sat a black man, taking toll of the comers-in, giving them in exchange for a coin or gold-dust (he had a rusty pair of scales to weigh the latter) a dirty ticket, which guaranteed them supper, a night's lodgings, and breakfast. I saw all this very quickly, and turned round upon my brother in angry despair. . . . [Dinner scene, involving travelers to and from California, without food resources; the group moves on and Mary Seacole stays.]

But it was destined that I should not be long in Cruces before my medicinal skill and knowledge were put to the test. Before the passengers for Panama had been many days gone, it was found that they had left one of their number behind them, and that one—the cholera. I believe that the faculty have not yet come to the conclusion that the cholera is contagious, and I am not presumptuous enough to forestall them; but my people have always considered it to be so, and the poor Cruces folks did not hesitate to say that this new and terrible plague had been a fellow-traveler with the Americans from New Orleans or some other of its favoured haunts. . . . [Brother's friend dying of cholera; treats her first cholera patient.]

For a few days the terrible disease made such slow progress amongst us that we almost hoped it had passed on its way and spared us; but all at once it spread rapidly, and affrighted faces and cries of woe soon showed how fatally the destroyer was at work. And in so great request were my services, that for days and nights together I scarcely knew what it was to enjoy two successive hours' rest. . . . [Expresses pride in her healing; meets with resistance in the community; many sick; steels herself to help the dying.]

I sat before the flickering fire, with my last patient in my lap—a poor, little, brown-faced orphan infant, scarce a year old, was dying in my arms. . . . [Stays on, prays for infant who dies.] I began to think—how the idea first arose in my mind I can hardly say—that, if it were possible to take this little child and examine it, I should learn more of the terrible disease which was sparing neither young nor old, and should know better how to do battle with it. . . . [With some doubts, designates infant corpse for autopsy.] It seems a strange deed to accomplish, and I am sure I could not wield the scalpel or the substitute I then used now, but at that time the excitement had strung my mind up to a high pitch of courage and determination; and perhaps the daily, almost hourly, scenes of death had made me somewhat callous. I need not linger on this scene, nor give the readers the results of my operation; a tough novel to me, and decidedly useful, they were what every medical man well knows.

We buried the poor little body beneath a piece of luxuriant turf, and stole back into Cruces like guilty things. But the knowledge I had obtained thus strangely was very valuable to me, and was soon put into practice. . . . [Describes medicines tried to cure widespread cholera; diagnoses symptoms;

elaborates on a case illustrating the epidemic and its power to equalize people; cannot avoid exposing herself to the disease.]

I hastened to my brother's house. When there, I felt an unpleasant chill come over me, and went to bed at once. Other symptoms followed quickly, and, before nightfall, I knew full well that my turn had come at last, and that the Cholera had attacked me, perhaps its greatest foe in Cruces.

When it became known that their "yellow doctress" had the cholera, I must do the people of Cruces the justice to say that they gave her plenty of sympathy. . . . [Cannot keep well-wishers away; recovers.]

After a few weeks, the first force of the cholera was spent, and although it lingered with us, as though loath to leave so fine a resting-place, for some months, it no longer gave us much alarm; and before long, life went on as briskly and selfishly as ever with the Cruces survivors, and the terrible past was conveniently forgotten. . . . [Americans retain her because of her reputation as medical assistant; establishes hotel, with restaurant and barber but no gambling; describes guests who pass through; discusses prevalence of thieving and her strategies against it.]

I remained at Cruces until the rainy months came to an end, and the river grew too shallow to be navigable by the boats higher up than Gorgona; and then we all made preparations for a flitting to that place. . . . [Describes parting visits, raucous Americans, and difficulty in establishing herself in Gorgona because of lateness of arrival; builds new hotel.] I soon grew as weary of my life in Gorgona as I had been at Cruces; and when I found my brother proof against all persuasion to quit the Isthmus, I began to entertain serious thoughts of leaving him. . . . [Discusses lack of desirable company and Americans; indigenous peoples' prejudice against Americans, informed by former slaves.] My readers can easily understand that when any Americans crossed the Isthmus, accompanied by their slaves, the Cruces and Gorgona people were restlessly anxious to whisper into their ears offers of freedom and hints how easy escape would be. Nor were the authorities at all inclined to aid in the recapture of a runaway slave. . . . [Gorgona comes to mean freedom for runaway slaves.] A young American woman, whose character can be best described by the word "vicious," fell ill at Gorgona, and was left behind by her companions under the charge of a young negro, her slave, whom she treated most inhumanly, as was evinced by the poor girl's frequent screams when under the lash. One night her cries were so distressing, that Gorgona could stand it no longer, but broke into the house and found the chattel bound hand and foot, naked, and being severely lashed. Despite the threats and astonishment of the mistress, they were both carried off on the following morning, before the alcalde, himself a man of color, and of a very humane disposition. When the particulars of the case were laid before him, he became strongly excited, and called upon the woman to offer an explanation of her cruelty. She treated it with the coolest unconcern—"The girl was her property, worth so many dollars, and a child at New Orleans; had misbehaved herself, and been properly corrected. The alcalde must be drunk or a fool, or both together, to interfere between an American and her property." Her coolness vanished, however, when the alcalde turned round to the girl and told her that she was free to leave her mistress when she liked. . . . [Mistress threatens but does not act against girl. Parallels between Gorgona and Cruces noted. Violence epitomized by colleague Dr. Casey, who shot a young boy but was not prosecuted. Floods in Gorgona.] Shortly after this, tired to death of life in Panama, I handed over my hotel to my brother, and returned to Kingston. . . . [Hated by passengers on American steamers; delays; waits for British steamer, arrives at Navy Bay, then Kingston.]

I stayed in Jamaica eight months out of the year 1853, still remembered in the island for its suffering and gloom. I returned just in time to find my services, with many others, needful; for the yellow fever never made a more determined effort to exterminate the English in Jamaica than it did in that dreadful year. So violent was the epidemic, that some of my people fell victims to its fury, a thing rarely heard of before. My house was full of sufferers—officers, their wives and children. . . . [Considers death, stressing relief for Christians.]

About eight months after my return to Jamaica, it became necessary that some one should go to the Isthmus of Panama to wind up the affairs of my late hotel; and having another fit of restlessness, I prepared to return there myself. I found Navy Bay but little altered. It was evening when I arrived there; and my friend Mr. H——, who came to meet me on the wharf, carefully piloted me through the wretched streets, giving me especial warning not to stumble over what looked like three long boxes, loosely covered with the *débris* of a fallen house. They had such a peculiar look about them that I stopped to ask what they were, receiving an answer which revived all my former memories of Darien life—"Oh, they're only three Irishmen, killed in a row a week ago, whom it's nobody's business to bury."

I went to Gorgona, wound up the affairs of the hotel, and, before returning to Navy Bay, took the occasion of accompanying my brother to the town of Panama. We did not go with the crowd, but rode alone on mules, taking with us three native guides on foot, and although the distance was not much over twenty miles, and we started at daybreak, we did not reach Panama until nightfall. But far from being surprised at this, my chief wonder was that we ever succeeded in getting over the journey. Through sand and mud, over hill and plain—through thick forests, deep gulleys, and over rapid streams, ran the track; the road sometimes being made of logs of wood laid transversely, with faggots stuffed between; while here and there we had to work our way through [a] tangled network of brushwood, and over broken rocks that seemed to have been piled together as stones for some giant's sling. We found Panama an old-fashioned, irregular town, with queer stone houses, almost all of which had been turned by the traders into stores.

On my return to Navy Bay—or Colon, as the New Granadans would have it called—I again opened a store, and stayed there for three months or so. I did not find that society had improved much in my absence; indeed, it appeared to have grown more lawless. . . . [In Escribanos, finds gold dust of questionable value and familiar struggles.]

Soon after this I left Escribanos, and stopping but a short time at Navy Bay, came on direct to England. I had claims on a Mining Company which are still unsatisfied; I had to look after my share in the Palmilla Mine speculation; and, above all, I had long been troubled with a secret desire to embark in a very novel speculation, about which I have as yet said nothing to the reader. . . . [Americans appropriate North Granada; Seacole is skeptical but understands why former slaves might favor "democracy."]

Before I left Jamaica for Navy Bay, as narrated in the last chapter, war had been declared against Russia, and we were all anxiously expecting news of a descent upon the Crimea. Now, no sooner had I heard of war somewhere, than I longed to witness it; and when I was told that many of the regiments I had known so well in Jamaica had left England for the scene of action, the desire to join them became stronger than ever. I used to stand for hours in silent thought before an old map of the world, in a little corner of which some one had chalked a red cross, to enable me to distinguish where the Crimea was; and as I traced the route thither, all difficulties would vanish. But when I came to talk over the project with my friends, the best scheme I could devise seemed so wild and improbable, that I was fain to resign my hopes for a time, and so started for Navy Bay.

But all the way to England, from Navy Bay, I was turning my old wish over and over in my mind; and when I found myself in London, in the autumn of 1854, just after the battle of Alma had been fought, and my old friends were fairly before the walls of Sebastopol, how to join them there took up far more of my thoughts than that visionary gold-mining speculation on the river Palmilla, which seemed so feasible to us in New Granada, but was considered so wild and unprofitable a speculation in London. And, as time wore on, the inclination to join my old friends of the 97th, 48th, and other regiments, battling with worse foes than yellow fever or cholera, took such exclusive possession of my mind, that I threw over the gold speculation altogether, and devoted all my energies to my new scheme.

Heaven knows it was visionary enough! I had no friends who could help in such a project—nay, who would understand why I desired to go, and what I desired to do when I got there. My funds, although they might, carefully husbanded, carry me over the three thousand miles, and land me at Balaclava, would not support me there long; while to persuade the public that an unknown Creole woman would be useful to their army before Sebastopol was too improbable an achievement to be thought of for an instant. Circumstances, however, assisted me.

As the winter wore on, came hints from various quarters of mismanagement, want, and suffering in the Crimea; and after the battle of Balaclava and Inkermann, and the fearful storm of the 14th of November, the worst anticipations were realized. Then we knew that the hospitals were full to suffocation, that scarcity and exposure were the fate of all in the camp, and that the brave fellows for whom any of us at home would have split our last shilling, and shared our last meal, were dying thousands of miles away from the active sympathy of their fellow-countrymen. Fast and thick upon the news of Inkermann, fought by a handful of fasting and enfeebled men against eight times their number of picked Russians, brought fresh and animated to the contest, and while all England was reeling beneath the shock of that fearful victory, came the sad news that hundreds were dying whom the Russian shot and sword had spared, and that the hospitals of Scutari were utterly unable to shelter, or their inadequate staff to attend to, the ship-loads of sick and wounded which were sent to them across the stormy Black Sea.

But directly England knew the worst, she set about repairing her past neglect. In every household busy fingers were working for the poor soldiers—money flowed in golden streams wherever need was—and Christian ladies, mindful of the sublime example, "I was sick, and ye visited me," hastened to volunteer their services by those sickbeds which only women know how to soothe and bless. . . . [Decides, after rationalizing her value, to go and help British forces in the Crimea.]

My first idea (and knowing that I was well fitted for the work, and would be the right woman in the right place, the reader can fancy my audacity) was to apply to the War Office for the post of hospital nurse. Among the diseases which I understood were most prevalent in the Crimea were cholera, diarrhoea, and dysentery, all of them more or less known in tropical climates; and with which, as the reader will remember, my Panama experience had made me tolerably familiar. Now, no one will accuse me of presumption, if I say that I thought (and so it afterwards proved) that my knowledge of these human ills would not only render my services as a nurse more valuable, but would enable me to be of use to the overworked doctors. . . . [Procures documents certifying her qualifications, and recommendations that validate her decision.]

So I made long and unwearied application at the War Office, in blissful ignorance of the labour and time I was throwing away. I have reason to believe that I considerably interfered with the repose of sundry messengers, and disturbed, to an alarming degree, the official gravity of some nice gentlemanly young fellows, who were working out their salaries in an easy, offhand way. But my ridiculous endeavours to gain an interview with the Secretary-at-War of course failed, and glad at last to oblige a distracted messenger, I transferred my attentions to the Quartermaster-General's department. Here I saw another gentleman, who listened to me with a great deal of polite enjoyment, and—his amusement ended—hinted, had I not better apply to the Medical Department; and accordingly I attached myself to their quarters with the same unwearying ardour. But, of course, I grew tired at last, and then I changed my plans. . . . [Speculates that rejection is based on gender, then race.]

The morrow, however, brought fresh hope. A good night's rest had served to strengthen my determination. Let what might happen, to the Crimea I would go. If in no other way, then would I upon my own responsibility and at my own cost. There were those there who had known me in Jamaica, who had been under my care; doctors who would vouch for my skill and willingness to aid them, and a general who had more than once helped me, and would do so still. Why not trust to their welcome and kindness, and start at once? If the authorities had allowed me, I would willingly have given them my services as a nurse; but as they declined them, should I not open an hotel for invalids in the Crimea in my own way? . . . [In advance, advertises her arrival and hotel that she will establish in the Crimea; bears in mind her primary desire, to nurse; tells of journey, old friends regained, impressions of Gibralter, Malta, Constantinople.]

BRITISH HOTEL
Mrs. Mary Seacole

(Late of Kingston, Jamaica),
Respectfully announced to her former kind friends, and to the Officers of the Army and Navy generally,

> That she has taken her passage in the screw-steamer "Hollander," to start from London on the 25th of January, intending on her arrival at Balaclava to establish a mess-table and comfortable quarters for sick and convalescent officers.

This bold programme would reach the Crimea in the end of January, at a time when any officer would have considered a stall in an English stable luxurious quarters compared to those he possesses, and had nearly forgotten the comforts of a mess-table. It must have read to them rather like a mockery, and yet, as the reader will see, I succeeded in redeeming my pledge.

While this new scheme was maturing, I again met Mr. Day in England. He was bound to Balaclava upon some shipping business, and we came to the understanding that (if it were found desirable) we should together open a store as well as an hotel in the neighbourhood of the camp. So was originated the well-known firm of Seacole and Day (I am sorry to say, the camp wits dubbed it Day and Martin), which for so many months, did business upon the now deserted high-road from the then busy harbour of Balaclava to the front of the British army before Sebastopol.

These new arrangements were not allowed to interfere in any way with the main object of my journey. A great portion of my limited capital was, with the kind aid of a medical friend, invested in medicines which I had reason to believe would be useful; with the remainder I purchased those home comforts which I thought would be most difficult to obtain away from England.

I had scarcely set my foot on board the "Hollander," before I met a friend. The supercargo was the brother of the Mr. S——, whose death in Jamaica the reader will not have forgotten, and he gave me a hearty welcome. . . .

It was afternoon when the boatmen set me down in safety at the landing-place of Scutari, and I walked up the slight ascent, to the great dull-looking hospital. Thinking of the many noble fellows who had been borne, or had painfully crept along this path, only to die within that dreary building, I felt rather dull; and directly I entered the hospital, and came up the long wards of sufferers lying there so quiet and still, a rush of tears came to my eyes, and blotted out the sight for a few minutes. But I soon felt at home, and looked about me with great interest. The men there were, many of them, very quiet. Some of the convalescent formed themselves into little groups around one who read a newspaper; others had books in their hands, or by their side, where they had fallen when slumber overtook the readers, while hospital orderlies moved to and fro, and now and then the female nurses, in their quiet uniform, passed noiselessly on some mission of kindness. . . .

One thought never left my mind as I walked through the fearful miles of suffering in that great hospital. If it is so here, what must it not be at the scene of war—on the spot where the poor fellows are stricken down by pestilence or Russian bullets, and days and nights of agony must be passed before a woman's hand can dress their wounds. And I felt happy in the conviction that I *must* be useful three or four days nearer to their pressing wants than this.

It was growing late before I felt tired, or thought of leaving Scutari, and Dr. S——, another Jamaica friend, who had kindly borne me company for the last half-hour, agreed with me that the caicque was not the safest conveyance by night on the Bosphorus, and recommended me to present my letter to Miss Nightingale, and perhaps a lodging for the night could be found for me. So, still under the Sergeant's patient guidance, we thread our way through passages and corridors, all used as sick wards, until we reach the corner tower of the building, in which are the nurses' quarters.

I think Mrs. B——, who saw me, felt more surprise than she could politely show (I never found women so quick to understand me as the men) when I handed her Dr. F——'s kind letter respecting me, and apologized for troubling Miss Nightingale. There is that in the Doctor's letter (he had been much at Scutari) which prevents my request being refused, and I am asked to wait until Miss Nightingale, whose every moment is valuable, can see me. Meanwhile Mrs. B—— questions me very kindly but with the same look of curiosity and surprise. . . . [Appeals to Nightingale for a night's stay, which is granted; employs "Jew Johnny" as a guide; begins trip to Balaclava but hears the situation is deteriorating; nurses en route; arrives, settles on the "Medora."]

What object has Mrs. Seacole in coming out? This is the purport of her questions. And I say, frankly, to be of use somewhere; for other considerations I had not, until necessity forced them upon me. Willingly, had they accepted me, I would have worked for the wounded, in return for bread and water. I fancy Mrs. B—— thought that I sought for employment at Scutari, for she said, very kindly—

"Miss Nightingale has the entire management of our hospital staff, but I do not think that any vacancy—"

"Excuse me, ma'am," I interrupt her with, "but I am bound for the front in a few days;" and my questioner leaves me, more surprised than ever. The room I waited in was used as a kitchen. Upon the stoves were cans of soup, broth, and arrow-root, while nurses passed in and out with noiseless tread and subdued manner. I thought many of them had that strange expression of the eyes which those who have gazed long on scenes of woe or horror seldom lose.

In half an hour's time I am admitted to Miss Nightingale's presence. A slight figure, in the nurses' dress; with a pale, gentle, and withal firm face, resting lightly in the palm of one white hand, while the other supports the elbow—a position which gives to her countenance a keen inquiring expression, which is rather marked. Standing thus in repose, and yet keenly observant—the greatest sign of impatience at any time a slight, perhaps unwitting motion of the grimly planted right foot—was Florence Nightingale—that English woman whose name shall never die, but sound like music on the lips of British men until the hour of doom.

She has read Dr. F——'s letter, which lies on the table by her side, and asks, in her gentle but eminently practical and business-like way, "What do you want, Mrs. Seacole—anything that we can do for you? If it lies in my power, I shall be very happy."

So I tell her of my dread of the night journey by caicque, and the improbability of my finding the "Hollander" in the dark; and, with some diffidence, threw myself upon the hospitality of Scutari, offering to nurse the sick for the night. Now unfortunately, for many reasons, room even for one in Scutari Hospital was at that time no easy matter to find; but at last a bed was discovered to be unoccupied at the hospital washerwomen's quarters.

My experience of washerwomen, all the world over, is the same—that they are kind soft-hearted folks. Possibly the soap-suds they almost live in find their way into their hearts and tempers, and soften them. This Scutari washerwoman is no exception to the rule, and welcomes me most heartily. With her, also, are some invalid nurses; and after they have gone to bed, we spend some hours of the night talking over our adventures, and giving one another scraps of our respective biographies. I hadn't long retired to my couch before I wished most heartily that we had continued our chat; for unbidden and most unwelcome companions took the washerwoman's place, and persisted not only in dividing my bed, but my plump person also. Upon my word, I believe the fleas are the only industrious creatures in all Turkey.

Some of their relatives would seem to have migrated into Russia; for I found them in the Crimea equally prosperous and ubiquitous.

In the morning, a breakfast is sent to my mangled remains, and a kind message from Mrs. B——, having reference to how I spent the night. And, after an interview with some other medical men, whose acquaintance I had made in Jamaica, I shake hands with the soft-hearted washerwoman, up to her shoulders in soap-suds already, and start for the "Hollander." . . .

I remained six weeks in Balaclava, spending my days on shore, and my nights on board ship. Over our stores, stacked on the shore, a few sheets of rough tarpaulin were suspended; and beneath these—my sole protection against the Crimean rain and wind—I spent some portion of each day, receiving visitors and selling stores.

But my chief occupation and one with which I never allowed any business to interfere, was helping the doctors to transfer the sick and wounded from the mules and ambulances into the transports that had to carry them to the hospitals of Scutari and Buyukdere. I did not forget the main object of my journey, to which I would have devoted myself exclusively had I been allowed; and very familiar did I become before long with the sick wharf of Balaclava. My acquaintance with it began very shortly after I had reached Balaclava. The very first day that I approached the wharf, a party of sick and wounded had just arrived. Here was work for me, I felt sure. With so many patients, the doctors must be glad of all the hands they could get. Indeed, so strong was the old impulse within me, that I waited for no permission, but seeing a poor artilleryman stretched upon a pallet, groaning heavily, I ran up to him at once, and eased the stiff dressings. Lightly my practised fingers ran over the familiar work, and well was I rewarded when the poor fellow's groans subsided into a restless uneasy mutter. God help him! He had been hit in the forehead, and I think his sight was gone. I stooped down, and raised some tea to his baked lips (here and there upon the wharf were rows of little pannikins containing this beverage). Then his hand touched mine, and rested there, and I heard him mutter indistinctly, as though the discovery had arrested his wandering senses—

"Ha! this is surely a woman's hand."

I couldn't say much, but I tried to whisper something about the hope and trust in God; but all the while I think his thoughts were running on this strange discovery. Perhaps I had brought to his poor mind memories of his home, and the loving ones there, who would ask no greater favour than the privilege of helping him thus; for he continued to hold my hand in his feeble grasp, and whisper "God bless you, *woman*—whoever you are, God bless you!"—over and over again.

I do not think that the surgeons noticed me at first, although, as this was my introduction to Balaclava, I had not neglected my personal appearance, and wore my favourite yellow dress, and blue bonnet, with the red ribbons; but I noticed one coming to me, who, I think, would have laughed very merrily had it not been for the poor fellow at my feet. As it was, he came forward, and shook hands very kindly, saying, "How do you do, ma'am? Much obliged to you for looking after my poor fellow; very glad to see you here." And glad they always were, the kind-hearted doctors, to let me help them look after the sick and wounded sufferers brought to that fearful wharf.

I wonder if I can ever forget the scenes I witnessed there? Oh! they were heartrending. I declare that I saw rough bearded men stand by and cry like the softest-hearted women at the sights of suffering they saw; while some who scorned comfort for themselves, would fidget about for hours before the long trains of mules and ambulances came in, nervous lest the most trifling thing that could minister to the sufferers' comfort should be neglected. I have often heard men talk and preach very learnedly and conclusively about the great wickedness and selfishness of the human heart; I used to wonder whether they would have modified those opinions if they had been my companions for one day of the six weeks I spent upon that wharf, and seen but one day's experience of the Christian sympathy and brotherly love shown by the strong to the weak. The task was a trying one, and familiarity, you might think, would have worn down their keener feelings of pity and sympathy; but it was not so. . . . [Scenes of recognition. Transfer of goods within triangle of boats: *Medora*, *Nonpareil*, *Albatross*. Store is built two miles from Balaclava. Brief friendship with Turks employed as carpenters. British Hotel at Spring Hill described in detail, including nuisances, vermin, and thieves.]

I hope the reader will give me credit for the assertion that I am about to make, viz., that I enter upon the particulars of this chapter with great reluctance; but I cannot omit them, for the simple reason that they strengthen my one and only claim to interest the public, viz., my services to the brave British army in the Crimea. But, fortunately, I can follow a course which will not only render it unnecessary for me to sound my own trumpet, but will be more satisfactory to the reader. I can put on record the written opinions of those who had ample means of judging and ascertaining how I fulfilled the great object which I had in view in leaving England for the

Crimea; and before I do so, I must solicit my readers' attention to the position I held in the camp as doctress, nurse, and "mother."

I have never been long in any place before I have found my practical experience in the science of medicine useful. Even in London I have found it of service to others. And in the Crimea, where the doctors were so overworked, and sickness was so prevalent, I could not be long idle; for I never forgot that my intention in seeking the army was to help the kind-hearted doctors, to be useful to whom I have ever looked upon and still regard as so high a privilege.

But before very long I found myself surrounded with patients of my own, and this for two simple reasons. In the first place, the men (I am speaking of the "ranks" now) had a very serious objection to going into hospital for any but urgent reasons, and the regimental doctors were rather fond of sending them there; and, in the second place, they could and did get at my store sick-comforts and nourishing food, which the heads of the medical staff would sometimes find it difficult to procure. These reasons, with the additional one that I was very familiar with the diseases which they suffered most from and successful in their treatment (I say this in no spirit of vanity), were quite sufficient to account for the numbers who came daily to the British Hotel for medical treatment.

That the officers were glad of me as a doctress and nurse may be easily understood. When a poor fellow lay sickening in his cheerless hut and sent down to me, he knew very well that I should not ride up in answer to his message empty-handed. And although I did not hesitate to charge him with the value of the necessaries I took him, still he was thankful enough to be able to *purchase* them. When we lie ill at home surrounded with comfort, we never think of feeling any special gratitude for the sick-room delicacies which we accept as a consequence of our illness; but the poor officer lying ill and weary in his crazy hut, dependent for the merest necessaries of existence upon a clumsy, ignorant soldier-cook, who would almost prefer eating his meat raw to having the trouble of cooking it (our English soldiers are bad campaigners), often finds his greatest troubles in the want of those little delicacies with which a weak stomach must be humoured into retaining nourishment. How often have I felt sad at the sight of poor lads who in England thought attending early parade a hardship, and felt harassed if their neckclothes set awry, or the natty little boots would not retain their polish, bearing, and bearing so nobly and bravely, trials and hardships to which the veteran campaigner frequently succumbed. Don't you think, reader, if you were lying, with parched lips and fading appetite, thousands of miles from mother, wife, or sister, loathing the rough food by your side, and thinking regretfully of that English home where nothing that could minister to your great need would be left untried—don't you think that you would welcome the familiar figure of the stout lady whose bony horse has just pulled up at the door of your hut, and whose panniers contain some cooling drink, a little broth, some homely cake, or a dish of jelly or blanc-mange—don't you think, under such circumstances, that you would heartily agree with my friend *Punch's* remark:—

> "That berry-brown face, with a kind heart's trace
> Impressed on each wrinkle sly,
> Was a sight to behold, through the snow-clouds rolled
> Across that iron sky."

I tell you, reader, I have seen many a bold fellow's eyes moisten at such a season, when a woman's voice and a woman's care have brought to their minds recollections of those happy English homes which some of them never saw again; but many did, who will remember their woman-comrade upon the bleak and barren heights before Sebastopol.

Then their calling me "mother" was not, I think, altogether unmeaning. I used to fancy that there was something homely in the word; and, reader, you cannot think how dear to them was the smallest thing that reminded them of home.

Some of my Crimean patients, who were glad of me as nurse and doctress, bore names familiar to all England, and perhaps, did I ask them, they would allow me to publish those names. I am proud to think that a gallant sailor, on whose brave breast the order of Victoria rests—a more gallant man can never wear it—sent for the doctress whom he had known in Kingston, when his arm, wounded on the fatal 18th of June, refused to heal, and I think that the application I recommended did it good; but I shall let some of my patients' letters, taken from a large bundle, speak for me. Of course I must suppress most of their names. Here are two from one of my best and kindest sons.

> "My dear Mamma,— Will you kindly give the bearer the bottle you promised me when you were here this morning, for my jaundice. Please let me know how much I am to take of it. Yours truly,"F.M., *C.E.*"

You see the medicine does him good, for a few days later comes another from the same writer:—

> "My dear Mrs. Seacole,— I have finished the bottle, which has done my jaundice a deal of good. Will you kindly send another by bearer. Truly yours, "F.M."

[Presents notes on cases, letters of thanks. Stresses her success as a woman despite weather's slowing her down. Weary soldiers come to hotel; visitors and dinner fare; daily life.]

In the last three chapters, I have attempted, without any consideration of dates, to give my readers some idea of my life in the Crimea. I am fully aware that I have jumbled up events strangely, talking in the same page, and even sentence, of events which occurred at different times; but I have three excuses to offer for my unhistorical inexactness. In the first place, my memory is far from trustworthy, and I kept no written diary; in the second place, the reader must have had more than enough of journals and chronicles of Crimean life, and I am only the historian of Spring Hill; and in the third place, unless I am allowed to tell the story of my life in my own way, I cannot tell it at all. . . . [Notes consolidation of her observations.]

My first experience of battle was pleasant enough. Before we had been long at Spring Hill, Omar Pasha got something for his Turks to do, and one fine morning they were marched away towards the Russian outposts on the road to Baidar. I accompanied them on horseback, and enjoyed the sight amazingly. English and French cavalry preceded the Turkish infantry over the plain yet full of memorials of the terrible Light Cavalry charge a few months before; and while one detachment of the Turks made a reconnaissance to the right of the Tchernaya, another pushed their way up the hill, towards Kamara, driving in the Russian outposts, after what seemed but a slight resistance. It was very pretty to see them advance, and to watch how every now and then little clouds of white smoke puffed up from behind bushes and the crests of hills, and were answered by similar puffs from the long line of busy skirmishers that preceded the main body. This was my first experience of actual battle, and I felt that strange excitement which I do not remember on future occasions, coupled with an earnest longing to see more of warfare, and to share in its hazards. It was not long before my wish was gratified.

I do not know much of the second bombardment of Sebastopol in the month of April, although I was as assiduous as I could be in my attendance at Cathcart's Hill. I could judge of its severity by the long trains of wounded which passed the British Hotel. I had a stretcher laid near the door, and very often a poor fellow was laid upon it, outwearied by the terrible conveyance from the front.

After this unsuccessful bombardment, it seemed to us that there was a sudden lull in the progress of the siege; and other things began to interest us. There were several arrivals to talk over. Miss Nightingale came to supervise the Balaclava hospitals, and before long, she had practical experience of Crimean fever. After her, came the Duke of Newcastle, and the great high priest of the mysteries of cookery, Mons. Alexis Soyer. He was often at Spring Hill, with the most smiling of faces and in the most gorgeous of irregular uniforms, and never failed to praise my soups and dainties. I always flattered myself that I was his match, and with our West Indian dishes could of course beat him hollow, and more than once I challenged him to a trial of skill; but the gallant Frenchman only shrugged his shoulders, and disclaimed my challenge with many flourishes of his jewelled hands, declaring that Madame proposed a contest where victory would cost him his reputation for gallantry, and be more disastrous than defeat. And all because I was a woman, forsooth. What nonsense to talk like that, when I was doing the work of half a dozen men. Then he would laugh and declare that, when our campaigns were over, we would render rivalry impossible, by combining to open the first restaurant in Europe. . . . [Notes cheerier moments, dinner scenes, amidst constant fighting.]

The deaths in the trenches touched me deeply, perhaps for this reason. It was very usual, when a young officer was ordered into the trenches, for him to ride down to Spring Hill to dine, or obtain something more than his ordinary fare to brighten his weary hours in those fearful ditches. They seldom failed on these occasions to shake me by the hand at parting, and sometimes would say, "You see, Mrs. Seacole, I can't say good-bye to the dear ones at home, so I'll bid you good-bye for them. Perhaps you'll see them some day, and if the Russians should knock me over, mother, just tell them I thought of them all—will you?" And although all this might be said in a light-hearted manner, it was rather solemn. I felt it to be so, for I never failed (although who was I, that I should preach?) to say something about God's providence and relying upon it; and they were very good. No army of parsons could be much better than my sons. They would listen very gravely, and shake me by the hand again, while I felt that there was nothing in the world I would not do for them. Then very often the men would say, "I'm going in with my master to-night, Mrs. Seacole; come and look after him, if he's hit;" and so often as this happened I would pass the night restlessly, awaiting with anxiety the morning, and yet dreading to hear the news it held in store for me. I used to think it was like having a large family of children ill with fever, and dreading to hear which one had passed away in the night. . . . [Extends sympathies to mourning families.]

Before I left the Crimea to return to England, the Adjutant-General of the British Army gave me a testimonial, which the reader has already read in Chapter 14, in which he stated that I had "frequently exerted myself in the most praiseworthy manner in attending wounded men, even in positions of great danger." The simple meaning of this sentence is that, in the discharge of what I conceived to be my duty, I was frequently "under fire." Now I am far from wishing to speak of this fact with any vanity or pride, because, after all, one soon gets accustomed to it, and it fails at last to create more than temporary uneasiness. Indeed, after Sebastopol was ours, you might often see officers and men strolling coolly, even leisurely, across and along those streets, exposed to the enemy's fire, when a little haste would have carried them beyond the reach of danger. The truth was, I believe, they had grown so habituated to being in peril from shot or shell, that they rather liked the sensation, and found it difficult to get on without a little gratuitous excitement and danger. . . . [Speaks of pervasive danger, gunshots nearby and around.]

In the first week of June, the third bombardment of Sebastopol opened, and the Spring Hill visitors had plenty to talk about. Many were the surmises as to when the assault would take place, of the success of which nobody entertained a doubt. Somehow or other, important secrets oozed out in various parts of the camp, which the Russians would have given much to know, and one of these places was the British Hotel. Some such whispers were afloat on the evening of Sunday the 17th June, and excited me strangely. Any stranger not in my secret would have considered that my conduct fully justified my partner, Mr. Day, in sending me home, as better fitted for a cell in Bedlam than the charge of an hotel in the Crimea. I never remember feeling more excited or more restless than upon that day, and no sooner had night fairly closed in upon us than, instead of making preparations for bed, this same stranger would have seen me wrap up—the nights were still cold—and start off for a long walk to Cathcart's Hill, three miles and a half away. I stayed there until past midnight, but when I returned home, there was no rest for me; for I had found out that, in the stillness of the night, many regiments were marching down to the trenches, and that the dawn of day would be the signal that should let them loose upon the Russians. . . . [On June 18, notes that British are repulsed at Redan. Relieves band of soldiers who, because of Redan, do not go forward. Helps at temporary hospital; while traveling, comes "under fire."] Several times in my wanderings on that eventful day, of which I confess to have a most confused remembrance, only knowing that I looked after many wounded men, I was ordered back, but each time my bag of bandages and comforts for the wounded proved my passport. While at the hospital I was chiefly of use looking after those, who, either from lack of hands or because their hurts were less serious, had to wait, pained and weary, until the kind-hearted doctors—who, however, *looked* more like murderers—could attend to them. And the grateful words and smile which rewarded me for binding up a wound or giving cooling drink was a pleasure worth risking life for at any time. It was here that I received my only wound during the campaign. I threw myself too hastily on the ground, in obedience to the command of those around me, to escape a threatening shell, and fell heavily on the thumb of my right hand, dislocating it. It was bound up on the spot and did not inconvenience me much, but it has never returned to its proper shape.

After this, first washing my hands in some sherry from lack of water, I went back to Cathcart's Hill, where I found my horse, and heard that the good-for-nothing lad, either frightened or tired of waiting, had gone away with the mules. I had to ride three miles after him, and then the only satisfaction I had arose from laying my horse-whip about his shoulders. After that, working my way round, how I can scarcely tell, I got to the extreme left attack, where General Eyre's division had been hotly engaged all day, and had suffered severely. I left my horse in charge of some men, and with no little difficulty, and at no little risk, crept down to where some wounded men lay, with whom I left refreshments. And then—it was growing late—I started for Spring Hill, where I heard all about the events of the luckless day from those who had seen them from posts of safety, while I, who had been in the midst of it all day, knew so little.

On the following day some Irishmen of the 8th Royals brought me, in token of my having been among them, a Russian woman's dress and a poor pigeon, which they had brought away from one of the houses in the suburb where their regiment suffered so severely.

But that evening of the 18th of June was a sad one, and the news that came in of those that had fallen were most heartrending. . . . [Gives her relation to men killed.]

On the following day, directly I heard of the armistice, I hastened to the scene of action, anxious to see once more the faces of those who had been so kind to me in life. That battle-field was a fearful sight for a woman to witness, and if I do not pray God that I may never see its like again, it is because I wish to be useful all my life, and it is in scenes of horror and distress that a woman can do so much. . . . [News of armistice; bodies; dying and dead arrive; presence of summer, flies; attends dying veterans of battle of Tchenaya, August 16, 1855. Watches bombardment of Sebastopol from Cathcart's Hill. Admitted to evacuated city to aid the wounded.]

It was very hazardous to pass along some of the streets exposed to the fire of the Russians on the north side of the harbour. We had to wait and watch our opportunity, and then gallop for it. Some of us had close shaves of being hit. More than this, fires still kept breaking out around; while mines and fougasses not unfrequently exploded from unknown causes. We saw two officers emerge from a heap of ruins, covered and almost blinded with smoke and dust, from some such unlooked-for explosion. With considerable difficulty we succeeded in getting into the quarter of the town held by the French, where I was nearly getting into serious trouble. . . . [Suspected as Russian spy; released upon former patient's recognition; given portrait of the Madonna.]

On the following day I again entered Sebastopol, and saw still more of its horrors. But I have refrained from describing so many scenes of woe, that I am loath to dwell much of these. The very recollection of that woeful hospital, where thousands of dead and dying had been left by the retreating Russians, is enough to unnerve the strongest and sicken the most experienced. I would give much if I had never seen that harrowing sight. I believe some Englishmen were found in it alive; but it was as well that they did not live to tell their fearful experience.

I made my way into the Redan also, although every step was dangerous, and took it some brown bread, which seemed to have been left in the oven by the baker when he fled.

Before many days were passed, some Frenchwomen opened houses in Sebastopol; but in that quarter of the town held by the English the prospect was not sufficiently tempting for me to follow their example, and so I saw out the remainder of the campaign from my old quarters at Spring Hill. . . . [Holiday festivities, during which Seacole notes various national attitudes; sick for a short time before Christmas; describes meal preparation.]

Before the New Year was far advanced we all began to think of going home, making sure that peace would soon be concluded. And never did more welcome message come anywhere than that which brought us intelligence of the armistice. . . . [Armistice signed by weary, not war-hating, men; friendships begin among strangers.] I was one of the first to ride down to the Tchernaya, and very much delighted seemed the Russians to see an English woman. I wonder if they thought they all had my complexion. . . . [After peace is concluded, exchanges take place with Russians. Takes trip to interior; anticipates leaving. War communities disperse.]

As the various regiments moved off, I received many acknowledgments from those who thought they owed me gratitude. Little presents, warm farewell words, kind letters full of grateful acknowledgments for services so small that I had forgotten them long, long ago—how easy it is to reach warm hearts!—little thoughtful acts of kindness, even from the humblest. . . . [Inserts letter of gratitude.]

But I had other friends in the Crimea—friends who could never thank me. Some of them lay in their last sleep, beneath indistinguishable mounds of earth; some in the half-filled trenches, a few beneath the blue waters of the Euxine. I might in vain attempt to gather the wild flowers which sprung up above many of their graves, but I knew where some lay, and could visit their last homes on earth. And to all the cemeteries where friends rested so calmly, sleeping well after a life's work nobly done, I went many times, lingering long over many a mound that bore the names of those whom I had been familiar with in life, thinking of what they had been, and what I had known of them. . . . [Considers graves, lost acquaintances. British Hotel looted; remains sold.]

We were among the last to leave the Crimea. Before going I borrowed a horse, easy enough now, and rode up the old well-known road—how unfamiliar in its loneliness and quiet—to Cathcart's Hill. I wished once more to impress the scene upon my mind. It was a beautifully clear evening, and we could see miles away across the darkening sea. I spent some time there with my companions, pointing out to each other the sites of scenes we all remembered so well. There were the trenches, already becoming indistinguishable, out of which, on the 8th of September we had seen the storming parties tumble in confused and scattered bodies, before they ran up the broken height of the Redan. There the Malakhoff, into which we had also seen the luckier French pour in one unbroken stream; below lay the crumbling city and the quiet harbour, with scarce a ripple on its surface, while around stretched away the deserted huts for miles. It was with something like regret that we said to one another that the play was fairly over, that peace had rung the curtain down, and that we, humble actors in some of its most stirring scenes, must seek engagements elsewhere.

I lingered behind, and stooping down, once more gathered little tufts of grass, and some simple blossoms from above the graves of some who in life had been very kind to me, and I left behind, in exchange, a few tears which were sincere.

A few days later, and I stood on board a crowded steamer, taking my last look at the shores of the Crimea. . . . Conclusion.

I did not return to England by the most direct route, but took the opportunity of seeing more of men and manners in yet other lands. Arrived in England at last, we set to work bravely at Aldershot to retrieve our fallen fortunes, and stem off the ruin originated in the Crimea, but all in vain; and at last defeated by fortune, but not I think disgraced, we were obliged to capitulate on very honourable conditions. In plain truth, the old Crimean firm of Seacole and Day was dissolved finally, and its partners had to recommence the world anew. And so ended *our* campaign. One of us started only the other day for the Antipodes, while the other is ready to take any journey to any place where a stout heart and two experienced hands may be of use.

Perhaps it would be right if I were to express more shame and annoyance than I really feel at the pecuniarily disastrous issue of my Crimean adventures, but I cannot—I really cannot. When I would try and feel ashamed of myself for being poor and helpless, I only experience a glow of pride at the other and more pleasing events of my career; when I think of the few whom I failed to pay in full (and so far from blaming me some of them are now my firmest friends), I cannot help remembering also the many who profess themselves indebted to me.

Let me, in as few words as possible, state the results of my Crimean campaign. To be sure, I returned from it shaken in health. I came home wounded, as many others did. Few constitutions, indeed, were the better for those winters before Sebastopol, and I was too hard worked not to feel their effects; for a little labour fatigues me now—I cannot watch by sick-beds as I could—a week's want of rest quite knocks me up now. Then I returned bankrupt in fortune. Whereas others in my position may have come back to England rich and prosperous, I found myself poor—beggared. So few words can tell what I have lost.

But what have I gained? I should need a volume to describe that fairly; so much is it, and so cheaply purchased by suffering ten times worse than what I have experienced. I have more than once heard people say that they would gladly suffer illness to enjoy the delights of convalescence, and so, by enduring a few days' pain, gain the tender love of relatives and sympathy of friends. And on this principle I rejoice in the trials which have borne me such pleasures as those I now enjoy, for wherever I go I am sure to meet some smiling face; every step I take in the crowded London streets may bring me in contact with some friend, forgotten by me, perhaps, but who soon reminds me of our old life before Sebastopol; it seems very long ago now, when I was of use to him and he to me.

Where, indeed, do I not find friends? In omnibuses, in river steamboats, in places of public amusement, in quiet streets and courts, where taking short cuts I lose my way oft-times, spring up old familiar faces to remind me of the months spent on Spring Hill. The sentries at Whitehall relax from the discharge of their important duty of guarding nothing to give me a smile of recognition; the very newspaper offices look friendly as I pass them by; busy Printing-house Yard puts on a cheering smile, and the *Punch* office in Fleet Street sometimes laughs outright. Now, would all this have happened if I had returned to England a rich woman? Surely not. [Acknowledgments follow.]

5

Harriet Ann Jacobs
(1813–1897)

■

Introduction

MANY BLACK U.S.-BORN WOMEN wrote major works in the mid-nineteenth century that accentuated freedom. In Carla Peterson's words, "The 1850s constitute a significant moment in the history of African-American literary production as they were the first decade to bear witness to the publication of full-length fictional narratives written by blacks, both male and female."[63] This was not surprising during the antebellum period when slavery, insurgency, and independence became prominent national issues.[64] That time frame saw passage of the Fugitive Slave Act and the Kansas-Nebraska Act, and the Supreme Court's *Dred Scott* decision. The Fugitive Slave Act (1850) stipulated that assisting escaped slaves was punishable.

The appearance of William Lloyd Garrison's *Liberator* in 1830, followed by Nat Turner's revolt in 1831, were landmarks that signaled the emergence of an intense struggle over abolition.[65] Britain's Emancipation Act of 1833/1834 also inspired the U.S. abolitionists. Between 1830 and 1840, many black autobiographies and biographies were published.[66] Newspapers, magazines, and books were more readily available. Among the most famous male slave narratives published in the prewar years were Frederick Douglass's autobiography and William Wells Brown's *Narrative of William Wells Brown, a Fugitive Slave, Written by Himself* (1847).[67] Among the most famous female slave narratives and fiction were the works of Harriet Ann Jacobs and Harriet E. Wilson.

From spiritual and secular narratives to autobiography and travel accounts, black women raised their voices to the world. Most often, they proclaimed their experiences in first person (though sometimes in third), but never surrendered their privilege and need to mask the distance, rearrange chronologies, and alter characters—all in the service of individual and collective representation and preservation. They always understood their struggle and their quest as political. The complexities of Harriet Jacobs's life, morever, politically necessitated a pseudonym, her persona part of her survival. Under a nom de plume, she could attack perpetrators of racist violence and sexual abuse with relative impunity. In the biographical narrative, however, I use her given name.

In earlier decades, as more African Americans escaped from the South, advertisements and posters calling for their return could be seen everywhere. Fugitive slaves, known or unknown, became an almost common Northern presence. The Colonization Society was founded in Ohio to return slaves and former slaves to Africa, and efforts were made to register African Americans under the Black Laws.[68]

In the 1840s, attempts to rescue fugitive slaves intensified. By the 1850s, in one critic's words, "escaping slaves were shooting up one street and slave hunters down another."[69] Racial prejudice was common, from which white abolitionists were by no means immune. In this highly charged milieu, Harriet Ann Jacobs, Jarena Lee, Harriet Wilson, Nancy Prince, and Mary Ann Shadd Cary penned their bold, controversial narratives.

■

Biographical Narrative

Harriet Jacobs was born in 1813 near Edenton, North Carolina, to Delilah and Daniel Jacobs. In her own words: "I was born a slave, raised in the Southern hot-bed until I was the mother of two children, sold at the early age of two and four years old."[70] Her father was a skilled carpenter, slave of Dr. Andrew Knox; her mother was owned by Margaret and John Horniblow, the latter a tavern-keeper in Edenton. Jacobs tells us her parents "were termed mulattoes."[71]

After 1819, when Jacobs's mother died, Jacobs and her younger brother, John, lived on the Norcom-Horniblow estate, where Mrs. Horniblow taught Jacobs to read, spell, and sew. Mrs. Horniblow died in 1825, having willed Harriet and John Jacobs to her three-year-old niece, Mary Matilda Norcom (Miss Emily Flint in Jacobs's *Incidents*). Disappointed that her first mistress did not free her as promised, Jacobs learned about owners' self-interest early on, the hard way. She relied for emotional support primarily on "my good grandmother and my affectionate brother."[72] Maternal grandmother Molly Horniblow, a freed slave, owned a house in Edenton, where she worked as a baker.[73] The grandmother's exceptional position in the town seems to have inspired Jacobs's quest for freedom. As exemplified in *Our Nig* and other texts, the close-knit family structure was a treasure and a means to self-empowerment.

Beginning in 1826, Jacobs lived with the Norcoms and suffered persistent attempts at rape by Dr. James Norcom (Dr. Flint in the text) over which she triumphed. Mrs. Norcom psychologically and repeatedly abused her.

Of Dr. Norcom, Jacobs states, "A razor was often held to my throat" (p. 31).[74] After he prevented Jacobs's marriage to a free black man, at fifteen she made a plucky decision to enter a voluntary sexual liaison with Samuel Tredwell Sawyer (Mr. Sands in the text), a neighbor and lawyer. In a situation that denied her power, Jacobs meant to assert herself.[75] "I knew what I did and I did it with deliberate calculation" (p. 54). Jacobs bore two children by Sawyer: Joseph and Louisa Matilda.

Jacobs's relationship with Sawyer pained her grandmother, even though she probably understood Jacobs's sabotage and her desire for a humane physical relationship: "It seemed to me a great thing to have such a friend," says Jacobs of Sawyer. "By degrees, a more tender feeling crept into my heart" (p. 55). Silently resonating is Jacobs's sense of security in having Sawyer as an ally, because she lives in a state of perpetual vulnerability to Dr. Norcom's rapacity. Choosing her own partner foreshadows her later decision to record these experiences; she believed in self-determination at all levels.

Around 1835, when Norcom threatened to remove Joseph and Louisa Matilda from Jacobs's grandmother's home and send them to Auburn, Jacobs ran with them from one escape house to another, finding intermittent respite. Then, incredibly, she managed to remain hidden in her grandmother's attic crawl space for seven years. Not long after, Sawyer bought the children. Elected to Congress, Sawyer did not fulfill his promise to Jacobs to emancipate their children. During her time in hiding, Jacobs sewed, wrote, and read the Bible. She received strength and support during this difficult period from her aunt Nancy:

> "She sent me word never to yield. She said if I persevered I might, perhaps, gain the freedom of my children; and even if I perished doing it, that was better than to leave them to groan under the same persecutions that had blighted my own life."[76]

After a protracted campaign of sabotage against Dr. Norcom that involved dispatching letters to him that purportedly came from her Northern redoubt, Jacobs escaped to the North in 1842 on a boat bound for

New York. There she became a nursemaid to the children of Mary Stace Willis and Nathaniel Parker Willis (Mr. and Mrs. Bruce in *Incidents*). She reestablished contact with her children; Sawyer had taken Louisa Matilda to a free state but had failed to keep his word about emancipating her and her brother. Then Jacobs had several lucky breaks.[77] Her employers entrusted their baby, Imogen, to her care, which provided her with a necessary cover during the era of the 1850 Fugitive Slave Law for traveling to New England. Without success, Dr. Norcom repeatedly went north to retrieve her.

Later, in Rochester, New York, she organized an anti-slavery reading room that put her in touch with abolitionists. Her fugitive brother, John, was also a radical activist. She became close friends with Amy Post but distrusted Harriet Beecher Stowe.[78] Early in 1852, to facilitate Jacobs's security, Mary Willis arranged to buy her for $300. Post urged Jacobs to write her autobiography, *Incidents in the Life of a Slave Girl. Written by Herself.,* which Jacobs brought out in 1861 on her own because of difficulty in finding a publisher. It appeared under the pseudonym Linda Brent, with a preface by Lydia Maria Child, who served as editor.

Similar to Mary Seacole in the Crimean War, Jacobs ministered to the wounded and dying slaves and freemen of the Union Army during the Civil War. She continued her work in Savannah from 1866 to 1868. She died on 7 March, 1897.[79] Her letters to Amy Post chronicle many of her concerns.[80]

Incidents is concerned with four issues: slavery, emancipation, female subjugation, and female self-empowerment. Using a distanced fictional persona, Jacobs presents her point of view; her subscription to democratic principles is evident throughout: legal freedom for all and an end to male tyranny. Although she apologizes profusely for her sexual behavior—"pity me, and pardon me, oh virtuous reader"—her discourse is always doubled. Her slave narrative testifies to experiences that overlap Mary Prince's, but in quite different locales: abuse at the hands of a second master and mistress with more explicit references to attempts at rape by the master and to punishment by a jealous mistress. Insisting on contextualizing her situation, accentuating that she has never been a free agent, she continually exposes differential cultural standards: "I feel that the slave woman ought not to be judged by the same standard as others" (p. 56). In other words, she challenges the concept of true womanhood and insists on comparative judgments. She realized that if she entered a relationship with another white man, there was a chance that she and her children would be manumitted. She is not, she declares, an "article" to be bought and sold, a piece of private property (p. 199).

Jacobs's fight for freedom was representative of thousands of others in her position. Like Mary Prince, she claims the critical vantage point of the ever-struggling oppressed individual. Like Douglass, Brown, and others, Jacobs links slavery to its "complex revolutionary heritage."[81] She also stresses that *Incidents* is a narrative about *her* actions, despite some assistance from white abolitionists.

Jacobs wrote when the abolition debate was at its height, and hers is the only first-person antebellum account by a female who was also a fugitive, a crucial status for slaves and plantocrats alike at mid-century. Her triumph is personal, but she gave voice to all slaves, and especially to sexually abused female slaves.

■

Chronology

1813	Born near Edenton, North Carolina, to parents Delilah (daughter of Molly Horniblow and slave of Margaret Horniblow, an Edenton tavern keeper) and Daniel Jacobs, a skilled carpenter and slave of Dr. Andrew Knox.
1815	John S. Jacobs, Harriet's brother, is born.
1819	Delilah Jacobs dies. Harriet lives with Margaret Horniblow.
1825	Margaret Horniblow wills Jacobs to Mary Matilda Norcom, three-year-old niece. Harriet and her brother move into the Dr. James Norcom household.
1826	Daniel Jacobs dies.
1829	Forbidden to marry and threatened with concubinage, she begins a voluntary sexual relationship with Samuel Tredwell Sawyer, a white neighborhood lawyer. She moves into her grandmother's house. Son Joseph is born.
1833	Louisa Matilda is born.
1835	Escapes to the home of her maternal grandmother, Molly Horniblow, after rejecting Norcom's sexual demands and being sent to a plantation.
1835–1842	Hides for seven years in grandmother's attic crawl space to escape detection. Sawyer buys Jacobs's brother and the children in 1835. The children live with their grandmother.

1842	Escapes to the North and becomes a nursemaid in New York to child Imogen of Mary Stace Willis and Nathaniel Parker Willis.
1843–1844	Fleeing slavecatchers, goes to Boston. Settles with Joseph and Louisa Matilda.
1845	Mrs. Willis dies. Goes with Mr. Willis to England as nursemaid to Imogen.
1849	Moves to Rochester and works in an Anti-Slavery Office and Reading Room run by her brother.
1850	During the period of the Fugitive Slave Law, she becomes close friends with Amy Post, returns to New York City and is reemployed by Mr. Willis. Norcom dies.
1852	Cornelia Grinnell Willis arranges to purchase Harriet Jacobs to set her free. Jacobs is free.
1853	Jacobs starts thinking about composing her life story.
1861	*Incidents in the Life of a Slave Girl. Written by Herself.* is published "for the author."
1862–1865	Nurses members of the Union Army's black military battalions.
1866–1868	Distributes supplies to the needy and organizes schools, nursing homes, and orphanages in Savannah.
1875	John S. Jacobs dies.
1885	Harriet and Louisa Matilda live in Washington, D.C.
1897	Dies.

■ ■ ■

FROM *INCIDENTS IN THE LIFE OF A SLAVE GIRL*

I was born a slave; but I never knew it till six years of happy childhood had passed away. My father was a carpenter, and considered so intelligent and skilful in his trade, that, when buildings out of the common line were to be erected, he was sent for from long distances, to be head workman. On condition of paying his mistress two hundred dollars a year, and supporting himself, he was allowed to work at his trade, and manage his own affairs. His strongest wish was to purchase his children; but, though he several times offered his hard earnings for that purpose; he never succeeded. In complexion my parents were a light shade of brownish yellow, and were termed mulattoes. They lived together in a comfortable home; and, though we were all slaves, I was so fondly shielded that I never dreamed I was a piece of merchandise, trusted to them for safe keeping, and liable to be demanded of them at any moment. I had one brother, William, who was two years younger than myself—a bright, affectionate child. I had also a great treasure in my maternal grandmother, who was a remarkable woman in many respects. She was the daughter of a planter in South Carolina, who, at his death, left her mother and his three children free, with money to go to St. Augustine, where they had relatives. It was during the Revolutionary War; and they were captured on their passage, carried back, and sold to different purchasers. Such was the story my grandmother used to tell me; but I do not remember all the particulars. She was a little girl when she was captured and sold to the keeper of a large hotel. I have often heard her tell how hard she fared during childhood. But as she grew older she evinced so much intelligence, and was so faithful, that her master and mistress could not help seeing it was for their interest to take care of such a valuable piece of property. She became an indispensable personage in the household, officiating in all capacities, from cook and wet nurse to seamstress. She was much praised for her cooking; and her nice crackers became so famous in the neighborhood that many people were desirous of obtaining them. In consequence of numerous requests of this kind, she asked permission of her mistress to bake crackers at night, after all the household work was done; and she obtained leave to do it, provided she would clothe herself and her children from the profits. Upon these terms, after working hard all day for her mistress, she began her midnight bakings, assisted by her two oldest children. The business proved profitable; and each year she laid by a little which was saved for a fund to purchase her children. Her master died, and the property was divided among his heirs. The widow had her dower in the hotel, which she continued to keep open. My grandmother remained in her service as a slave; but her children were divided among her master's children. As she had five, Benjamin, the youngest one, was sold in order that each heir might have an equal portion of dollars and cents. There was so little difference in our ages that he seemed more like my brother than my uncle. He was a bright handsome lad, nearly white; for he inherited the complexion my grandmother had derived from Anglo-Saxon ancestors. Though only ten years old, seven hundred and twenty dollars were paid for him. His sale was a terrible blow to my grandmother; but she was naturally hopeful, and she went to work with renewed energy, trusting in time to be able to purchase some of her children. She had laid up three hundred dollars, which her mistress one day begged as a loan, promising to pay her soon. The reader probably knows that no promise or writing given to a slave is legally binding; for, according to Southern laws, a slave, *being property*, can *hold* no property. When my grandmother lent her hard earnings to her mistress, she trusted solely to her honor. The honor of a slaveholder to a slave!

To this good grandmother I was indebted for many comforts. My brother Willie and I often received portions of the crackers, cakes, and preserves, she made to sell; and after we ceased to be children we were indebted to her for many more important services.

Such were the unusually fortunate circumstances of my early childhood. When I was six years old, my mother died; and then, for the first time, I learned, by the talk around me, that I was a slave. My mother's mistress was the daughter of my grandmother's mistress. She was the foster sister of my mother; they were both nourished at my grandmother's breast. In fact, my mother had been weaned at three months old, that the babe of the mistress might obtain sufficient food. They played together as children; and, when they became women, my mother was a most faithful servant to her whiter foster sister. On her death-bed her mistress promised that her children would never suffer for any thing; and during her lifetime she kept her word. They all spoke kindly of my dead mother, who had been a slave merely in name, but in nature was noble and womanly. I grieved for her, and my young mind was troubled with the thought who would now take care of me and my little brother. I was told that my home was now to be with her mistress; and I found it a happy one. No toilsome or disagreeable duties were imposed upon me. My mistress was so kind to me that I was always glad to do her bidding, and proud to labor for her as much as my young years would permit. I would sit by her side for hours, sewing diligently, with a heart as free from care as that of any freeborn white child. When she thought I was tired, she would send me out to run and jump and away I bounded, to gather berries or flowers to decorate her room. Those were happy days—too happy to last. The slave child had no thought for the morrow; but there came that blight, which too surely waits on every human being born to be a chattel.

When I was nearly twelve years old, my kind mistress sickened and died. As I saw the cheek grow paler, and the eye more glassy, how earnestly I prayed in my heart that she might live! I loved her; for she had been almost like a mother to me. My prayers were not answered. She died, and they buried her in the little churchyard where, day after day, my tears fell upon her grave.

I was sent to spend a week with my grandmother. I was now old enough to begin to think of the future; and again and again I asked myself what they would do with me. I felt sure I should never find a mistress so kind as the one who was gone. She had promised my dying mother that her children should never suffer for any thing; and when I remembered that, and recalled her many proofs of attachment to me, I could not help having some hopes that she had left me free. My friends were almost certain it would be so. They thought she would be sure to do it, on account of my mother's love and faithful service. But, alas! we all know that the memory of a faithful slave does not avail much to save her children from the auction block.

After a brief period of suspense, the will of my mistress was read, and we learned that she had bequeathed me to her sister's daughter, a child of five years old. So vanished our hopes. My mistress had taught me the precepts of God's Word: "Thou shalt love thy neighbor as thyself." "Whatsoever ye would that men should do unto you, do ye even so unto them." But I was her slave, and I suppose she did not recognize me as her neighbor. I would give much to blot out from my memory that one great wrong. As a child, I loved my mistress; and, looking back on the happy days I spent with her, I try to think with less bitterness of this act of injustice. While I was with her, she taught me to read and spell; and for this privilege, which so rarely falls to the lot of a slave, I bless her memory.

She possessed but few slaves; and at her death those were all distributed among her relatives. Five of them were my grandmother's children, and had shared the same milk that nourished her mother's children. Notwithstanding my grandmother's long and faithful service to her owners, not one of her children escaped the auction block. These God-breathing machines are no more, in the sight of their masters, than the cotton they plant, or the horses they tend. . . . [Describes "The New Master & Mistress."]

Dr. Flint, a physician in the neighborhood, had married the sister of my mistress, and I was now the property of their little daughter. It was not without murmuring that I prepared for my new home; and what added to my unhappiness, was the fact that my brother William was purchased by the same family. My father, by his nature, as well as by the habit of transacting business as a skilful mechanic, had more of the feelings of a freeman that is common among slaves. My brother was a spirited boy; and being brought up under such influences, he early detested the name of master and mistress. . . . [Cold new home; William acts defiantly.]

I had been there nearly a year, when a dear little friend of mine was buried. I heard her mother sob, as the clods fell on the coffin of her only child, and I turned away from the grave, feeling thankful that I still had something left to love. I met my grandmother, who said, "Come with me, Linda;" and from her tone I knew that something sad had happened. She led me apart from the people, and then said, "My child, your father is dead." Dead! How could I believe it? He had died so suddenly I had not even heard that he was sick. I went home with my grandmother. My heart rebelled against God, who had taken from me mother, father, mistress and friend. The good grandmother tried to comfort me. "Who knows the ways of God?" said she. "Perhaps they have been kindly taken from the evil days to come." Years afterwards I often thought of this. She promised to be a mother to her grandchildren, so far as she might be permitted to do so; and strengthened by her love, I returned to my master's [Poor conditions; William protests injustice; little care for slaves' food.]

On the appointed day, the customary advertisement was posted up, proclaiming that there would be a "public sale of negroes, horses, &c." Dr. Flint called to tell my grandmother that he was unwilling to wound her feelings by putting her up at auction, and that he would prefer to dispose of her at private sale. My grandmother saw through his hypocrisy; she understood very well that he was ashamed of the job. She was a very spirited woman, and if he was base enough to sell her, when her mistress intended she should be free, she was determined the public should know it. She had for a long time supplied many families with crackers and preserves; consequently, "Aunt Marthy," as she was called, was generally known, and every body who knew her respected her intelligence and good character. Her long and faithful service in the family was well known, and the intention of her mistress to leave her free. When the day of sale came, she took her place among the chattels, and at the first call, she sprang upon the auction-block. Many voices called out, "Shame! Shame! Who is going to sell *you*, aunt Marthy? Don't stand there! That is no place for *you*." Without saying a word, she quietly awaited her fate. No one bid for her. At last, a feeble voice said, "Fifty dollars." It came from a maiden lady, seventy years old, the sister of my grandmother's deceased mistress. She had lived forty years under the same roof with my grandmother; she knew how faithfully she had served her owners, and how cruelly she had been defrauded of her rights; and she resolved to protect her. The auctioneer waited for a higher bid; but her wishes were respected; no one bid above her. . . . [Grandmother set free.]

At that time, my grandmother is just fifty years old. Laborious years had passed since then; and now my brother and I were slaves to the man who had defrauded her of her money, and tried to defraud her of her freedom. One of my mother's sisters, called Aunt Nancy, was also a slave in his family. She was a kind, good aunt to me; and supplied the place of both housekeeper and waiting maid to her mistress. She was, in fact, at the beginning and end of everything.

Mrs. Flint, like many southern women, was totally deficient in energy. She had not strength to superintend her household affairs; but her nerves were so strong, that she could sit in her easy chair and see a woman whipped, till the blood trickled from every stroke of the lash. She was a member of the church; but partaking of the Lord's supper did not seem to put her in a Christian frame of mind. If dinner was not served at the exact time on that particular Sunday, she would station herself in the kitchen, and wait till it was dished, and then spit in all the kettles and pans that had been used for cooking. She did this to prevent the cook and her children from eking out their meager fare with the remains of the gravy and other scrapings. The slave could get nothing to eat except what she chose to give them. Provisions were weighed out by the pound and once, three times a day. I can assure you she gave them no chance to eat wheat bread from her flour barrel. She knew how many biscuits a quart of flour would make, and exactly what size they ought to be.

Dr. Flint was an epicure. The cook never sent a dinner to his table without fear and trembling; for if there happened to be a dish not to his liking, he would either order her to be whipped, or compel her to eat every mouthful of it in his presence. The poor, hungry creature might not have objected to eating it; but she did object to having her master cram it down her throat till she choked. . . . [The Flints' brutal treatment of slaves; grandmother offers spiritual comfort; Dr. Flint preys sexually on Jacobs/Brent.]

I remember the first time I was punished. It was in the month of February. My grandmother had taken my old shoes, and replaced them with a new pair. I needed them; for several inches of snow had fallen, and it still continued to fall. When I walked through Mrs. Flint's room, their creaking grated harshly on her refined nerves. She called me to her, and asked what I had about me that made such a horrid noise. I told her it was my new shoes. "Take them off," said she, "and if you put them on again, I'll throw them into the fire."

I took them off, and my stockings also. She then sent me a long distance, on an errand. As I went through the snow, my bare feet tingled. That night I was very hoarse, and I went to bed thinking the next day would find me sick, perhaps dead. What was my grief on waking to find myself quite well!

I had imagined if I died, or was laid up for some time, that my mistress would feel a twinge of remorse that she had so hated "the little imp," as she styled me. It was my ignorance of that mistress that gave rise to such extravagant imaginings.

Dr. Flint occasionally had high prices offered for me; but he always said, "She don't belong to me. She is my daughter's property, and I have no right to sell her." Good, honest man! . . . [Uncle Benjamin escapes, is recaptured, and jailed six months. Grandmother intervenes, Benjamin then escapes to New York, meets brother Philip, who returns home. His freedom is purchased by grandmother.]

Every where the years bring to all enough of sin and sorrow; but in slavery the very dawn of life is darkened by these shadows. Even the little child, who is accustomed to wait on her mistress and her children, will learn, before she is twelve years old, why it is that her mistress hates such and such a one among the slaves. Perhaps the child's own mother is among those hated ones. She listens to violent outbreaks of jealous passion, and cannot help understanding what is the cause. She will become prematurely knowing in evil things. Soon she will learn to tremble when she hears her master's footfall. She will be compelled to realize that she is no longer a child. If God has bestowed beauty upon her, it will prove her greatest curse. That which commands admiration in the white woman only hastens the degradation of the female slave. I know that some are too much brutalized by slavery to feel the humiliation of their position; but many slaves feel it most acutely, and shrink from the memory of it. I cannot tell how much I suffered in the presence of these wrongs, nor how I am still pained by the retrospect. My master met me at every turn, reminding me that I belonged to him, and swearing by heaven and earth that he would compel me to submit to him. If I went out for a breath of fresh air, after a day of unwearied toil, his footsteps dogged me. If I knelt by my mother's grave, his dark shadow fell on me even there. The light heart which nature had given me became heavy with sad forebodings. The other slaves in my master's house noticed the change. Many of them pitied me; but none dared to ask the cause. They had no need to inquire. They knew too well the guilty practices under that roof; and they were aware that to speak of them was an offence that never went unpunished.

I longed for some one to confide. I would have given the world to have laid my head on my grandmother's faithful bosom, and told her all my troubles. But Dr. Flint swore he would kill me, if I was not silent as the grave. Then, although my grandmother was all in all to me, I feared her as well as loved her. I had been accustomed to look up to her with a respect bordering upon awe. I was very young, and felt shamefaced about telling her such impure things, especially as I knew her to be very strict on such subjects. Moreover, she was a woman of high spirit. She was usually very quiet in her demeanor; but if her indignation was once roused, it was not very easily quelled. I had been told that she once chased a white gentleman with a loaded pistol, because he insulted one of her daughters. I dreaded the consequences of a violent outbreak; and both pride and fear kept me silent. But though I did not confide in my grandmother, and even evaded her vigilant watchfulness and inquiry, her presence in the neighborhood was some protection to me. Though she had been a slave, Dr. Flint was afraid of her. . . . [Injustice of slavery repeated; Dr. Flint harasses Jacobs/Brent—Mrs. Flint is jealous. Dr. Flint threatens death when Jacobs/Brent wants to leave.]

I had entered my sixteenth year, and every day it became more apparent that my presence was intolerable to Mrs. Flint. Angry words frequently passed between her and her husband. He had never punished me himself, and he would not allow any body else to punish me. In that respect, she was never satisfied; but, in her angry moods, no terms were too vile for her to bestow upon me. Yet I, whom she detested so bitterly, had far more pity for her than he had, whose duty it was to make her life happy. I never wronged her, or wished to wrong her; and one word of kindness from her would have brought me to her feet.

After repeated quarrels between the doctor and his wife, he announced his intention to take his youngest daughter, then four years old, to sleep in his apartment. It was necessary that a servant should sleep in the same room, to be on hand if the child stirred. I was selected for that office, and informed for what purpose that arrangement had been made. By managing to keep within sight of people, as much as possible, during the day time, I had hitherto succeeded in eluding my master, though a razor was often held to my throat to force me to change this line of policy. At night I slept by the side of my great aunt, where I felt safe. He was too prudent to come into her room. She was an old woman, and had been in the family many years. Moreover, as a married man, and a professional man, he deemed it necessary to save appearances in some degree. But he resolved to remove the obstacle in the way of his scheme; and he thought he had planned it so that he should evade suspicion. He was well aware how much I prized my refuge at the side of my old aunt, and he determined to dispossess me of it. The first night the doctor had the little child in his room alone. The next morning, I was ordered to take my station as nurse the following night. A kind Providence interposed in my favor. During the day Mrs. Flint heard of this new arrangement, and a storm followed. I rejoiced to hear it rage.

After a while my mistress sent for me to come to her room. Her first question was, "Did you know you were to sleep in the doctor's room?"

"Yes, ma'am."

"Who told you?"

"My master."

"Will you answer truly all the questions I ask?"

"Yes, ma'am."

"Tell me, then, as you hope to be forgiven, are you innocent of what I have accused you?"

"I am."

She handed me a Bible, and said, "Lay your hand on your heart, kiss this holy book, and swear before God that you tell me the truth."

I took the oath she required, and I did it with a clear conscience.

"You have taken God's holy word to testify your innocence," said she. "If you have deceived me, beware! Now take this stool, sit down, look me directly in the face, and tell me all that has passed between your master and you."

I did as she ordered. As I went on with my account her color changed frequently, she wept, and sometimes groaned. She spoke in tones so sad, that I was touched by her grief. The tears came to my eyes; but I soon convinced that her emotions arose from anger and wounded pride. She felt that her marriage vows were desecrated, her dignity insulted; but she had no compassion for the poor victim of her husband's perfidy. She pitied herself as a martyr; but she was incapable of feeling for the condition of shame and misery in which her unfortunate, helpless slave was placed.

Yet perhaps she had some touch of feeling for me; for when the conference was ended, she spoke kindly, and promised to protect me. I should have been much comforted by this assurance if I could have had confidence in it; but my experiences in slavery had filled me with distrust. She was not a very refined woman, and had not much control over her passions. I was an object of her jealousy, and consequently, of her hatred; and I knew I could not expect kindness and confidence from her under the circumstances in which I was placed. I could not blame her. Slaveholders' wives feel as other women would under similar circumstances. The fire of her temper kindled from small sparks, and now the flame became so intense that the doctor was obliged to give up his intended arrangement. . . . [Dr. Flint refuses to allow Jacobs/Brent to marry a free carpenter who wants to buy her freedom. Beaten for being presumptuous.]

And now, reader, I come to a period in my unhappy life, which I would gladly forget if I could. The remembrance fills me with sorrow and shame. It pains me to tell you of it; but I have promised to tell you the truth, and I will do it honestly, let it cost me what it may. I will not try to screen myself behind the plea of compulsion from a master; for it was not so. Neither can I plead ignorance or thoughtlessness. For years, my master had done his utmost to pollute my mind with foul images, and to destroy the pure principles inculcated by my grandmother, and the good mistress of my childhood. The influences of slavery had had the same effect on me that they had on other young girls; they had made me prematurely knowing, concerning the evil ways of the world. I knew what I did, and I did it with deliberate calculation. . . . [She deplores how slavery robs an individual of purity and security.]

I have told you that Dr. Flint's persecutions and his wife's jealousy had given rise to some gossip in the neighborhood. Among others, it chanced that a white unmarried gentleman had obtained some knowledge of the circumstances in which I was placed. He knew my grandmother, and often spoke to me in the street. He became interested in me, and asked questions about my master, which I answered in part. He expressed a great deal of sympathy, and a wish to aid me. He constantly sought opportunities to see me, and wrote to me frequently. I was a poor slave girl, only fifteen years old.

So much attention from a superior person was, of course, flattering; for human nature is the same in all. I also felt grateful for his sympathy, and encouraged by his kind words. It seemed to me a great thing to have such a friend. By degrees, a more tender feeling crept into my heart. He was an educated and eloquent gentleman; too eloquent, alas, for the poor slave girl who trusted in him. Of course I saw whither all this was tending. I knew the impassable gulf between us; but to be an object of interest to a man who is not married, and who is not her master, is agreeable to the pride and feelings of a slave, if her miserable situation has left her any pride or sentiment. It seems less degrading to give one's self, than to submit to compulsion. There is something akin to freedom in having a lover who has no control over you, except that which he gains by kindness and attachment. A master may treat you as rudely as he pleases, and you dare not speak; moreover, the wrong does not seem so great with an unmarried man, as with one who has a wife to be made unhappy. There may be sophistry in all this; but the condition of a slave confuses all principles of morality, and, in fact, renders the practice of them impossible.

When I found that my master had actually begun to build the lonely cottage, other feelings mixed with those I have described. Revenge, and calculations of interest, were added to flattered vanity and sincere gratitude for kindness. I knew nothing would enrage Dr. Flint so much as to know that I favored another; and it was something to triumph over my tyrant even in that small way. I thought he would revenge himself by selling me, and I was sure my friend, Mr. Sands, would buy me. He was a man of more generosity and feelings than my master, and I thought my freedom could be easily obtained from him. The crisis of my fate now came so near that I was desperate. I shuddered to think of being the mother of children that would be owned by my old tyrant. I knew that as soon as a new fancy took him, his victims were sold far off to get rid of them; especially if they had children. I had seen several women sold, with his babies at the breast. He never allowed his offspring by slaves to remain long in sight of himself and his wife. Of a man who was not my master I could ask to have my children well supported; and in this case, I felt confident I should obtain the boon. I also felt quite sure that they would be made free. With all these thoughts revolving in my mind, and seeing no other way of escaping the doom I so much dreaded, I made a headlong plunge. . . . [She takes a white lover, Mr. Sands, which causes her deep anguish.] Pity me, and pardon me, O virtuous reader! You never knew what it is to be a slave; to be entirely unprotected by law or custom; to have the laws reduce you to the condition of a chattel, entirely subject to the will of another. You never exhausted your ingenuity in avoiding the snares, and eluding the power of a hated tyrant; you never shuddered at the sound of his footsteps, and trembled within hearing of his voice. I know I did wrong. No one can feel it more sensibly than I do. The painful and humiliating memory will haunt me to my dying day. Still, in looking back, calmly, on the events of my life, I feel that the slave woman ought not to be judged by the same standard as others. . . .

The months passed on. I had many unhappy hours. I secretly mourned over the sorrow I was bringing on my grandmother, who had tried to shield me from harm. I knew that I was the greatest comfort of her old age, and that it was a source of pride to her that I had not degraded myself, like most of the slaves. I wanted to confess to her that I was no longer worthy of her love; but could not utter the dreaded words.

As for Dr. Flint, I had a feeling of satisfaction and triumph in the thought of telling *him*. From time to time he told me of his intended arrangements, and I was silent. At last, he came and told me the cottage was completed, and ordered me to go to it. I told him I would never enter it. He said, "I have heard enough of such talk as that. You shall go, if you are carried by force; and you shall remain there."

I replied, "I will never go there. In a few months I shall be a mother."

He stood and looked at me in dumb amazement, and left the house without a word. I thought I should be happy in my triumph over him. But now that the truth was out, and my relatives would hear of it, I felt wretched. . . .

I went to my grandmother. . . . She exclaimed, "O Linda! has it come to this? I had rather see you dead than to see you as you now are. You are a disgrace to your dead mother." She tore from my fingers my mother's wedding ring and her silver thimble. "Go away!" she exclaimed, "and never come to my house again.". . . [Receives solace from mother's friend and returns to her grandmother's house. Flint persists. Nat Turner insurrection provokes fear and retribution; Christianity is a comfort.]

My children [by lover Mr. Sands] grew finely; and Dr. Flint would often say to me, with an exulting smile, "These brats will bring me a handsome sum of money one of these days.". . . [She returns, out of fear that her children will be sold. Children remain with grandmother; Jacobs/Brent plans an escape.]

Again and again I had traversed those dreary twelve miles, to and from the town; and all the way, I was meditating upon some means of escape that ingenuity could devise to effect our purchase, but all their plans had proved abortive. . . . [Dr. Flint is suspicious. Jacobs/Brent visits parents' gravesites. Young Mr. Flint marries.]

My plan was to conceal myself at the house of a friend, and remain there a few weeks till the search was over. My hope was that the doctor would get discouraged, and, for fear of losing my value, and also of subsequently finding my children among the missing, he would consent to sell us; and I knew somebody would buy us. . . . [Grandmother counsels to endure; Jacobs/Brent discovers children will be "broken" in. Flees to a friend's house.]

My grandmother's house was searched from top to bottom. As my trunk was empty, they concluded I had taken my clothes with me. Before ten o'clock every vessel northward bound was thoroughly examined, and the law against harboring fugitives was read to all on board. . . . [Dr. Flint posts notice of reward for finder of Jacobs/Brent.]

The search for me was kept up with more perseverance than I had anticipated. I began to think that escape was impossible. . . . [Friend of grandmother's aids her escape North.]

I received a message to leave my friend's house at such an hour, and go to a certain place where a friend would be waiting for me. As a matter of prudence no names were mentioned. I had no means of conjecturing who I was to meet, or where I was going. I did not like to move thus blindfolded, but I had no choice. It would not do for me to remain where I was. I disguised myself, summoned up courage to meet the worst, and went to the appointed place. My friend Betty was there; she was the last person I expected to see. We hurried along in silence. The pain in my leg was so intense that it seemed as if I should drop, but fear gave me strength. We reached the house and entered unobserved. Her first words were: "Honey, now you is safe. Dem devils ain't coming to search *dis* house. When I get you into missis' safe place, I will bring some nice hot supper. I specs you need it after all dis skeering." Betty's vocation led her to think eating the most important thing in life. She did not realize that my heart was too full for me to care much about supper.

The mistress came to meet us, and led me upstairs to a small room over her own sleeping apartment. "You will be safer here, Linda," she said; "I keep this room to store away things that are out of use. The girls are not accustomed to be sent to it, and they will not suspect any thing unless they hear some noise. I always keep it locked, and Betty shall take care of the key. But you must be very careful, for my sake as well as your own; and you must never tell my secret; for it would ruin me and my family. . . . [Stowed away.]

I was daily hoping to hear that my master had sold my children; for I knew who was on the watch to buy them. But Dr. Flint cared even more for revenge than he did for money. My brother William, and the good aunt who had served his family twenty years, and my little Benny, and Ellen, who was a little over two years old, were thrust into jail, as a means of compelling my relatives to give some information about me . . . . [Dr. Flint goes to New York in pursuit. William saved from trader by Uncle Philip. Children safe. Philip arrested.]

The search for me was renewed. Something had excited suspicions that I was in the vicinity. They searched the house I was in. I heard their steps and their voices. At night, when all were asleep, Betty came to release me from my place of confinement. The fright I had undergone, the constrained posture, and the dampness of the ground, made me ill for several days. My uncle was soon after taken out of prison; but the movements of all my relatives, and of all our friends, were very closely watched. We all saw that I could not remain where I was much longer. . . . [Escapes in disguise, by boat, with help of old friends.]

A small shed had been added to my grandmother's house years ago. Some boards were laid across the joints at the top, and between these boards and the roof was a very small garret, never occupied by any thing but rats and mice. It was a pent roof, covered with nothing but shingles, according to the southern custom for such buildings. The garret was only nine feet long and seven wide. The highest part was three feet high, and sloped down abruptly to the loose board floor. There was no admission for either light or air. My uncle Philip, who was a carpenter, had very skillfully made a concealed trap-door, which communicated with the storeroom. He had been doing this while I was waiting in the swamp. The storeroom opened upon a piazza. To this hole I was conveyed as soon as I entered the house. The air was stifling; the darkness total. A bed had been spread on the floor. I could sleep quite comfortably on one side; but the slope was so sudden that I could not turn on the other without hitting the roof. The rats and mice ran over my bed; but I was weary, and I slept such a sleep as the wretched may, when a tempest has passed over them. Morning came. I knew it only by the noises I heard; for in my small den day and night were all the same. I suffered for air even more than for light. But I was not comfortless. I heard the voices of my children. There was joy and there was sadness in the sound. It made my tears flow. How I longed to speak to them! I was eager to look on their faces; but there was no hole, no crack through which I could peep. This continued darkness was oppressive. It seemed horrible to sit or lie in a cramped position day after day, without one gleam of light. Yet I would have chosen this, rather than my lot as a slave, though white people considered it an easy one; and it was so compared with the fate of others. I was never cruelly over worked; I was never lacerated with the whip from head to foot; I was never so beaten and bruised that I could not turn from one side to the other; I never had my heel-strings cut to prevent my running away; I was never chained to a log and forced to drag it about, while I toiled in the fields from morning till night; I was never branded with hot iron, or torn by bloodhounds. On the contrary, I had always been kindly treated, and tenderly cared for, until I came into the hands of Dr. Flint. I had never wished for freedom till then. But though my life in slavery was comparatively devoid of hardships, God pity the woman who is compelled to lead such a life!

My food was passed up to me through the trap-door my uncle had contrived; and my grandmother, my uncle Phillip, and aunt Nancy would seize such opportunities as they could, to mount up there and chat with me at the opening. But of course this was not safe in the daytime. It must all be done in darkness. It was impossible for me to move in an erect position, but I crawled about my den for exercise. One day I hit my head against something, and found it was a gimlet. My uncle had left it sticking there when he made the trap-door. I was as rejoiced as Robinson Crusoe could have been at finding a treasure. It put a lucky thought into my head. I said to myself, "Now I will have some light. Now I will see my children." I did not dare to begin my work during the daytime, for fear of attracting attention. But I groped around; and having found the side next to the street, where I could frequently see my children, I stuck the gimlet in and waited for evening. I bored three rows of holes, one above another; then I bored out the interstices between. I thus succeeded in making one hole about an inch long and an inch broad. I sat by it till late into the night, to enjoy the little whiff of air that floated in. In the morning I watched for my children. The first person I saw in the street was Dr. Flint. I had a shuddering, superstitious feeling that it was a bad omen. Several familiar faces passed by. At last I heard the merry laugh of children, and presently two sweet little faces were looking up at me, as though they knew I was there, and were conscious of the joy they imparted. How I longed to *tell* them I was there!

My condition was now a little improved, but for weeks I was tormented by hundreds of little red insects fine as a needle's point, that pierced through my skin and produced an intolerable burning. The good grandmother gave me her tease and cooling medicines, and finally I got rid of them. The heat of my den was intense, for nothing but thin shingles protected me from the scorching summer's sun. But I had my consolations. Through my peeping-hole I could watch the children, and when they were near enough, I could hear their talk. Aunt Nancy brought me all the news she could hear at Dr. Flint's. From her I learned that the doctor had written to New York to a colored woman, who had been born and raised in our neighborhood, and had breathed his contaminating atmosphere. He offered her a reward if she could find out anything about me. . . . [Elaborate foils to confuse Dr. Flint. Jacobs/Brent glimpses scenes of Christmas from her peep hole.]

I hardly expect that the reader will credit me, when I affirm that I lived in that little dismal hole, almost deprived of light and air, and with no space to move my limbs, for nearly seven years. . . . [Fanny, a friend, stowed away nearby; Peter offers chance to escape.] I was to escape in a vessel. . . . For the last time I went to my nook. Its desolate appearance no longer chilled me, for the light of hope had risen in my soul. Yet, even with the blessed prospect of freedom before me, I felt very sad at leaving forever that old homestead, where I had been sheltered so long by the dear old grandmother; where I had dreamed my first young dream of love; and where, after that had faded away, my children came to twine themselves so closely round my desolate heart. As the hour approached for me to leave, I again descended to the storeroom. My grandmother and Benny were there. She took me by the hand, and said, "Linda, let us pray." We knelt down together, with my child pressed to my heart, and my other arm round the faithful, loving friend I was about to leave forever. On no other occasion has it ever been my lot to listen to so fervent a supplication for mercy and protection. It thrilled through my heart, and inspired me with trust in God. . . . [Waylaid in Philadelphia. She is taken in by the Durhams, antislavery friends; reaches New York.]

When we arrived in New York, I was half crazed by the crowd of coachmen calling out, "Carriage, ma'am?". . . [Parts with Fanny; meets daughter Ellen.] So there was quite a company of us, all from my grandmother's neighborhood. These friends gathered round me and questioned me eagerly. They laughed, they cried, and they shouted. They thanked God that I had got away from my persecutors and was safe on Long Island. It was a day of great excitement. How different from the silent days I had passed in my dreary den. . . . [Asks Dr. Flint her selling price; he wants her to return and be sold.]

My greatest anxiety now was to obtain employment. . . . [Taken in by Bruces to nurse their newborn; Bruces' kindness; visits Ellen; son Benny arrives in New York; vacations with Bruces; Flint pursues her to New York; she escapes to Boston, temporarily, with children.]

[But] I could not feel safe in New York, and I accepted the offer of a friend, that we should share expenses and keep house together. I represented to Mrs. Hobbs that Ellen [her daughter] must have some schooling, and must remain with me for that purpose. She felt ashamed of being unable to read, or spell at her age, so instead of sending her to school with Benny, I instructed her myself till she was fitted to enter an intermediate school. The winter passed pleasantly, while I was busy with my needle, and my children with their books. . . . [Mrs. Bruce dies. Having ensured children's safety, Jacobs/Brent accompanies Mr. Bruce and child to England for ten-month stay.]

We had a tedious winter passage [from England], and from the distance specters seemed to rise up on the shores of the United States. It is a sad feeling to be afraid of one's native country. We arrived in New York safely, and I hastened to Boston to look after my children. . . . [Benny leaves trade profession. Emily Flint, now Mrs. Dodge, still tries to bait Jacobs/Brent home.]

For two years my daughter and I supported ourselves comfortably in Boston. At the end of that time, my brother William offered to send Ellen to a boarding school It required a great effort for me to consent to part with her, for I had few near ties, and it was her presence that made my two little rooms seem home-like. But my judgment prevailed over my selfish feelings. I made preparations for her departure. . . . [Ellen attends school in New York; Jacobs/Brent returns to service with Bruce family (new wife, new baby). William goes to California. Jacobs/Brent has problematic "slave status" in free state; Dr. Flint still vigilant. Grandmother's letters. Dr. Flint dies. Jacobs/Brent fears Dodge family will claim her. Flees again to Northeast. Jacobs/Brent finally free.]

My grandmother lived to rejoice in my freedom; but not long after, a letter came with a black seal. She had gone "where the wicked cease from troubling, and the weary are at rest."

Time passed on, and a paper came to me from the south, containing an obituary notice of my uncle Phillip. It was the only case I ever knew of such a honor conferred upon a colored person. It was written by one of his friends, and contained these words: "Now that death has laid him low, they call him a good man and a useful citizen; but what are eulogies to the black man, when the world has faded from his vision? It does not require man's praise to obtain rest in God's kingdom." So they called a colored man a citizen! Strange words to be uttered in that region!

Reader, my story ends with freedom; not in the usual way, with marriage. I and my children are not free! We are as free from the power of the slaveholders as are the white people of the north; and though that, according to my ideas, is not saying a great deal, it is a vast improvement in my condition. The dream of my life is not yet realized. I do not sit with my children in a home of my own. I still long for a hearthstone of my own, however humble. I wish it for my children's sake far more than for my own. But God so orders circumstances as to keep me with my friend Mrs. Bruce. Love, duty, gratitude, also bind me to her side. It is a privilege to serve her who pities my oppressed people, and who has bestowed the inestimable boon of freedom on me and my children.

It has been painful for me, in many ways, to recall the dreary years I passed in bondage. I would gladly forget them if I could. Yet the retrospection is not altogether without solace; for with those gloomy recollections come tender memories of my good old grandmother, like light, fleecy clouds floating over a dark and troubled sea.

6

Harriet E. Adams Wilson (1824 or 1828–1868/1870?)

■

Introduction

THE STRUGGLE TO RESCUE Harriet E. Adams Wilson from obscurity is paradigmatic of the larger struggle to give the accomplishments and texts of black writers their appropriate place in history. Wilson's is a particularly good case in point because virtually nothing was known about her until Henry Louis Gates, Jr., published a contemporary edition of her novel, *Our Nig*, that included a complex reconstruction of Wilson's life. Several years later, Barbara White's additions to the reconstruction made the context of *Our Nig* yet more comprehensible, especially regarding the double standard of such white abolitionists as the Hayward family members. Compellingly requestioning the status of *Our Nig* as fiction based on the biographical data she has uncovered, White sketches important parallels between *Incidents* and *Our Nig* that call for a reclassification of the work. Like Jacobs, Wilson used changed names to protect herself, and hence her writing was pronounced fiction. White convincingly speculates that the shifting point of view from third person to occasional first person could be the result of the rewriting of an earlier first-person draft.[82]

In terms of the African American cultural tradition, *Our Nig* is remarkably innovative. Henry Louis Gates, Jr. declared:

> *Our Nig* is a major example of generic fusion in which a woman writer appropriated black male (the slave narrative) and white female (the sentimental novel) forms and revised these into a synthesis at once peculiarly black and female. For Harriet Wilson is not only the first black woman novelist in the tradition, she is also the first major innovator of fictional narrative form.

Wilson's work ventilates the question of black women's authority and whether fiction or autobiography was more effective in publicizing the complexity of black cultural lives.

Moreover, the title of the work parodies "authenticating" statements by friends as well as white society itself. *Our Nig* tells white society/readers: "You think you own heroines like Frado and can speak of them disrespectfully, but I will expose that false belief and claim." The "authenticating" documents, that is, hold a racist society up to ridicule. It is a society without vision, short on self-knowledge, that will not voluntarily recognize its own members.

■

Biographical Narrative

Harriet E. Adams was born in Milford, New Hampshire, (or possibly in Virginia), probably between 1824 and 1828. She spent her childhood as an indentured servant in the household of Nehemiah Hayward, a farming family. She is listed as a "free colored person" in the 1840 Milford census. By the time she was eighteen, according to a corroborating acquaintance mentioned in *Our Nig*, her health was seriously impaired because of harsh servitude, a condition she shared with at least Mary Prince and Nancy Prince. The 1850 "Report of the Overseers of the Poor" shows that a family with whom Harriet Adams lived was reimbursed $43.84 by the town (the Haywards had left Milford in 1845). In 1851, Harriet Adams married Thomas Wilson. In late May or early June 1852, George Mason Wilson was born in Goffstown, probably at the Hillsborough County Farm, a pauper facility. Wilson and her son remained at Hillsborough after George was born until Thomas Wilson returned briefly, brought them to another town, then left again. Wilson gave her son up for adoption at this point.

By 1855, the list of "Support of Poor not at Pauper Farm" contains an entry for Harriet E. Wilson, $45.55. George Wilson, aged three, was admitted to the Hillsborough County Farm in August 1855; conditions there were deplorable, especially after the 1853 smallpox epidemic. Economic straits forced Wilson to move to Boston to find a means to an income that would permit her to retrieve her son. She took up dressmaking and also wrote a novel that recorded her experiences, *Our Nig; or, Sketches from the Life of a Free Black, In a Two-Story White House, North. Showing That Slavery's Shadows Fall Even There* by "Our Nig" (1859). Tellingly close to home, she documents the racial and psychological brutality suffered by an indentured black or mulatto woman named Frado, who lives in the North.[83]

On 18 August 1859, Wilson registered the copyright of her work, which was published on 5 September. She was probably the first African American to publish a novel in the United States and "one of the first of the two black women to publish a novel in any language."[84] George Mason Wilson died in February 1860 of "fever." His parents named in the death records are Thomas and Harriet E. Wilson; his "color" is designated "black."

Hailed by the *New York Times* in 1982 as a "black literary landmark," *Our Nig* draws from the white, sentimental tradition while flouting its conventions about homogeneous womanhood. Poignantly yet boldly sharing difficulties she encountered trying to bring the work to the market, she accentuates the importance she attached to possessing plural identities: mother, writer, impoverished person, innovator, unwell person. "Deserted by kindred, disabled by failing health, I am forced to some experiment which shall aid me in maintaining myself and my child without extinguishing this feeble life" (p. x).

Written in a shifting third person that affords authorial distance, *Our Nig* tells the story of Frado, a free mulatto woman who grows up in a relatively well-to-do New England household as an indentured servant. It graphically documents young Frado's life under the "she-devil" Mrs. Bellmont, who is "wholly imbued with *Southern* principles." Further, it illumines the great similiarity between the experiences of slaves and of indentured servants.[85] The scenario stresses the problematics of Frado's supposedly "free" status and the license it affords employers. Permanent injury and an autonomous will are the telling consequences.

White's evidence regarding the Hayward family shows that Wilson's accounts in *Our Nig* are literally true; only the names are changed. Ironically, it seems, given their behavior, the Hayward family had abolitionist connections. Such information makes Jacobs's seemingly puzzling critique of abolitionists' racism much more focal than it has been thought. Jonas Hayward, for example (Lewis Bellmont in *Our Nig*), was selling tickets to abolitionist concerts while his parents kept a slave at home. Thus Wilson is rendering an accurate account of white female hypocrisy, of pseudoabolitionists who brutalize their domestic servant with impunity. Jacobs's famous reservations about Harriet Beecher Stowe take on a different resonance in light of these new findings about Harriet Wilson.[86] Did Jacobs think that the Haywards and Stowe had shared certain unspoken attitudes?

Let me back up for a moment and sketch the action of *Our Nig*. A white woman, Meg Smith, is married to Jim, a "kind-hearted African." She gives birth to a "beautiful mulatto" named Frado and one other child, but Jim dies of consumption and Mag finds herself in straitened circumstances. She marries Seth Shipley, Jim's colleague, and they decide to leave the town and give the children to the Bellmont family who live in the house designated in the book's title.

Perhaps because of her high spirits, Frado incenses Mrs. Bellmont and her daughter Mary, and the conflicts seriously disrupt the family; sometimes Mr. Bellmont, sometimes his sister Abby, and, most likely, his son James take Frado's part. Her off-rhyme name that combines the words "free" and "do" resonates in these early scenes when Frado defends herself.

While learning to read, write, spell, and do arithmetic, by the time she is fourteen Frado is not only washing, ironing, baking and [doing] "the common etcetera of household duties" (p. 63), but being persistently scolded and whipped by Mrs. Bellmont. Schoolbooks are her refuge (p. 115).

The years of brutality take a hard physical toll, despite Frado's independent spirit and efforts to claim agency. Even when she leaves at eighteen, she has difficulty making a living because of protracted maltreatment and has to return. Still in very poor health, she marries Samuel, who later deserts his pregnant wife. Eventually, "a plain, poor single woman" taught Frado, a now "invalid mulatto," to sew with some expertise. She learns to make straw bonnets, a skill that brings about her self-sufficiency. Liberation through sewing and economic independence is furthered by Wilson's other avenue of creativity—writing. She chronicles her life to try to retrieve her son from the poorhouse. But she is unsuccessful.

Wilson seems in the last chapter to speak in her own voice. It is as if she and the third-person narrator speak separately and then as one. Whether this movement from first to third person and back is deliberate is unclear. Could Wilson have cleverly surmised that this ambiguity would "give the game away," that shifting as if from an earlier first-person draft to a later, more assured third-person draft would provide the firmest code to her authentic identity? Such a doubled narrative technique, in any event, serves her well. That careful voice joins the voices of the three others who write corroborative appendices to "authenticate," for disbelievers, Wilson's creativity and her personal "reality."[87]

Utilizing fiction as an appropriate mask for a harsh quotidian existence, *Our Nig* initiates a tradition of black female chronicles in that hundred-year period of the earliest writings. Treading a precarious tightrope between fiction and autobiography, Wilson boldly introduces a black man married to a white woman, then in an act of daring political integrity, places the protagonist, their daughter, in a heavily encoded two-faced abolitionist household.

A rich contemporary debate continues about the role played by Frado in the text, whether her character confronts white bigotry and/or to what extent she is able to develop a self-identity.[88]

That debate aside, Wilson's overt reason for writing—to earn enough to take her son out of the county pauper farm—has now been incontrovertibly confirmed. Arguably too, Wilson's title, *Our Nig*, gives her the last word, as it were, on the cover, as do the book's final pages.

Wilson's name appears in the *Boston City Listing* for 1863, but has not been found in any subsequent record. Her death is conjectured to have occurred in 1868 or 1870.

▪

Chronology

Between 1824 and 1828	Born in New Hampshire or Virginia. Possibly spent childhood as a servant indentured to the well-to-do farming family headed by Nehemiah Hayward, some members of which were abolitionists. Receives harsh treatment detrimental to her health.
1840	Appears in Milford Census as a "free colored person" working for the Hayward family.
1851	Marries Thomas Wilson of Virginia, who subsequently goes to sea.
1852	Gives birth to George Mason Wilson in Goffstown, New Hampshire, probably at the Hillsborough County Farm, a home for paupers.
1853	Smallpox outbreak in Goffstown; Thomas Wilson returns briefly and moves family to another town.
1853–1855	George Wilson temporarily given to foster parents.
1855	George Wilson admitted to the Hillsbough County Farm.
1856–1863	Harriet Wilson moves to Boston and lives there seven years; listed in Boston City Directory as widowed.
18 August 1859	Registers the copyright of *Our Nig*.
5 September 1859	*Our Nig* published by George E. Rand and Avery Company, Boston.

1860	George Mason Wilson dies "of bilious fever."
1868 or 1870	Information about Wilson's last years is incomplete and under some debate.

■ ■ ■

FROM *OUR NIG; OR, SKETCHES FROM THE LIFE OF A FREE BLACK, IN A TWO-STORY WHITE HOUSE, NORTH. SHOWING THAT SLAVERY'S SHADOWS FALL EVEN THERE.*

Lonely Mag Smith! See her as she walks with downcast eyes and heavy heart. It was not always thus. She *had* a loving, trusting heart. Early deprived of parental guardianship, far removed from relatives, she was left to guide her tiny boat over life's surges alone and inexperienced. As she merged into womanhood, unprotected, uncherished, uncared for, there fell on her ear the music of love, awakening an intensity of emotion long dormant. It whispered of an elevation before unaspired to; of ease and plenty her simple heart had never dreamed of as hers. She knew the voice of her charmer, so ravishing, sounded far above her. It seemed like an angel's, alluring her upward and onward. She thought she could ascend to him and become an equal. She surrendered to him a priceless gem, which he proudly garnered as a trophy, with those of other victims, and left her to her fate. The world seemed full of hateful deceivers and crushing arrogance. Conscious that the great bond of union to her former companions was severed, that the disdain of others would be insupportable, she determined to leave the few friends she possessed, and seek an asylum among strangers. Her offspring came unwelcomed, and before its nativity numbered weeks, it passed from earth, ascending to a purer and better life.

"God be thanked," ejaculated Mag, as she saw its breathing cease; "no one can taunt *her* with my ruin."

Blessed release! may we all respond. How many pure, innocent children not only inherit a wicked heart of their own, claiming life-long scrutiny and restraint, but are heirs also of parental disgrace and calumny, from which only long years of patient endurance in paths of rectitude can disencumber them.

Mag's new home was soon contaminated by the publicity of her fall; she had a feeling of degradation oppressing her; but she resolved to be circumspect, and try to regain in a measure what she had lost. Then some foul tongue would jest of her shame, and averted looks and cold greetings disheartened her. She saw she could not bury in forgetfulness her misdeed, so she resolved to leave her home and seek another in the place she at first fled from.

Alas, how fearful are we to be first in extending a helping hand to those who stagger in the mires of infamy; to speak the first words of hope and warning to those emerging into the sunlight of morality! Who can tell what numbers, advancing just far enough to hear a cold welcome and join in the reserved converse of professed reformers, disappointed, disheartened, have chosen to dwell in unclean places, rather than encounter these "holier-than-thou" of the great brotherhood of man!

Such was Mag's experience; and disdaining to ask favor or friendship from a sneering world, she resolved to shut herself up in a hovel she had often passed in better days, and which she knew to be untenanted. She vowed to ask no favors of familiar faces; to die neglected and forgotten before she would be dependent on any. Removed from the village, she was seldom seen except as upon your introduction, gentle reader, with downcast visage, returning her work to her employer, and thus providing herself with the means of subsistence. In two years many hands craved the same avocation; foreigners who cheapened toil and clamored for a livelihood, competed with her, and she could not thus sustain herself. She was now above no drudgery. Occasionally old acquaintances called to be favored with help of some kind, which she was glad to bestow for the sake of the money it would bring her; but the association with them was such a painful reminder of bygones, she returned to her hut morose and revengeful, refusing all offers of a better home than she possessed. Thus she lived for years, hugging her wrongs, but making no effort to escape. She had never known plenty, scarcely competency; but the present was beyond comparison with those innocent years when the coronet of virtue was hers.

Every year her melancholy increased, her means diminished. At last no one seemed to notice her, save a kind-hearted African, who often called to inquire after her health and to see if she needed any fuel, he having the responsibility of furnishing that article, and she in return mending or making garments.

"How much you earn dis week, Mag?" asked he one Saturday evening.

"Little enough, Jim. Two or three days without any dinner. I washed for the Reeds, and did a small job for Mrs. Bellmont; that's all. I shall starve soon, unless I can get more to do. Folks seem as afraid to come here as if they expected to get some awful disease. I don't believe there is a person in the world but would be glad to have me dead and out of the way."

"No, no, Mag! don't talk so. You shan't starve so long as I have barrels to hoop. Peter Greene boards me cheap. I'll help you, if nobody else will."

A tear stood in Mag's faded eye. "I'm glad," she said, with a softer tone than before, "if there is *one* who isn't glad to see me suffer. I b'lieve all Singleton wants to see me punished, and feel as if they could tell when I've been punished long enough. It's a long day ahead they'll set it, I reckon."

After the usual supply of fuel was prepared, Jim returned home. Full of pity for Mag, he set about devising measures for her relief. "By golly!" said he to himself one day—for he had become so absorbed in Mag's interest that he had fallen into a habit of musing aloud—"By golly! I wish she'd *marry* me."

"Who?" shouted Pete Greene, suddenly starting from an unobserved corner of the rude shop.

"Where you come from, you sly nigger!" exclaimed Jim.

"Come, tell me, who is't?" said Pete; Mag Smith, you want to marry?"

"Git out, Pete! and when you come in dis shop again, let a nigger know it. Don't steal in like a thief."

Pity and love know little severance. One attends the other. Jim acknowledged the presence of the former, and his efforts in Mag's behalf told also of a finer principle.

This sudden expedient which he had unintentionally disclosed, roused his thinking and inventive powers to study upon the best method of introducing the subject to Mag.

He belted his barrels, with many a scheme revolving in his mind, none of which quite satisfied him, or seemed, on the whole, expedient. He thought of the pleasing contrast between her fair face and his own dark skin; the smooth, straight hair, which he had once, in expression of pity, kindly stroked on her now wrinkled but once fair brow. There was a tempest gathering in his heart, and at last, to east his pent-up passion, he exclaimed aloud, "By golly!" Recollecting his former exposure, he glanced around to see if Pete was in hearing again. Satisfied on this point, he continued: "She'd be as much of a prize to me as she'd fall short of coming up to the mark with white folks. I don't care for past things. I've done things 'fore now I's 'shamed of. She's good enough for me, any how."

One more glance about the premises to be sure Pete was away.

The next Saturday night brought Jim to the hovel again. The cold was fast coming to tarry its apportioned time. Mag was nearly despairing of meeting its rigor.

"How's the wood, Mag?" asked Jim.

"All gone; and no more to cut, any how," was the reply.

"Too bad!" Jim said. His truthful reply would have been, I'm glad.

"Anything to eat in the house?" continued he.

"No," replied Mag.

"Too bad!" again, orally, with the same *inward* gratulation as before.

"Well, Mag," said Jim, after a short pause, "you's down low enough. I don't see but I've got to take care of ye. 'Sposin' we marry!"

Mag raised her eyes, full of amazement, and uttered a sonorous "What?"

Jim felt abashed for a moment. He knew well what were her objections.

"You's had trial of white folks, any how. They run off and left ye, and now none of 'em come near ye to see if you's dead or alive. I's black outside, I know, but I's got a white heart inside. Which you rather have, a black heart in a white skin, or a white heart in a black one?"

"Oh, dear!" sighed Mag; "Nobody on earth care for *me*—"

"I do," interrupted Jim.

"I can do but two things," said she, "beg my living, or get it from you."

"Take me, Mag. I can give you a better home than this, and not let you suffer so."

He prevailed; they married. You can philosophize, gentle reader, upon the impropriety of such unions, and preach dozens of sermons on the evils of amalgamation. Want is a more powerful philosopher and preacher. Poor Mag. She has sundered another bond which held her to her fellows. She has descended another step down the ladder of infamy. . . . [Chapter 2, "My Father's Death"; misery.]

Jim, proud of his treasure,—a white wife,—tried hard to fulfil his promises; and furnished her with a more comfortable dwelling, diet, and apparel. It was comparatively a comfortable winter she passed after her marriage. When Jim could work, all went on well. Industrious, and fond of Mag, he was determined she should not regret her union to him. Time levied an additional charge upon him, in the form of two pretty mulattos, whose infantile pranks amply repaid the additional toil. A few years, and a severe cough and pain in his side compelled him to be an idler for weeks together, and Mag had thus a reminder of by-gones. She cared for him only as a means to subserve her own comfort; yet she nursed him faithfully and true to marriage vows till death released her. He became the victim of consumption. He loved Mag to the last. So long as life continued, he stifled his sensibility to pain, and toiled for her sustenance long after he was able to do so.

A few expressive wishes for her welfare; a hope of better days for her; an anxiety lest they should not all go to the "good place;" brief advice about their children; a hope expressed that Mag would not be neglected as she used to be; the manifestation of Christian patience; these were *all* the legacy of miserable Mag. A feeling of cold desolation came over her, as she turned from the grave of one who had been truly faithful to her.

She was now expelled from companionship with white people; this last step—her union with a black—was the climax of repulsion.

Seth Shipley, a partner in Jim's business, wished her to remain in her present home; but she declined, and returned to her hovel again, with obstacles threefold more insurmountable than before. Seth accompanied her, giving her a weekly allowance which furnished most of the food necessary for the four inmates. After a time, work failed; their means were reduced.

How Mag toiled and suffered, yielding to fits of desperation, bursts of anger, and uttering curses too fearful to repeat. When both were supplied with work, they prospered; if idle, they were hungry together. In this way their interests became united; they planned for the future together. Mag had lived an outcast for years. She had ceased to feel the gushings of penitence; she had crushed the sharp agonies of an awakened conscience. She had no longings for a pure heart, a better life. Far easier to descend lower. She entered the darkness of perpetual infamy. She asked not the rite of civilization or Christianity. Her will made her the wife of Seth. Soon followed scenes familiar and trying.

"It's no use," said Seth one day; "we must give the children away, and try to get work in some other place."

"Who'll take the black devils?" snarled Mag.

"They're none of mine," said Seth; "what you growling about?"

"Nobody will want any thing of mine, or yours either," she replied.

"We'll make 'em, p'raps," he said. "There's Frado's six years old, and pretty, if she is yours, and white folks'll say so. She'd be a prize somewhere," he continued, tipping his chair back against the wall, and placing his feet upon the rounds, as if he had much more to say when in the right position.

Frado, as they called one of Mag's children, was a beautiful mulatto, with long, curly black hair, and handsome, roguish eyes, sparkling with an exuberance of spirit almost beyond restraint.

Hearing her name mentioned, she looked up from her play, to see what Seth had to say of her.

"Wouldn't the Bellmonts take her?" asked Seth.

"Bellmonts?" shouted Mag. "His wife is a right she-devil! and if—"

"Hadn't they better be all together?" interrupted Seth, reminding her of a like epithet used in reference to her little ones.

Without seeming to notice him, she continued, "She can't keep a girl in the house over a week; and Mr. Bellmont wants to hire a boy to work for him, but he can't find one that will live in the house with her; she's so ugly, they can't."

"Well, we've got to make a move soon," answered Seth; "if you go with me, we shall go right off. Had you rather spare the other one?" asked Seth, after a short pause.

"One's as bad as t'other," replied Mag. "Frado is such a wild, frolicky thing, and means to do jest as she's a mind to; she won't go if she don't want to. I don't want to tell her she is to be given away."

"I will," said Seth. "Come here, Frado?"

The child seemed to have some dim fore-shadowing of evil, and declined.

"Come here," he continued; "I want to tell you something."

She came reluctantly. He took her hand and said: "We're going to move, by-'m-bye; will you go?"

"No!" screamed she; and giving a sudden jerk which destroyed Seth's equilibrium, left him sprawling on the floor, while she escaped through the open door.

"She's a hard one," said Seth, brushing his patched coat sleeve. "I'd risk her at Bellmont's."

They discussed the expediency of a speedy departure. Seth would first seek employment, and then return for Mag. They would take with them what they could carry, and leave the rest with Pete Greene, and come for them when they were wanted. They were long in arranging affairs satisfactorily, and were not a little startled at the close of their conference to find Frado missing. They thought approaching night would bring her. Twilight passed into darkness, and she did not come. They thought she had understood their plans, and had, perhaps, permanently withdrawn. They could not rest without making some effort to ascertain her retreat. Seth went in pursuit, and returned without her. They rallied others when they discovered that another little colored girl was missing, a favorite playmate of Frado's. All effort proved unavailing. Mag felt sure her fears were realized, and she might never see her again. Before her anxieties became realities, both were safely returned, and from them and their attendant they learned that they went to walk, and not minding the direction soon found themselves lost. They had climbed fences and walls, passed through thickets and marshes, and when night approached selected a thick cluster of shrubbery as a covert for the night. They were discovered by the person who now restored them, chatting of their prospects, Frado attempting to banish the childish fears of her companion. As they were some miles from home, they were kindly cared for until morning. Mag was relieved to know her child was not driven to desperation by their intentions to relieve themselves of her, and she was inclined to think severe restraint would be helpful.

The removal was all arranged; the few days necessary for such migrations passed quickly, and one bright summer morning they bade farewell to their Singleton hovel, and with budgets and bundles commenced their weary march. As they neared the village, they heard the merry shouts of children gathered around the schoolroom, awaiting the coming of their teacher.

"Halloo!" screamed one, "Black, white and yeller!" "Black, white and yeller," echoed a dozen voices.

It did not grate so harshly on poor Mag as once it would. She did not even turn her head to look at them. She had passed into an insensibility no childish taunt could penetrate, else she would have reproached herself as she passed familiar scenes, for extending the separation once so easily annihilated by steadfast integrity. Two miles beyond lived the Bellmonts, in a large, old fashioned, two-story white house, environed by fruitful acres, and embellished by shrubbery and shade trees. Years ago a youthful couple consecrated it as home; and after many little feet had worn paths to favorite fruit trees, and over its green hills, and mingled at last with brother man in the race which belongs neither to the swift or strong, the sire became grey-haired and decrepid, and went to his last repose. His aged consort soon followed him. The old homestead thus passed into the hands of a son, to whose wife Mag had applied the epithet "she-devil," as may be remembered. John, the son, had not in his family arrangements departed from the example of the father. The pastimes of his boyhood were ever freshly revived by witnessing the games of his own sons as they rallied about the same goal his youthful feet had often won; as well as by the amusements of his daughters in their imitations of maternal duties.

At the time we introduce them, however, John is wearing the badge of age. Most of his children were from home; some seeking employment; some were already settled in homes of their own. A maiden sister shared with him the estate on which he resided, and occupied a portion of the house.

Within sight of the house, Seth seated himself with his bundles and the child he had been leading, while Mag walked onward to the house leading Frado. A knock at the door brought Mrs. Bellmont, and Mag asked if she would be willing to let that child stop there while she went to the Reed's house to wash, and when she came back she would call and get her. It seemed a novel request, but she consented. Why the impetuous child entered the house, we cannot tell; the door closed, and Mag hastily departed. Frado waited for the close of day, which was to bring back her mother. Alas! it never came. It was the last time she ever saw or heard of her mother. . . . [Chapter 3, "A New Home For Me."]

As the day closed and Mag did not appear, surmises were expressed by the family that she never intended to return. Mr. Bellmont was a kind, humane man, who would not grudge hospitality to the poorest wanderer, nor fail to sympathize with any sufferer, however humble. The child's desertion by her mother appealed to his sympathy, and he felt inclined to succor her. To do this in opposition to Mrs. Bellmont's wishes, would be like encountering a whirlwind charged with fire, daggers and spikes. She was not as susceptible of fine emotions as her spouse. Mag's opinion of her was not without foundation. She was self-willed, haughty, undisciplined, arbitrary and severe. In common parlance, she was a *scold*, a thorough one. Mr. B. remained silent during the consultation which follows, engaged in by mother, Mary and John, or Jack, as he was familiarly called.

"Send her to the County House," said Mary, in reply to the query what should be done with her, in a tone which indicated self-importance in the speaker. She was indeed the idol of her mother, and more nearly resembled her in disposition and manners than the others.

Jane, an invalid daughter, the eldest of those at home, was reclining on a sofa apparently un-interested.

"Keep her," said Jack. "She's real handsome and bright, and not very black, either."

"Yes," rejoined Mary; "that's just like you, Jack. She'll be of no use at all these three years, right under foot all the time."

"Poh! Miss Mary; if she should stay, it wouldn't be two days before you would be telling the girls about *our* nig, *our* nig!" retorted Jack.

"I don't want a nigger 'round *me*, do you mother?" asked Mary.

I don't mind the nigger in the child. I should like a dozen better than one," replied her mother. "If I could make her do my work in a few years, I would keep her. I have so much trouble with girls I hire, I am almost persuaded if I have one to train up in my way from a child, I shall be able to keep them awhile. I am tired of changing every few months."

"Where could she sleep?" asked Mary. "I don't want her near me."

"In the L chamber," answered the mother.

"How'll she get there?" asked Jack. "She'll be afraid to go through that dark passage, and she can't climb the ladder safely."

"She'll have to go there; it's good enough for a nigger," was the reply. . . . [Jack ascertains that Frado's family has departed; Frado is put in uncomfortable, small room and steels herself to tarry until mother returns; the family is reluctant to accept this behavior but intend to put her to use.]

Frado was called early in the morning by her new mistress. Her first work was to feed the hens. She was shown how it was *always* to be done, and in no other way; any departure from this rule to be punished by a whipping. She was then accompanied by Jack to drive the cows to pasture, so she might learn the way. Upon her return she was allowed to eat her breakfast, consisting of a bowl of skimmed milk, with brown bread crusts, which she was told to eat, standing, by the kitchen table, and must not be over ten minutes about it. Meanwhile the family were taking their morning meal in the dining-room. This over, she was placed on a cricket to wash the common dishes; she was to be in waiting always to bring wood and chips, to run hither and thither from room to room. . . . [The work load increases, and there is physical and verbal abuse.]

At first she wept aloud, which Mrs. Bellmont noticed by apply a rawhide, always at hand in the kitchen. It was a symptom of discontent and complaining which must be "nipped in the bud," she said.

Thus passed a year. No intelligence of Mag. It was now certain Frado was to become a permanent member of the family. Her labors were multiplied; she was quite indispensable, although but seven years old. She had never learned to read, never heard of a school until her residence in the family.

Mrs. Bellmont was in doubt about the utility of attempting to educate people of color, who were incapable of elevation. This subject occasioned a lengthy discussion in the family. Mr. Bellmont, Jane and Jack arguing for Frado's education; Mary and her mother objecting. At last Mr. Bellmont declared decisively that she *should* go to school. . . . [The decision holds, despite protests of haughty daughter Mary.]

The opening day of school came. Frado sauntered in far in the rear of Mary, who was ashamed to be seen "walking with a nigger."... [Teased and hated by the students, despondent. Teacher takes her by the hand.] Miss March inquired if the children knew "any cause for the sorrow of that little girl?" pointing to Frado.... [Teacher recommends kind words, no prejudice.]

Example rendered her words efficacious. Day by day there was a manifest change of deportment towards, "Nig." Her speeches often drew merriment from the children; no one could do more to enliven their favorite pastimes than Frado. Mary could not endure to see her thus noticed, yet knew not how to prevent it. . . . [Mary's antagonism grows; Frado and Mary walk home across field intersected with stream.]

It occurred to Mary that it would be a punishment to Nig to compel her to cross over; so she dragged her to the edge, and told her authoritatively to go over. Nig hesitated, resisted. Mary placed herself behind the child, and, in the struggle to force her over, lost her footing and plunged into the stream. Some of the larger scholars being in sight, ran, and thus prevented Mary from drowning and Frado from falling. Nig scampered home fast as possible, and Mary went to the nearest house, dripping, to procure a change of garments. She came loitering home, half crying, exclaiming, "Nig pushed me into the stream!". . . [Frado protests, incensing Mrs. Bellmont, whose husband refuses to punish Frado and leaves.]

No sooner was he out of sight than Mrs. B. and Mary commenced beating her inhumanly; then propping her mouth open with a piece of wood, shut her up in a dark room, without any supper. . . . [Mr. Bellmont tends cows for Frado.] At dark Jack came in, and seeing Mary, accosted her with, "So you thought you'd vent your spite on Nig, did you? Why can't you let her alone? It was good enough for you to get a ducking, only you did not stay in half long enough.". . . [Jack opposes mother's protests and threat of father's anger in verifiying Frado's version. Mr. Bellmont's stoic sympathy. Jack pities and comforts Frado.]

He resolved to do what he could to protect her from Mary and his mother. He bought her a dog, which became a great favorite with both. The invalid, Jane, would gladly befriend her; but she had not the strength to brave the iron will of her mother. . . . [Jane silently sympathizes. Frado is chatty; her antics are appreciated at school and by farm workers, though restrained at home. Three months pass. Mrs. Bellmont forbids Frado's shielding herself from the sun so as to "exaggerate" her natural color.]

She could now read and spell, and knew the elementary steps in grammar, arithmetic, and writing. Her education completed, as *she* said, Mrs. Bellmont felt that her time and person belonged solely to her. She was under her in every sense of the word. What an opportunity to indulge her vixen nature! No matter what occurred to ruffle her, or from what source provocation came, real or fancied, a few blows on Nig seemed to relieve her of a portion of ill-will. . . . [Fido, Jack's gift, is Frado's closest confidante. Preparations are made for son James's arrival. Frado beaten over wrong size firewood; she hides out and invokes sympathies of Jane, James, Jack, Mr. Bellmont, and Aunt Abby (who lives with the Bellmont's but in a separate apartment), and thereby causes family rift between her supporters and Mrs. Bellmont and Mary.]

After a suitable interval she [Jane] was married to George, and removed to his home in Vermont. Thus another light disappeared from Nig's horizon. Another was soon to follow. Jack was anxious to try his skill in providing for his own support; so a situation as clerk in a store was procured in a Western city, and six months after Jane's departure, was Nig abandoned to the tender mercies of Mary and her mother. As if to remove the last vestige of earthly joy, Mrs. Bellmont sold the companion and pet of Frado, the dog Fido. . . . [Mr. Bellmont retrieves Fido. Mr. and Mrs. Bellmont leave to visit James and wife. Mary is mistress of the house, Aunt Abby remains. Frado cherishes hope of being sent for by James.]

She was now able to do all the washing, ironing, baking, and the common *et cetera* of household duties, though but fourteen. Mary left all for her to do, though she affected great responsibility. She would show herself in the kitchen long enough to relieve herself of some command, better withheld; or insist upon some compliance to her wishes in some department which she was very imperfectly acquainted with, very much less than the person she was addressing; and so impetuous till her orders were obeyed, that to escape the turmoil, Nig would often go contrary to her own knowledge to gain a respite.

Nig was taken sick! What could be done[?] The *work*, certainly, but not by Miss Mary. So Nig would work while she could remain erect, than sink down upon the floor, or a chair, till she could rally for a fresh effort. Mary would look in upon her, chide her for her laziness, threaten to tell mother when she came home, and so forth.

"Nig!" screamed Mary, one of her sickest days, "come here, and sweep these threads from the carpet." She attempted to drag her weary limbs along, using the broom as support. Impatient of delay, she called again, but with a different request. "Bring me some wood, you lazy jade, quick." Nig rested the broom against the wall, and started on the fresh behest.

Too long gone. Flushed with anger, she rose and greeted her with, "What are you gone so long, for? Bring it in quick I say."

"I am coming as quick as I can," she replied, entering the door.

"Saucy, impudent nigger, you! is this the way you answer me?" and taking a large carving knife from the table, she hurled it, in her rage, at the defenseless girl.

Dodging quickly, it fastened in the ceiling a few inches from where she stood. There rushed on Mary's mental vision a picture of bloodshed, in which she was the perpetrator, and the sad consequences of what was so nearly an actual occurrence.

"Tell anybody of this, if you dare. If you tell Aunt Abby, I'll certainly kill you," said she, terrified. She returned to her room, brushed her threads herself; was for a day or two more guarded, and so escaped deserved and merited penalty. . . . [Mr. and Mrs. Bellmont return, and the latter's abuse resumes, against which Aunt Abby is powerless.]

The first of spring a letter came from James, announcing declining health. He must try northern air as a restorative; so Frado joyfully prepared for this agreeable increase of the family, this addition to her cares.

He arrived feeble, lame, from his disease, so changed Frado wept at his appearance, fearing he would be removed from her forever. He kindly greeted her, took her to the parlor to see his wife and child, and said many things to kindle smiles on her sad face.

Frado felt so happy in his presence, so safe from maltreatment! He was to her a shelter. He observed, silently, the ways of the house a few days; Nig still took her meals in the manner as formerly, having the same allowance of food. He, one day, bade her not remove the food, but sit down to the table and eat.

"She *will*, mother," said he, calmly, but imperatively; I'm determined; she works hard; I've watched her. Now, while I stay, she is going to sit down *here*, and eat such food as we eat.". . . [Frado is excluded from religious practices by Mary and Mrs. Belmont. Aunt Abby and James expose Frado to religion. James extends his sympathies to Frado; repeats promise to Frado that she will be taken along when he goes home, despite his frail health.]

Susan now came for her long absent husband, and they returned home to their room.

The month of November was one of great anxiety on James's account. He was rapidly wasting away.

A celebrated physician was called, and performed a surgical operation, as a last means. Should this fail, there was no hope. Of course he was confined wholly to his room, mostly to his bed. With all his bodily suffering, all his anxiety for his family, whom he might not live to protect, he did not forget Frado. He shielded her from many beatings, and every day imparted religious instructions. No one, but his wife, could move him so easily as Frado; so that in addition to her daily toil she was often deprived of her rest at night.

Yet she insisted on being called; she wished to show her love for one who had been such a friend to her. Her anxiety and grief increased as the probabilities of his recovery became doubtful.

Mrs. Bellmont found her weeping on his account, shut her up, and whipped her with the raw-hide, adding an injunction never to be seen snivelling again because she had a little work to do. She was very careful never to shed tears on his account, in her presence, afterwards. . . . [James continues to fail. Frado falls ill; is beaten to near-death by Mrs. Bellmont; turns to the Bible. James's last words to Frado. Frado questions her suitability for Heaven. Mrs. Bellmont and Aunt Abby argue. Frado and Aunt Abby excluded from prayers for James; Frado eavesdrops; mourns.]

The family, gathered by James' decease, returned to their homes. Susan and Charles returned to Baltimore. Letters were received from the absent, expressing their sympathy and grief. The father bowed like a "bruised reed," under the loss of his beloved son. He felt desirous to die the death of the righteous; also, conscious that he was unprepared, he resolved to start on the narrow way, and some time solicit entrance through the gate which leads to the celestial city. He acknowledged his too ready acquiescence with Mrs. B., in permitting Frado to be deprived of her only religious privileges for weeks together. He accordingly asked his sister to take her to meeting once more, which she was ready at once to do.

The first opportunity they once more attended meeting together. The minister conversed faithfully with every person present. He was surprised to find the little colored girl so solicitous, and kindly directed her to the flowing fountain where she might wash and be clean. He inquired of the origin of her anxiety, of her progress up to this time, and endeavored to make Christ, instead of James, the attraction of Heaven. He invited her to come to his house, to speak freely her mind to him, to pray much, to read her Bible often.

The neighbors, who were at meeting,—among them Mrs. Reed,—discussed the opinions Mrs. Bellmont would express on the subject. Mrs. Reed called and informed Mrs. B. that her colored girl "related her experience the other night at the meeting."

"What experience?" asked she, quickly, as if she expected to hear the number of times she had whipped Frado, and the number of lashes set forth in plain Arabic numbers.

"Why, you know she is serious, don't you? She told the minister about it."

Mrs. B. made no reply, but changed the subject adroitly. Next morning she told Frado she "should not go out of the house for one while, except on errands; and if she did not stop trying to be religious, she would whip her to death."

Frado pondered; her mistress was a professor of religion; was *she* going to heaven? then she did not wish to go. If she could be near James, even, she could not be happy with those fiery eyes watching her ascending path. She resolved to give over all thought of the future world, and strove daily to put her anxiety far from her.

Mr. Bellmont found himself unable to do what James or Jack could accomplish for her. He talked with her seriously, told her he had seen her many times punished undeservedly; he did not wish to have her saucy or disrespectful, but when she was *sure* she did not deserve a whipping, to avoid it if she could. "You are looking sick," he added, "you cannot endure beating as you once could."

It was not long before an opportunity offered of profiting by his advice. She was sent for wood, and not returning as soon as Mrs. B. calculated, she followed her, and, snatching from the pile a stick, raised it over her.

"Stop!" shouted Frado, "strike me, and I'll never work a mite more for you;" and throwing down what she had gathered, stood like one who feels the stirring of free and independent thoughts.

By this unexpected demonstration, her mistress, in amazement, dropped her weapon, desisting from her purpose of chastisement. Frado walked towards the house, her mistress following with the wood she herself was sent after. She did not know, before, that she had a power to ward off her assaults. Her triumph in seeing her enter the door with *her* burden, repaid her for much of her former suffering.

It was characteristic of Mrs. B. never to rise in her majesty, unless she was sure she should be victorious.

This affair never met with an "after clap," like many others.

Thus passed a year. The usual amount of scolding, but fewer whippings. Mrs. B. longed once more for Mary's return, who had been absent over a year. . . . Another letter brought tidings that Mary was seriously ill; her mother's presence was solicited.

She started without delay. Before she reached her destination, a letter came to the parents announcing her death. . . . [Mr. Bellmont and Aunt Abby commiserate. Frado cannot help rejoicing.]

The family returned from their sorrowful journey, leaving the dead behind. Nig looked for a change in her tyrant; what could subdue her, if the loss of her idol could not? . . . [Mrs. Bellmont mourns.]

A few weeks revived the former tempests, and so at variance did they seem with chastisement sanctified, that Frado felt them to be unbearable. She determined to flee. But where? Who would take her? Mrs. B. had always represented her ugly. Perhaps every one thought her so. Then no one would take her. She was black, no one would love her. She might have to return, and then she would be more in her mistress' power than ever.

She remembered her victory at the wood-pile. She decided to remain to do as well as she could; to assert her rights when they were trampled on; to return once more to her meeting in the evening, which had been prohibited. She had learned how to conquer; she would not abuse the power while Mr. Bellmont was at home.

But had she not better run away? Where? She had never been from the place far enough to decide what course to take. She resolved to speak to Aunt Abby. *She* mapped the dangers of her course, her liability to fail in finding so good friends as John and herself. Frado's mind was busy for days and nights. She contemplated administering poison to her mistress, to rid herself and the house of so detestable a plague.

But she was restrained by an overruling Providence; and finally decided to stay contentedly through her period of service, which would expire when she was eighteen years of age.

In a few months Jane returned home with her family, to relieve her parents, upon whom years and affliction had left the marks of age. The years intervening since she had left her home, had, in some degree, softened the opposition to her unsanctioned marriage with George. . . . [Jane follows Jack west, asking weary Frado to follow when released.]

Darkness before day. Jane left, but Jack was now to come again. After Mary's death he visited home, leaving a wife behind. An orphan whose home was with a relative, gentle, loving, the true mate of kind, generous Jack. His mother was a stranger to her, of course, and had perfect right to interrogate:

"Is she good looking, Jack?" asked his mother.

"Looks well to me," was the laconic reply.

"Was her *father* rich?"

"Not worth a copper, as I know of; I never asked him," answered Jack.

"Hadn't she any property? What did you marry her for," asked his mother.

"Oh, she's *worth a million* dollars, mother, though not a cent of it is in money.". . . [Jack returns home and then his new wife arrives. Mrs. Bellmont tries to sabotage the marital relationship while Jack is gone on business with Lewis. Susan (James's wife) and child visit.]

Frado had merged into womanhood, and, retaining what she had learned, in spite of the few privileges enjoyed formerly, was striving to enrich her mind. Her school-books were her constant companions, and every leisure moment was applied to them. Susan was delighted to witness her progress, and some little book from her was a reward sufficient for any task imposed, however difficult. She had her book always fastened open near her, where she could glance from toil to soul refreshment. The approaching spring would close the term of years which Mrs. B. claimed as the period of her servitude. Often as she passed the way-marks of former years did she pause to ponder on her situation, and wonder if she *could* succeed in providing for her own wants. Her health was delicate, yet she resolved to try.

Soon she counted the time by days which should release her. Mrs. B. felt that she could not well spare one who could so well adapt herself to all departments—man, boy, housekeeper, domestic, etc. She begged Mrs. Smith to talk with her, to show her how ungrateful it would appear to leave a home of such comfort—how wicked it was to be ungrateful! But Frado replied that she had had enough of such comforts; she wanted some new ones; and as it was so wicked to be ungrateful, she would go from temptation; Aunt Abby said "we mustn't put ourselves in the way of temptation."

Poor little Fido! She shed more tears over him than over all beside.

The morning for departure dawned. Frado engaged to work for a family a mile distant. Mrs. Bellmont dismissed her with the assurance that she would soon wish herself back again, and a present of a silver half dollar.

Her wardrobe consisted on one decent dress, without any superfluous accompaniments. A Bible from Susan she felt was her greatest treasure.

Now was she alone in the world. The past year had been one of suffering resulting from a fall, which had left her lame.

The first summer passed pleasantly, and the wages earned were expended in garments necessary for health and cleanliness. Though feeble, she was well satisfied with her progress. Shut up in her room, after her toil was finished, she studied what poor samples of apparel she had, and, for the first time, prepared her own garments.

Mrs. Moore, who employed her, was a kind friend to her, and attempted to heal her wounded spirit by sympathy and advice, burying the past in the prospects of the future. But her failing health was a cloud no kindly human could dissipate. A little light work was all she could accomplish. A clergyman, whose family was small, sought her, and she was removed there. Her engagement with Mrs. Moore finished in the fall. Frado was anxious to keep up her reputation for efficiency, and often pressed far beyond prudence. In the winter she entirely gave up work, and confessed herself thoroughly sick. Mrs. Hale, soon overcome by additional cares, was taken sick also, and now it became necessary to adopt some measures for Frado's comfort, as well as to relieve Mrs. Hale. Such dark forebodings as visited her as she lay, solitary and sad, no moans or sighs could relieve. . . . [Frado is broken down and sick, her prognosis pessimistic; moved to shelter near the Bellmonts' home, then to Aunt Abby's apartment.]

Not that she was well, or ever would be; but she had recovered so far as rendered it hopeful she might provide for her own wants. The clergyman at whose house she was taken sick, was now seeking some one to watch his sick children, and as soon as he heard of her recovery, again asked for her services.

What seemed so light and easy to others, was too much for Frado; and it became necessary to ask once more where the sick should find an asylum.

All felt that the place where the declining health began, should be the place of relief; so they applied once more for a shelter.

"No," exclaimed the indignant Mrs. B.; "She shall never come under this roof again; never! never!" she repeated, as if each repetition were a bolt to prevent admission.

One only resource; the public must pay the expense. So she was removed to the home of two maidens, (old,) who had principle enough to be willing to earn the money a charitable public disburses.

Three years of weary sickness wasted her, without extinguishing a life apparently so feeble. Two years had these maidens watched and cared for her, and they began to weary, and finally to request the authorities to remove her.

Mrs. Hoggs was a lover of gold and silver, and she asked the favor of filling her coffers by caring for the sick. The removal caused severe sickness.

By being bolstered in the bed, after a time she could use her hands, and often would ask for sewing to beguile the tedium. She had become very expert with her needle the first year of her release from Mrs. B., and she had forgotten none of her skill. Mrs. H. praised her, and as she improved in health, was anxious to employ her. She told her she could in this way replace her clothes, and as her board would be paid for, she would thus gain something.

Many times her hands wrought when her body was in pain; but the hope that she might yet help herself, impelled her on.

Thus she reckoned her store of means by a few dollars, and was hoping soon to come in possession, when she was startled by the announcement that Mrs. Hoggs had reported her to the physician and town officers as an impostor. That she was, in truth, able to get up and go to work.

This brought on a severe sickness of two weeks, when Mrs. Moore again sought her, and took her to her home. She had formerly had wealth at her command, but misfortune had deprived her of it, and unlocked her heart to sympathies and favors she had never known while it lasted. Her husband, defrauded of his last means by a branch of the Bellmont family, had supported them by manual labor, gone to the West, and left his wife and four young children. But she felt humanity required her to give a shelter to one she knew to be worthy of a hospitable reception. Mrs. Moore's physician was called, and pronounced her a very sick girl, and encouraged Mrs. M. to keep her and care for her, and he would see that the authorities were informed of Frado's helplessness, and pledged assistance.

Here she remained till sufficiently restored to sew again. Then came the old resolution to take care of herself, to cast off the unpleasant charities of the public.

She learned that in some towns in Massachusetts, girls make straw bonnets—that it was easy and profitable. But how should *she*, black, feeble and poor, find any one to teach her. But God prepares the way, when human agencies see no path. Here was found a plain, poor, simple woman, who could see merit beneath a dark skin; and when the invalid mulatto told her sorrows, she opened her door and her heart, and took the stranger in. Expert with the needle, Frado soon equalled her instructress; and she sought also to teach her the value of useful books; and while one read aloud to the other of deeds historic and names renowned, Frado experienced a new impulse. She felt herself capable of elevation; she felt that this book information supplied an undefined dissatisfaction she had long felt, but could not express. Every leisure moment was carefully applied to self-improvement, and a devout and Christian exterior invited confidence from the villagers. Thus she passed months of quiet, growing in the confidence of her neighbors and new found friends. . . .

A few years ago, within the compass of my narrative, there appeared often in some of our New England villages, professed fugitives from slavery, who recounted their personal experience in homely phrase, and awakened the indignation of non-slaveholders against brother Pro. Such a one appeared in the new home of Frado; and as people of color were rare there, was it strange she should attract her dark brother; that he should inquire her out; succeed in seeing her; feel a strange sensation in his heart towards her; that he should toy with her shining curls, feel proud to provoke her to smile and expose the ivory concealed by thin, ruby lips; that her sparkling eyes should fascinate; that he should propose; that they should marry? A short acquaintance was indeed an objection, but she saw him often, and thought she knew him. He never spoke of his enslavement to her when alone, but she felt that, like her own oppression, it was painful to disturb oftener than was needful.

He was a fine, straight negro, whose back showed no marks of the lash, erect as if it never crouched beneath a burden. There was a silent sympathy which Frado felt attracted her, and she opened her heart to the presence of love—that arbitrary and inexorable tyrant.

She removed to Singleton, her former residence, and there was married. Here were Frado's first feelings of trust and repose on human arm. She realized, for the first time, the relief of looking to another for comfortable support. Occasionally he would leave her to "lecture."

Those tours were prolonged often to weeks. Of course he had little spare money. Frado was again feeling her self-dependence, and was at last compelled to resort alone to that. Samuel was kind to her when at home, but made no provision for his absence, which was at last unprecedented.

He left her to her fate—embarked at sea, with the disclosure that he had never seen the South, and that his illiterate harangues were humbugs for hungry abolitionists. Once more alone! Yet not alone. A still newer companionship would soon force itself upon her. No one wanted her with such prospects. Herself was burden enough; who would have an additional one?

The horrors of her condition nearly prostrated her, and she was again thrown upon the public for sustenance. Then followed the birth of her child. The long absent Samuel unexpectedly returned, and rescued her from charity. Recovering from her expected illness, she once more commenced toil for herself and child, in a room obtained of a poor woman, but with better fortune. One so well known would not be wholly neglected. Kind friends watched her when Samuel was from home, prevented her from suffering, and when the cold weather pinched the warmly clad, a kind friend took them in, and thus preserved them. At last Samuel's business became very engrossing, and after long desertion, news reached his family that he had become a victim of yellow fever, in New Orleans.

So much toil as was necessary to sustain Frado, was more than she could endure. As soon as her babe could be nourished without his mother, she left him in charge of a Mrs. Capon, and procured an agency, hoping to recruit her health, and gain an easier livelihood for herself and child. This afforded her better maintenance that she had yet found. She passed into the various towns of the State she lived in, then into Massachusetts. Strange were some of her adventures. Watched by kidnappers, maltreated by professed abolitionists, who didn't want slaves at the South, nor niggers in their own houses, North. Faugh! to lodge one; to eat with one; to admit one through the front door; to sit next one; awful!

Traps slyly laid by the vicious to ensnare her, she resolutely avoided. In one of her tours, Providence favored her with a friend who, pitying her cheerless lot, kindly provided her with a valuable recipe, from which she might herself manufacture a useful article for her maintenance. This proved a more agreeable, and an easier way of sustenance.

And thus, to the present time, may you see her busily employed in preparing her merchandise; then sallying forth to encounter many frowns, but some kind friends and purchasers. Nothing turns her from her steadfast purpose of elevating herself. Reposing on God, she has thus far journeyed securely. Still an invalid, she asks your sympathy, gentle reader. Refuse not, because some part of her history is unknown, save by the Omniscient God. Enough has been unrolled to demand your sympathy and aid.

Do you ask the destiny of those connected with her *early* history? A few years only have elapsed since Mr. and Mrs. B. passed into another world. As age increased, Mrs. B. became more irritable, so that no one, even her own children, could remain with her; and she was accompanied by her husband to the home of Lewis, where, after an agony in death unspeakable, she passed away. Only a few months since, Aunt Abby entered heaven. Jack and his wife rest in heaven, disturbed by no intruders; and Susan and her child are yet with the living. Jane has silver locks in place of auburn tresses, but she has the early love of Henry still, and has never regretted her exchange of lovers. Frado has passed from their memories, as Joseph from the butler's, but she will never cease to track them till beyond mortal vision.

7

Jarena Lee
(1783–after 1849)

■

Introduction

The focus on slavery in the 1830s to the 1850s was complemented, not coincidentally, by a new concentration on spiritual freedom. This stress on Christianity and Christian values enabled women like Maria W. Stewart, the first black female political writer born in the United States, deeply religious, abolitionist, and committed to women's rights; Zilpha Elaw, gospel missionary who wrote her memoirs; and Jarena Lee to see themselves as agents with power of their own.[89] Lee and Elaw wrote their spiritual autobiographies while Stewart spoke out publicly on a wide range of issues. Religion was frequently a goal and a tool, as well as a fortification. During this tumultuous era, black churchgoers were independently restructuring their institutions: "The first separate denominations to be formed by African Americans in the U.S. were Methodist and organized by free black people in the North. . . . It was the first effective stride toward freedom by African Americans"[90]

In 1784, U.S. Methodist societies splintered from British Methodism and were united. The Philadelphia Free African Society was founded in 1787 by the Reverend Richard Allen and Absolom Jones, a Methodist lay minister. In 1794, Allen and his followers established the Bethel African Methodist Episcopal Church in Philadelphia.[91] Allen was consecrated as the first bishop in 1816.[92]

These new religious institutions with male leadership challenged such religiously active women as Jarena Lee because their taboos were firm against female participation. Since its inception in 1816, the African Methodist Episcopal Church's refusal to license and ordain women preachers had meant that women could never attain a position of authority within it. Lee resolutely challenged the male hegemony. Using personally inspired spiritual dictates, she insisted on the right of women to preach and helped to foment debate and rebellion in the church's ranks.[93] Meanwhile, she kept a religious journal, which became the basis of her two autobiographical publications. In this she makes it clear that some of her difficulties stemmed from being both an African American and a woman. Her spiritual autobiographies attest to her knowledge that a crucial aspect of black female history was in the making.[94] By the end of her life, Jarena Lee had become both a preacher and a representative voice, encouraging and committed on a range of issues concerning gender and race.

■

Biographical Narrative

Born in Cape May in southern New Jersey in 1783, to free black parents, Jarena Lee, a contemporary of Maria Stewart and Sojourner Truth, discloses few details of her childhood. At age seven, she was separated from her family and lived as a servant maid to a Mr. Sharp. Such silence follows a traditional format in spiritual autobiography, where the "world" scarcely matters. Most of the known data about Lee derives from her spiritual-autobiographical narratives, *The Life and Religious Experience of Jarena Lee* (1836) and *Religious Experience and Journal of Mrs. Jarena Lee* (1849). Her autobiography was possibly the "next separately published volume by an African American woman after that by Phillis Wheatley."[95] It stamps her as the "first female preacher of the first African Methodist Episcopal Church" to challenge the traditional roles for women in her practices and writings. Her struggle underscores the tight control that a religious patriarchy exercised over female church members.

The special attraction that Wesleyan Methodism held for Lee paralleled its attraction for the Hart sisters. The egalitarian message of salvation for all was especially empowering in the antebellum period.[96] The tenets of Methodism offered a logical movement from religious equality to social practice and spoke simultaneously about abolition.

Largely self-taught, Lee was drawn in earnest at the age of twenty-one to a spiritual life, when an itinerant Protestant missionary made her feel the overwhelming "weight" of her sins. Lee had suffered from both spiritual doubts and poor health for about four years and had contemplated suicide on three occasions. Her embrace of "the entire sanctification of the soul to God"[97] soon rendered her confident again. Her spiritual experiences and evangelical calling released a repressed sense of subjugation.

Five years later, in 1809, Lee's move to Philadelphia proved to be a crucial turning point. First, a sermon delivered by the founder of the African Methodist Episcopal Church, Richard Allen, brought her to new spiritual realizations about her power and calling. Allen was also an inaugural member of the African Freemason Lodge of Philadelphia.[98] This introduction to positive black Freemason ideas probably influenced Lee's quest for spiritual freedom. Second, in 1811, Jarena married Joseph Lee, the pastor of a black church in a rural community outside Philadelphia. She reluctantly bows to the propriety of moving from her own spiritual community to Snow Hill, her husband's. She never discloses her maiden name. For religious reasons, she soon felt the need to relocate, but Joseph Lee declined to leave, whereupon Jarena became very ill; her desire to move was closely tied to her need to begin preaching: "I fell into a state of general debility."[99]

A semimystical experience inspired Lee to disobey the rules and start preaching, reasoning to herself that her holy condition of sanctification was implicit legitimation. "Did not Mary *first* preach the risen Saviour?" (p. 36). She refers to herself during this spiritual and political struggle as God's "poor coloured female instrument" (p. 37). By then tragedy had come to her: her husband and two of their children died within six years.

Widowed in 1817, the mother of two small children, Lee returned to Philadephia in 1818. Again she approached Allen, now a bishop, asking to hold prayer meetings in her home. Allen granted the request; at some point, he had heard Lee's fiery address and considered her calling valid (possibly when she preached to her husband's congregation). Then in her midthirties, despite frequent illness, Lee began traveling and preaching throughout the Northeast. She left her one remaining child in the care of friends and committed herself to preaching the Gospel to whites, blacks, and Indians in churches, schoolhouses, bush arbors, markets, private homes, and camp meetings.

Returning to Philadelphia in 1823, Lee accepted a position at Bethel, tendered by Allen despite church opposition to her appointment. Allen also made provision for Lee's son's education. Lee described herself as the first female preacher of the First African Methodist Episcopal Church. The opportunity to join the newly formed African Methodist Episcopal church fostered her determination to include issues of race, implicitly and explicitly, in her autobiographical writings.[100] Moreover, she concurrently considered herself rooted in a rememberable cultural past. She was careful, for example, to mark ethnically any individual whom she met and any difficult experiences of her own.

In 1836, when whe was thirty-three, *The Life and Religious Experience of*

Jarena Lee appeared as a twenty-four page pamphlet. Between this early spiritual charting and publication in 1849 of an expanded version, Lee joined the American Anti-slavery Society.[101] The second memoir, *Religious Experience and Journal of Mrs. Jarena Lee,* included a journal sequence of twenty-five pages and was underwritten by Lee. Apparently, the African Methodist Episcopal Church was reluctant to pay the cost of the undertaking; the administrators considered it not in the best interests of the Methodist Connection[102]—financial reasons were one thing, but put bluntly, and just as realistically, because female preaching was contrary to church doctrine. Female preaching also, ironically, embodied principles of democracy inscribed in the new U.S. Constitution. All are equal, Lee insisted, and invited anyone to gainsay that principle and remain politically consistent.

The memoir starts with a brief description of Lee's birth and childhood, then details the period from her conversion to 1842, when she had been evangelizing for twenty years. For the most part, she preached on the East Coast and in Illinois and Ohio, and for a short time in Canada. As did John Wesley, she walked great distances to preach: "This day I walked six miles, and preached twice to large congregations, both in the morning and evening."[103]

Issues of gender and class, as well as race and religion, figure in her autobiographical writings. She insists on her right—and by implication the right of all women—to preach. Her belief that proselytizing is paramount enables her to abandon women's prescribed roles, especially those of homemaker and ever-present mother.

She located herself on a continuum of women writers, of historical chroniclers, of community spokeswomen, and of itinerant preachers (like Jesus): "And why should it be thought impossible, heterodox, or improper for a woman to preach, seeing the Saviour died for the woman as well as the man? . . . Did not Mary *first* preach the risen Saviour, and is not the doctrine of the resurrection the very climax of Christianity . . . ? Then did not Mary, a woman, preach the gospel? For she preached the resurrection of the crucified Son of God."[104] Subscribing to church beliefs that argue equal spiritual opportunities for the lowliest, she highlights the idea of a spiritual democracy (pp. 157–58). Each individual soul has the right to her or his own voice. Lee's literary models are probably spiritual autobiographers in general, journal writers, and sinner memoirists.

The date of Lee's death is unknown.

■

CHRONOLOGY

1783	Born Cape May, South Jersey, 11 February, to free black parents.
1787	Free African Society organized by the Reverend Richard Allen and Absalom Jones.
1790	Servant maid to a Mr. Sharp.
ca. 1804–1805	Deeply moved by Presbyterian missionary's preaching, contemplates suicide. Conversion to Christ. Attends a white Methodist church in Philadelphia for three months; then joins Allen's congregation, known as the Free African Society. Her sanctification follows in the next few years.
1809	Moves to Philadelphia; hears the well-known Reverend Richard Allen preaching; denied permission to preach, but permitted to exhort and hold prayer meetings.
1811	Marries Joseph Lee, a pastor, and moves to Snow Hill, six miles from Philadelphia where Lee is pastor of a "Coloured Society." Despite being refused, preaches for the next few years.
1816	Richard Allen is the first consecrated Bishop of the African Methodist Episcopal Church, the first independent black denomination, an outgrowth of the Free African Society.
1817	Husband, two children die.
1818–19	Returns to Philadelphia, where Bishop Allen now gives permission for Lee to preach; first female preacher of the African Methodist Episcopal Church, publicly praised as preacher by Allen.
1818 and later	Itinerant preaching in East as far south as Maryland and as far west as Illinois, her success resulting in more church roles for women. Keeps journal while circuit riding.
1831	Convention movement founded through which African Americans debated critical issues of the day, such as slavery, civil rights, the desirability of emigration.
1833	American Anti-Slavery Society formed, in part led by Abraham Shadd, Mary Anne Shadd Cary's father. Richard Allen's autobiography published posthumously.
1836	*The Life and Religious Experience of Jarena Lee* published.

1840 Joined American Anti-Slavery Society.

1849 *Religious Experience and Journal of Mrs. Jarena Lee* published.

■ ■ ■

FROM *RELIGIOUS EXPERIENCE AND JOURNAL OF MRS. JARENA LEE*

> "And it shall come to pass . . . that I will pour out my Spirit upon all flesh; and your sons, and your daughters shall prophecy."
>
> —Joel 2:28

I was born February 11th, 1783, at Cape May, State of New Jersey. At the age of seven years I was parted from my parents, and went to live as a servant maid, with a Mr. Sharp, at the distance of about sixty miles from the place of my birth.

My parents being wholly ignorant of the knowledge of God, had not therefore instructed me in any degree in this great matter. Not long after the commencement of my attendance on this lady, she had bid me do something respecting my work, which in a little while after she asked me if I had done, when I replied, Yes—but this was not true.

At this awful point, in my early history, the Spirit of God moved in power through my conscience, and told me I was a wretched sinner. On this account so great was the impression, and so strong were the feelings of guilt, that I promised in my heart that I would not tell another lie.

But notwithstanding this promise my heart grew harder, after a while, yet the Spirit of the Lord never entirely forsook me, but continued mercifully striving with me, until his gracious power converted my soul.

The manner of this great accomplishment, was as follows: In the year 1804, it so happened that I went with others to hear a missionary of the Presbyterian order preach. It was an afternoon meeting, but few were there, the place was a school room; but the preacher was solemn, and in his countenance the earnestness of his master's business appeared equally strong, as though he were about to speak to a multitude.

At the reading of the Psalms, a ray of renewed conviction darted into my soul. These were the words, composing the first verse of the Psalms for the service:

"Lord, I am vile, conceived in sin,
Born unholy and unclean.
Sprung from man, whose guilty fall
Corrupts the race, and taints us all."

This description of my condition struck me to the heart, and made me to feel in some measure, the weight of my sins, and sinful nature. But not knowing how to run immediately to the Lord for help, I was driven of Satan, in the course of a few days, and tempted to destroy myself.

There was a brook about a quarter of a mile from the house, in which there was a deep hole, where the water whirled about among the rocks; to this place it was suggested, I must go and drown myself.

At the time I had a book in my hand; it was on a Sabbath morning, about ten o'clock; to this place I resorted, where on coming to the water I sat down on the bank, and on my looking into it, it was suggested that drowning would be an easy death. It seemed as if some one was speaking to me, saying put your head under, it will not distress you. But by some means, of which I can give no account, my thoughts were taken entirely from this purpose, when I went from the place to the house again. It was the unseen arm of God which saved me from self-murder.

But notwithstanding this escape from death, my mind was not at rest—but so great was the labor of my spirit and the fearful oppressions of a judgment to come, that I was reduced as one extremely ill, on which account a physician was called to attend me, from which illness I recovered in about three months.

But as yet I had not found Him of whom Moses and the prophets did write, being extremely ignorant: there being no one to instruct me in the way of life and salvation as yet. After my recovery, I left the lady, who, during my sickness, was exceedingly kind, and went to Philadelphia. From this place I soon went a few miles into the country, where I resided in the family of a Roman Catholic. But my anxiety still continued respecting my poor soul, on which account I used to watch my opportunity to read in the Bible; and this lady observing this, took the Bible from me and hid it, giving me a novel in its stead—which when I perceived, I refused to read.

Soon after this I again went in the city of Philadelphia, and commenced going to the English Church, the pastor of which was an Englishman, by the name of Pilmore, one of the number who at first preached Methodism in America in the city of New York.

But while sitting under the ministration of this man, which was about three months, and at the last time, it appeared that there was a wall between me and a communion with that people, which was higher than I could possibly see over, and seemed to make this impression upon my mind, this is not the people for you.

But on returning home at noon I inquired of the head cook of the house respecting the rules of the Methodists, as I knew she belonged to that society, who told me what they were; on which account I replied, that I should not be able to abide by such strict rules not even one year—however, I told her that I would go with her and hear what they had to say.

The man who was to speak in the afternoon of that day, was the Rev. Richard Allen, since bishop of the African Episcopal Methodists in America. During the labors of this man that afternoon, I had come to the conclusion, that this is the people to which my heart unites, and it so happened, that as soon as the service closed he invited such as felt a desire to flee the wrath to come, to unite on trial with them—I embraced the opportunity. Three weeks from that day, my soul was gloriously converted to God, under preaching, at the very outset of the sermon. The text was barely pronounced, which was "I perceive thy heart is not right in the sight of God," when there appeared to my view, in the centre of the heart, one sin; and this was malice against one particular individual, who had strove deeply to injure me, which I resented. At this discovery I said, Lord I forgive every creature. That instant, it appeared to me as if a garment, which had entirely enveloped my whole person, even to my fingers; ends split at the crown of my head, and was stripped away from me, passing like a shadow from my sight—when the glory of God seemed to cover me in its stead.

That moment, though hundreds were present, I did leap to my feet and declare that God, for Christ's sake, had pardoned the sins of my soul. Great was the ecstacy of my mind, for I felt that not only the sin of malice was pardoned, but all other sins were swept away together. That day was the first when my heart had believed, and my tongue had made confession unto salvation—the first words uttered, a part of that song, which shall fill eternity with its sound, was glory to God. For a few moments I had power to exhort sinners, and to tell of the wonders and of the goodness of Him who had clothed me with His salvation. During this the minister was silent, until my soul felt its duty had been performed, when he declared another witness of the power of Christ to forgive sins on earth, was manifest in my conversion.

From the day on which I first went to the Methodist Church, until the hour of my deliverance, I was strangely buffetted by that enemy of all righteousness—the devil.

I was naturally of a lively turn of disposition; and during the space of time from my first awakening until I knew my peace was made with God, I rejoiced in the vanities of this life, and then again sunk back into sorrow.

For four years I had continued in this way, frequently laboring under the awful apprehension, that I could never be happy in this life. This persuasion was greatly strengthened during the three weeks, which was the last of Satan's power over me, in this peculiar manner, on which account I had come to the conclusion that I had better be dead than alive. Here I was again tempted to destroy my life by drowning; but suddenly this mode was changed—and while in the dusk of the evening, as I was walking to and from in the yard of the house, I was beset to hang myself with a cord suspended from the wall enclosing the secluded spot.

But no sooner was the intention resolved on in my mind, than an awful dread came over me, when I ran into the house; still the tempter pursued me. There was standing a vessel of water—into this I was strangely impressed to plunge my head, so as to extinguish the life which God had given me. Had I done this, I have been always of the opinion, that I should have been unable to have released myself; although the vessel was scarcely large enough to hold a gallon of water. Of me may it not be said, as written by Isaiah, (chap. 65, verses 1, 2.) "I am sought of them that asked not for me; I am found of them that sought me not." Glory be to God for his redeeming power, which saved me from the violence of my own hands, from the malice of Satan, and from eternal death; for had I have killed myself, a great ransom could not have delivered me; for it is written—"No murderer hath eternal life abiding in him." How appropriately can I sing—

"Jesus sought me when a stranger,
Wandering from the fold of God
He to rescue me from danger,
Interposed his precious blood."

But notwithstanding the terror which seized upon me, when about to end my life, I had no view of the precipice on the edge of which I was tottering, until it was over, and my eyes were opened. Then the awful gulf of hell seemed to be open beneath me, covered only, as it were, by a spider's web, on which I stood. I seemed to hear the howling of the damned, to see the smoke of the bottomless pit, and to hear the rattling of those chains, which hold the impenitent under clouds of darkness to the judgment of the great day.

I trembled like Belshazzar, and cried out in the horror of my spirit, "God be merciful to me a sinner." That night I formed a resolution to pray; which, when resolved upon, there appeared, sitting in one corner of the room, Satan, in the form of a monstrous dog, and in a rage, as if in pursuit, his tongue protruding from his mouth to a great length, and his eyes looked like two balls of fire; it soon, however, vanished out of my sight. From this state of terror and dismay, I was happily delivered under the preaching of the Gospel as before related.

This view which I was permitted to have of Satan, in the form of a dog, is evidence, which corroborates in my estimation, the Bible account of a hell of fire, which burneth with brimstone, called in Scripture the bottomless pit; the place where all liars, who repent not, shall have their portion; as also the Sabbath breaker, the adulterer, the fornicator, with the fearful, the abominable, and the unbelieving, this shall be the portion of their cup.

This language is too strong and expressive to be applied to any state of suffering in time. Were it to be thus applied, the reality could no where be found in human life; the consequence would be, that this scripture would be found a false testimony. But when made to apply to an endless state of perdition, in eternity, beyond the bounds of human life, then this language is found not to exceed our views of a state of eternal damnation.

During the latter part of my state of conviction, I can now apply to my case, as it then was, the beautiful words of the poet:

> "The more I strove against its power,
> I felt its weight and guilt the more;
> 'Till late I heard my Saviour say,
> Come hither soul, I am the way."

This I found to be true, to the joy of my disconsolate and despairing heart, in the hour of my conversion to God.

During this state of mind, while sitting near the fire one evening, after I had heard Rev. Richard Allen, as before related, a view of my distressed condition so affected my heart, that I could not refrain from weeping and crying aloud; which caused the lady with whom I then lived, to inquire, with surprise, what ailed me; to which I answered, that I knew not what ailed me. She replied that I ought to pray. I arose from where I was sitting, being in an agony, and weeping convulsively, requested her to pray for me; but at the very moment when she would have done so, some person wrapped heavily at the door for admittance; it was but a person of the house, but this occurrence was sufficient to interrupt us in our intentions; and I believe to this day, I should then have found salvation to my soul. This interruption was, doubtless, also the work of Satan.

Although at this time, when my conviction was so great, yet I knew not that Jesus Christ was the Son of God, the second person in the adorable Trinity. I knew him not in the pardon, that my lot must inevitably be damnation. If I would pray—I knew not how. I could form no connexion of ideas into words; but I knew the Lord's prayer; this I uttered with a loud voice, and with all my might and strength. I was the most ignorant creature in the world; I did not even know that Christ had died for the sins of the world, and to save sinners. Every circumstance, however, was so directed as still to continue and increase the sorrows of my heart, which I now know to have been a Godly sorrow which wrought repentance, which is not to [be] repented of. Even the falling of the dead leaves from the forests, and dried spires of the mown grass, showed me that I too must die in like manner. But my case was awfully different from that of the grass of the field, or the wide spread decay of a thousand forests, as I felt within me a living principle, an immortal spirit, which cannot die, and must forever either enjoy the smiles of its Creator, or feel the pangs of ceaseless damnation.

But the Lord led me on; being gracious, he took pity on my ignorance; he heard my wailings, which had entered into the ear of the Lord of Sabaoth. Circumstances so transpired that I soon came to a knowledge of the being and character of the Son of God, of whom I knew nothing.

My strength had left me. I had become feverish and sickly through the violence of my feelings, on which account I left my place of service to spend a week with a colored physician, who was a member of the Methodist society, and also to spend this week in going to places where prayer and supplication was statedly made for such as me.

Through this means I had learned much, so as to be able in some degree to comprehend the spiritual meaning of the text, which the minister took on the Sabbath morning, as before related, which was "I perceive thy heart is not right in the sight of God."—Acts, chap. 8, verse 21. . . . [Lee doubts she is worthy of the blessing of sanctification; retreats for three months, struggles with Satan, and is sanctified.]

Between four and five years after my sanctification, on a certain time, an impressive silence fell upon me, and I stood as if some one was about to speak to me, yet I had no such thought in my heart.—But to my utter surprise there seemed to sound a voice which I thought I distinctly heard, and most certainly understand, which said to me, "Go preach the Gospel!" I immediately replied aloud, "No one will believe me." Again I listened, and again the same voice seemed to say—"Preach the Gospel; I will put words in your mouth, and will turn your enemies to become your friends."

At first I supposed that Satan had spoken to me, for I had read that he could transform himself into an angel of light for the purpose of deception. Immediately I went into a secret place, and called upon the Lord to know if he had called me to preach, and whether I was deceived or not; when there appeared to my view the form and figure of a pulpit, with a Bible lying thereon, the back of which was presented to me as plainly as if it had been a literal fact.

In consequence of this, my mind became so exercised, that during the night following, I took a text and preached in my sleep. I thought there stood before me a great multitude, while I expounded to them the things of religion. So violent were my exertions and so loud were my exclamations, that I awoke from the sound of my own voice, which also awoke the family of the house where I resided. Two days after I went to see the preacher in charge of the African Society, who was the Rev. Richard Allen, the same before named in these pages, to tell him that I felt it my duty to preach the gospel. But as I drew near the street in which his house was, which was in the city of Philadelphia, my courage began to fail me; so terrible did the cross appear, it seemed that I should not be able to bear it. Previous to my setting out to go to see him, so agitated was my mind, that my appetite for my daily food failed me entirely. Several times on my way there, I turned back again; but as often I felt my strength again renewed, and I soon found that the nearer I approached to the house of the minister, the less was my fear. Accordingly, as soon as I came to the door, my fears subsided, the cross was removed, all things appeared pleasant—I was tranquil.

I now told him, that the Lord had revealed it to me, that I must preach the gospel. He replied, by asking, in what sphere I wished to move in? I said, among the Methodists. He then replied, that a Mrs. Cook, a Methodist lady, had also some time before requested the same privilege; who, it was believed, had done much good in the way of exhortation, and holding prayer meetings; and who had been permitted to do so by the verbal license of the preacher in charge at the time. But as to women preaching, he said that our Discipline knew nothing at all about it—that it did not call for women preachers. This I was glad to hear, because it removed the fear of the cross—but no sooner did this feeling cross my mind, than I found that a love of soul had in a measure departed from me; that holy energy which burned within me, as a fire, began to be smothered. This I soon perceived. . . . [Lee speculates on the prohibition against women preachers; the efficacy of women preachers; fears of falling from grace; visions and faith in God's redemption.]

In the year 1811, I changed my situation in life, having married Mr. Joseph Lee, pastor of a Society at Snow Hill, about six miles from the city of Philadelphia. It became necessary therefore for me to remove. This was a great trial at first, as I knew no person at Snow Hill, except my husband, and to leave my associates in the society, and especially those who composed the band of which I was one. None but those who have been in sweet fellowship with such as really love God, and have together drank bliss and happiness from the same fountain, can tell how dear such company is, and how hard it is to part from them.

At Snow Hill, as was feared, I never found that agreement and closeness in communion and fellowship, that I had in Philadelphia, among my young companions, nor ought I to have expected it. The manners and customs at this place were somewhat different, on which account I became discontented in the course of a year, and began to importune my husband to remove to the city. But this plan did not suit him, as he was the Pastor of the Society, he could not bring his mind to leave them. This afflicted me a little. But the Lord showed me in a dream what his will was concerning this matter.

I dreamed that as I was walking on the summit of a beautiful hill, that I saw near me a flock of sheep, fair and white, as if but newly washed; when there came walking toward me a man of a grave and dignified countenance, dressed entirely in white, as it were in a robe, and looking at me, said emphatically, "Joseph Lee must take care of these sheep, or the wolf will come and devour them." When I awoke I was convinced of my error, and immediately, with a glad heart, yielded to the right spirit in the Lord. This also greatly strengthened my faith in his care over them, for fear the wolf should by some means take any of them away. The following verse was beautifully suited to our condition, as well as to all the little flocks of God scattered up and down this land:

"Us into thy protection take,
And gather with Thine arm;
Unless the fold we first forsake,
The wolf can never harm."

After this, I fell into a state of general debility, and in an ill state of health, so much so, that I could not sit up; but a desire to warn sinners to flee the wrath to come, burned vehemently in my heart, when the Lord would send sinners into the house to see me. Such opportunities I embraced to press home on their consciences the things of eternity, and so effectual was the word of exhortation made through the Spirit, that I have seen them fall to the floor crying aloud for mercy.

From this sickness I did not expect to recover, and there was but one thing which bound me to earth, and this was, that I had not as yet preached the gospel to the fallen sons and daughters of Adam's race, to the satisfaction of my mind. I wished to go from one end of the earth to the other, crying, Behold, behold the lamb! To this end I earnestly prayed the Lord to raise me up, if consistent with his will. He condescended to hear my prayer, and to give me a token in a dream, that in due time I should recover my health. The dream was as follows: I thought I saw the sun rise in the morning, and ascend to an altitude of about half an hour high, and then become obscured by a dense black cloud, which continued to hide its rays for about one-third part of the day, and then it burst forth again with renewed splendor.

This dream I interpreted to signify my early life, my conversion to God, and this sickness, which was a great affliction, as it hindered me, and I feared would forever hinder me from preaching the gospel, was signified by the cloud; and the bursting forth of the sun, again, was the recovery of my health, and being permitted to preach.

I went to the throne of grace on this subject, where the Lord made this impressive reply in my heart, while on my knees: "Ye shall be restored to thy health again, and worship God in full purpose of heart."

This manifestation was so impressive, that I could but hide my face as if some one was gazing upon me, to think of the great goodness of the Almighty God to my poor soul and body. From that very time I began to gain strength of body and mind, glory to God in the highest, until my health was fully recovered.

For six years from this time I continued to receive from above, such baptisms of the Spirit as mortality could scarcely bear. About that time I was called to suffer in my family, by death—five, in the course of about six years, fell by his hand; my husband being one of the number, which was the greatest affliction of all.

I was now left alone in the world, with two infant children, one of the age of about two years, the other six months, with no other dependence than the promise of Him who hath said—I will be the widow's God, and a father to the fatherless. . . . [Acknowledges friends and God's bounty.]

It was now eight years since I had made application to be permitted to preach the gospel, during which time I had only been allowed to exhort, and even this privilege but seldom. This subject now was renewed afresh in my mind; it was as a fire shut up in my bones. About thirteen months passed on, while under this renewed impression. During this time, I had solicited of the Rev. Bishop, Richard Allen, who at this time had become Bishop of the African Episcopal Methodists in America, to be permitted the liberty of holding prayer meetings in my own hired house, and of exhorting as I found liberty, which was granted me. By this means, my mind was relieved, as the house soon filled when the hour appointed for prayer had arrived. . . . [Lee is called on by the dying to pray; visions of redeeming Christ.]

Soon after this, as above related, the Rev. Richard Williams was to preach at Bethel Church, where I with others were assembled. He entered the pulpit, gave out the hymn, which was sung, and then addressed the throne of grace; took his text, passed through the exordium, and commenced to expound it. The text he took is in Jonah, 2d chap. 9th verse,—"Salvation is of the Lord." But as he proceeded to explain, he seemed to have lost the spirit; when in the same instant, I sprang, as by altogether supernatural impulse, to my feet, when I was aided from above to give an exhortation on the very text which my brother Williams had taken.

I told them I was like Jonah; for it had been then nearly eight years since the Lord had called me to preach his gospel to the fallen sons and daughters of Adam's race, but that I had lingered like him, and delayed to go at the bidding of the Lord, and warn those who are as deeply guilty as were the people of Ninevah.

During the exhortation, God made manifest his power in a manner sufficient to show the world that I was called to labor according to my ability, and the grace given unto me, in the vineyard of the good husbandman.

I now sat down, scarcely knowing what I had done, being frightened. I imagined, that for this indecorum, as I feared it might be called, I should be expelled from the church. But instead of this, the Bishop rose up in the assembly, and related that I had called upon him eight years before, asking to be permitted to preach, and that he had put me off; but that he now as much believed that I was called to that work, as any of the preachers present. These remarks greatly strengthened me, so that my fears of having given an offence, and made myself liable as an offender, subsided, giving place to a sweet serenity, a holy joy of a peculiar kind, untasted in my bosom until then. . . . [Lee begins holding meetings at various homes; conversions;

travels along the East Coast; is finally sponsored by Allen, who at times is her traveling companion; is appointed to Bethel Church, Philadelphia; also opens small schools along her way to earn money to keep going; health declines.]

After my return to Urbanna, Ohio, I took stage for Springfield, and from there to Columbus, and spoke several times. The Elder's class consisted of about twenty; a young man and myself led the class in 1829. The Elder W. C. ordered a camp-meeting for the Cincinnati people, and the brother at Cap-teen and Rev. Bishop Brown, held a conference, and we had a very large camp-meeting, and manifestations of great good, and at the close of the Love-feast, there were thirty-two or three testified that they experienced the love of God. The people of color came out forcibly, and the preachers preached in power. My health was much destroyed by speaking so often and laboring so very hard, having a heavy fever preying upon my system. I was called upon to speak at a camp-meeting, I could scarcely accomplish the task, and I was obliged to take my bed (having also lost my appetite) as soon as my sermon was over. After a while my particular friends conveyed me to Mount Pleasant in a carriage; the day was pleasant, but in the woods at night we were overtaken by a dreadful storm of thunder, wind and rain, but through the will of Providence I escaped the inclemency of the weather and stopped at brother and sister Hance's; after being medically renovated, I fulfilled an appointment, and commenced to visit the sick in that place, but was arrested by a heavy fever. A physician was called, and by daybreak my senses left me, so severe was the disease, which caused the physician to visit me two and three times a day, which proved to be the bilious fever. After my mind returned and became calm, I was convinced that it would not terminate in death at that time. I had faith in the Lord. Eleven days I lived on rice water and chicken tea without salt, at the end of which time I felt an appetite to eat. I had been under a deep salivation which proved a blessing in effecting a cure. After a lapse of four weeks I was enabled to get out of that house, but very weak; my money was short; I left seven dollars with them hoping the Lord may bless them; then I returned to brother Hance, and was well treated. I commenced preaching, though very weak, and I accepted an appointment on Sabbath in the white Methodist Episcopal church, to a well-behaved congregation, about ten miles distance. I had to be carried to the carriage in a blanket and returned the same way, and was well taken care of by brother and sister Moor and family, for which may the Lord bless them in basket and store. Elder Jones gave me an invitation to go to Pittsburgh and try to gather a little strength, which I accepted, and was kindly taken care of by brother Lewis and wife, which I very much profited by the assistance of his family doctor, which he called in amid the blessings of Providence; this was in May, 1830. I then commenced to labor amid the souls of the people, which are precious. After gaining strength in body and mind in my recovery, I spoke to a good number of colored friends on the Hill, and they were about to build a church for worship as they owned the property. When I was able to travel, one of the preacher's wives and a kind brother conducted me on to Washington, from which I took stage for Mount Pleasant; labored for them, enjoyed a love-feast with them, and in a few days left for St. Clairsville and the next successive place; then took stage for Zanesville, continuing to labor around the circuit, and then went to Columbus. I was invited to attend a quarterly meeting at Urbana; we had quite a profitable waiting upon the Lord; it makes me glad when they say let us go up to the house of the Lord. After trying to rest myself four or five weeks, a brother preacher, in company with brother Steward's widow and myself, visited the Indians, she having lived nine years in Sandusky. We heard them preach in their language, but I could only understand when he said Jesus Christ or God, and the interpreter had gone to conference. I spoke to them in English, was entertained in an indian family, and that very kindly, after which I shook the dust off my feet and left them in peace. Thank the Lord for Urbana. The Elder appointed a camp-meeting at Hillsborough; it was nothing to boast off; after which I turned towards Philadelphia. Brother Rains paid my stage fare on to Springfield; there I endeavoured to speak to a small and very quiet congregation; from thence to Columbus and paid seven dollars and a half, and left for Wheeling; stopped at a camp-meeting at the request of the Wheeling friends, but it seemed that both the golden wedge and Babalonish garment was there, as the wheel could not turn, for Christ said I could not do many mighty works on account of your unbelief; the Devil was at work, but the Lord was above. . . . [More traveling and preaching; son James takes up trade; discusses her financial situation.]

I then left for Little York in Canada, which was one day's sail across the Lakes; the passage was very rough that day. I was directed to Brother Brown's, the preacher, and was kindly received by himself and wife. I preached on Sabbath morning and afternoon, and that day we had a shout in the Camp of Israel. Praise God, the mission was both owned and received. After speaking several times and holding prayer meetings, I left them for Niagara, spoke three times. From there to St. David, and preached to a respectable congregation of whites and coloured persons. Six years before this I visited Niagara and there was a large society of the A.M.E.

Connexion, but at this time the very Chapel was gone, the minister dead, the people scattered and backslid. I, finding only two or three members at this time and no school, and children coming up in sin, then left for St. Catharine; spoke three times, but no particular revival, there were some who wished to be lords among God's heritage, and the work seemed stagnated, but they used me well, and I left them with peace of mind, in discharging my duty, Fort George, and spoke on Sabbath morning to a white and colored congregation in a schoolhouse—wonderful time indeed—some shouted, some mourned, others sought for mercy and I felt the Holy Ghost upon me, glory, glory, glory to God. After I helped to lead the class, I was insisted upon specially to preach a child's funeral sermon, before the corps left the incident: Seven years before I had preached in the neighborhood, to a great mixed multitude, after which I was invited to dine by this person, on which visit this child was born, or on that day; after some little hesitation on my part, I accepted the invitation and preached from the 2d book of Samuel, "I shall go to him, but he shall not return to me." It was a very solemn time—the corpse was then taken to the Church of England, and laid before the altar, the clergy spake over it, and very much to the purpose, without partiality, and then committed it to the breathless grave. On Thursday night I filled an appointment at a brother's house, the Lord was there. On the next Sabbath I rode seven miles, preached and helped to lead class, and the next week I left in stage for Little York, but stopped in Niagara, preached several times and paid a visit to a new society of Wesleyan Methodists, also then returned to York again, and preached for a society of Baptists, a very quiet and attentive congregation, with one exception. Text, by grace ye are saved through faith, that's not of yourselves, it's the gift of God. The Devil is always busy in his agency as in the following: a schoolteacher was present in the congregation who, after I concluded my subject, arose to contradict my argument, he became very much excited and red in his face, but while he was on his feet I expressed a desire of the congregation not to notice his reply, and they accordingly treated it with contempt, which caused him to desist with all his prejudices against women. The people were very kind. From thence by steamboat, I proceeded to Hambleton, which was 50 miles; I found no colored society in that place, but the children went to school; about two miles from there I found a class, and, by permission of the trustees, on Wednesday evening, I spoke in the Methodist Chapel, to a small congregation, from a very short notice, but the Lord owned His Word. After the close of the meeting, an English gentleman and his lady invited me to go home and lodge one night at their house, which I did, and they exhibited a great degree of benevolence towards me; may God reward them for it. On Sabbath morning I spoke to my own people, and afterwards led class and found the same one God owned them in worship also. I saw that seed must be sown accordingly. I spoke in the afternoon, and the Lord made himself manifest by His Spirit in great display; the people, though very poor, were exceedingly kind; one of the brother preachers, conveyed me to Dundee and Flamburg, west. I preached to a large congregation in the white Methodist Chapel. We had an humble waiting upon the Lord. From there I went to Lancaster, there the Lord prepared a friend to take care of me through the winter. I preached several times and met many friends whom I had seen in Cincinnati; some gifted preachers there, but no elder to preside. There were many of our society there, called from place to place, which had been scattered like sheep without a shepherd—it truly was heart-rending to hear them lamenting the loss of their shepherd who was deceased. The brethren kept a watch meeting on Christmas eve. We enjoyed the meeting and spent the night like St. Paul; the next day it fell to my lot to fill an appointment which I did with both life and liberty, (praise God for it) from the 2nd chap. of St. Luke, verses 10, 11. I felt my mind lead me to a village called Ammonsburg, on Lake Ontario, on what was called the Bush side, but I kept it with myself and the Lord, and kept travelling and preaching as the Lord gave ability. Brother S. Lewis was much interested at my anxiety for that people's welfare, and also Brother Wm. Edwards, a gospel preacher, who had been instrumental in civilizing and christianizing many of the natives whom I saw in Brentford, an Indian town on the Mohawk river, where a number of the natives lived along the river side, in the woods formed churches of societies of different denominations, ours excepted, and having no Methodist Church, a gentleman, seeing the necessity of a place of worship for us, gave us the privilege of a large house to worship in several times; truly it was cold, but we had many comfortable meetings, and very many solemn impressions made on a number of the minds of those present; afterwards I left for Buffalo. The road was so rough that it caused me to be quite sick. I could not stand it to ride 200 miles that cold weather, and I continued to preach in and out of town to different denominations through frost and snow. A gentleman came to me after the sermon was over, and wished me God's speed in a very friendly manner, then quietly withdrew with his ladies in company with him, with politeness. My mind was on Buffalo, Brother Edwards had not yet formed any society. I particularly desired him to take my appointment, which he did, and also read the discipline with proper explanations, wishing to know who would be subject to the government of the same, and there were ten persons came forward and consented to be subject as members of our Discipline. I went to Ancaster, stopped at brother Lewis' and wife, and although she was a young married woman, she was very much like a mother to me. My mind was exercised to go to Ammonsburg, through a gloomy winter; that night, after serious meditation, I fell asleep, and suddenly awoke and received the witness that I must go. Next morning I informed brother Lewis that I must go, and, he, feeling interested for me, had me conveyed, in a private carriage, that I might travel comfortably. In the middle of February I left for Chatham, and arrived there on the 26th of the same month, where I found a society scattered, without a shepherd; some living in the faith of Christ, while others had gone back to the beggarly elements of the world. Mr. Lightfoot received me very kindly; his house was open for worship, where I had large gatherings some five or six times, for a new place. The house being quite commodious, and Mr. Lightfoot used every endeavor to send me on with the gospel to others. In April I left for Ammonsburg, there the believers seemed much strengthened; backsliders reclaimed, and sinners converted to God. Among which was a woman that had belonged to the Methodists by profession, having the form of godliness but was destitute of the power, until the Spirit of God arrested her at this time. After which she ceased her carnal amusements; quit dancing and went to praying, at which time she arose on her feet and said that she never saw that dancing was wrong before now—but she had resolved to serve God in spirit and truth—praise God for the victory. For three days in Ammonsburg we could scarcely get any rest, from the effects of the outpouring of the spirit of God, on both white and colored. I was still more confirmed in mind that my visit was accepted of my God, who gave me this mission in Christ Jesus. I stopped with a brother, Jas. McKinney, and his affectionate wife, who had suffered much in the fear of Jesus. Brother made an appointment for the next evening for me, which I tried to fill. Text as follows: 16th chap. of St. Matthew's Gospel, 26th verse. I was in a strange part of God's vineyard, but his power was manifest even there; after which another appointment was made for Sunday morning, which was alike prosperous, and I helped to lead class; then spoke in the afternoon and at night with equal success. My mind was much exercised, seeing the need of schools. I counted 25 children and some young people whom I loved. I lamented their obscurity, and advised them to get a white man to teach them, and endeavoured to shew them, that, without the advantages of education they never would be a moral people, and, in the course of time, their own children could, by proper advancement, become teachers for themselves. So I continued in all the towns, finally they caught the spirit and commenced in the following places; in Ancaster they chose their trustees to build a house for school, and likewise to preach in, at Brantford, at Chatham, and St. Catharine. Some went to St. David's and Toronto, to Sabbath Schools, and in the week also; colored and white, all went together. After the course of two or three weeks, a colored teacher came to the last named place and established a school of between 30 or 40 scholars (after being examined and found competent) which improved the manners of the people very much, and they worshipped in their own Chapels. Their own preachers, exhorters, and class-leaders (colored.) There was a young sister that wished to travel with me a little way, and brother McKinney furnished us with a driver and conveyance, and the friends received us very kindly, and, to my astonishment, we were given appointments by the trustees of the Church. I spoke from the following text, By grace ye are saved through faith, that is not of yourselves, but it is the gift of God. A Friend, W——, was there, who was ever ready to oppose the Methodists; he was a Baptist preacher, and would invite the Methodists to preach for them, and then get up and contradict them; he wished me to come and preach for them, but I felt no spirit of contention in religion and I declined. Our own people were talking of forming a union with the Canadian Methodists who were a branch of the Old Episcopal Methodists, that was raised by the missionaries from America; this being the time of the split, but some would leave to the Wesleyan Methodists. I preached five or six different times in this village for several Sabbaths two sermons a day, in which the Lord gave ability. We continued our meetings as usual, and invited the old ministers to visit us, which they did; and one of them gave an exhortation after me, and God's power filled the house and the guilty were alarmed, while believers rejoiced in hope of a better resurrection. I left that morning, rode five miles with a friend, and on Wednesday afternoon preached again—signs and wonders followed—after which I continued to visit the sick the remainder of the week; and on Sabbath day I rode five miles again to the Chapel, and filled an appointment in the afternoon for the last time as I thought, but the Lord seen best, and I was retained another week; the next Sabbath I filled an appointment from the following text: Finally, brethren, pray for us that the word of the Lord have free course and be glorified even as it is with you; which was my Farewell Sermon. After which I returned to Ammonsburg in the fear of God; where I preached several times and saw many manifestations of the operations of the Spirit of grace, and, on the following Sabbath, Brother A—— made an appointment for me six miles distant, and one also for 6 o'clock in the evening; we had a very hard ride through the swamp, and met a large gathering both in and out of doors, and sinners were cut to the heart, and cried aloud for mercy, which was a joyful sound to believers in Christ Jesus. The next evening I spoke again from Isaiah, chap. 59 ver. 1; and several of the nobility taking into consideration my necessities, contributed to me the sum of $5. We had a quiet waiting upon the Lord; after which I and a sister that was with me, called on Mr. Gardiner and he collected some subscriptions and added to the former sum, for which, I trust, God will reward all the cheerful givers, as they were very generous. I held prayer-meetings, visited the sick, and passed many joyful moments of sweet communion especially in one sister's company, who was a member of the National Church in Ammonsburg.

But in affliction she enjoyed the Spirit's grace, and, in May, 1834, we parted as for eternity, and I trust to meet her where parting will be no more, neither will any of us shake the parting hand, for we have had sweet communion together, in spiritual exercises. Dear reader, think not that I am going to heaven as in golden slippers, for I have various trials to encounter while travelling over this world so wide, but I feel willing to suffer for the cause of God, after which I shall (if faithful) meet many of my friends that have communed with me in the Spirit, where we never, never shall shake the parting hand—these are the consolations in affliction as described in Rev. chap. 12, 11th verse. And they overcame him by the Blood of the Lamb, and by the word of their testimony, and they loved not their lives unto death; and whilst I move my pen my soul rejoices in God my Redeemer. Having filled my mission I parted with my friends in joy. I sailed for Detroit city, 18 miles, then bid adieu to British shores, not knowing that I should ever step on them again. I was kindly received on American possessions by a respectable family from Cincinnati, a Mr. D——. I felt there was a work for me to do in that part of God's vineyard. I arrived on Tuesday and on Thursday evening we had a comfortable meeting at the usual place. I met with much encouragement in laboring for the Lord, and many impressions were made on the minds of the hearers. The evening previous to my landing I saw some of the American affliction towards the people of color, such as mobbing, theft and destruction. Wo [*sic*] unto the inhabitants of the earth and the sea, for the Devil is come down unto you. On the following Sabbath morning, 10 o'clock, I preached again, then lead class—a soul reviving time, indeed—at 7 o'clock, P.M. I preached again, and the house was crowded to overflowing, it not being sufficient to hold the people. Text as follows: And the gospel of the kingdom shall be preached unto all the world for a witness, and then shall the end come. After which we visited a prayer meeting held by the stationed minister in the white Church, which was truly comfortable. On the next Sabbath I had an appointment made for me on the British side in a dwelling house, but, it not being sufficient to hold the people, the Episcopal Methodists opened their session-room which was larger and well crowded with various denominations. Text, 1st chap. St. John; ver. 45. The Lord touched my tongue as with a live coal from his altar, and we had a good time as from the hand of the Lord, and the Amens of the preachers, elders, and leaders, helped to swell the theme of rejoicing. Glory to God, we had all things common. But now feeling my mission ended I waited for the first opportunity and took passage for Buffalo. Three hundred and sixty miles on Lake Ontario, and, I must say, the most uncomfortable passage I ever experienced, although the boat was commodious, yet they treated the people of color very indifferently indeed, as regards their accommodation, and yet charged them a high price, I having paid $4.50. After two uncomfortable days' and nights' sail, we arrived at Buffalo wharf about six o'clock, A.M. . . . [Six years pass in Buffalo; mingling with various friends and Anti-Slavery Society members; longs to return to Philadelphia; resumes preaching agenda at AME church, catalogue of travels, including Canada; opponents of female preaching.]

I was then sent for to return again to Owego, a distance of 38 miles, and they would pay my way on to Montrose, on my way to Philadelphia. I obeyed the request and found things very prosperous indeed. At night we had prayer meetings, and the Lord continued to pour out his spirit upon the people, and we had a meeting every night. Mr. J. H., formerly of Columbia, whose lot was cast as in a strange land, where there were only a few people that were members of the M.E. church; several husbands, strangers to God until now, and their wives, servants of the most High God, and two daughters of Mr. J. H., were justified through faith—three joined the church previously. I was selected to make a class book, and did so, as I wanted to see how many were for us. The Baptists had held an anxious meeting, after which five joined them. I made the trial by special invitation, and thirteen joined us. I had preached on Sabbath morning and night, and then held prayer meetings every night afterwards that week, except Saturday night; a man and his wife fell to the floor and cried for mercy, and both arose in the same hour soundly converted, giving God the glory. I preached on the next Sabbath morning and then led class, and at night again—text, Judges iv. 25, 26. They all marvelled at a woman taking such a deep subject, but the Lord assisted the organ of clay, and we had the victory, as there were twenty-one persons joined from that revival, and nearly all of them evinced justifying grace. On 3d day night we wound up, as I was to start on my journey on next day, which I did—brother paid my passage. I rode 28 miles in good company with a lady and gentleman who were going to New York. She said she was sorry to part; we had a heavy thunder storm with rain, and it was very dark, but we had a very careful driver, and we arrived safe at Montrose and took supper—between 12 and 1 o'clock at night I took stage for Wilkesbarre and arrived there at 8 next morning, and there I crossed the Susquehanna; I was very hungry, and having a little time I went to the house and asked the lady for breakfast and I would pay her. She said she had nothing, but would try and get me a good breakfast and take no pay, which she did. I truly feel thankful to God that he had proved himself a table in the wilderness. About 4 o'clock in the afternoon I arrived safe and was kindly received, and preached on Sabbath morning and night. Between the two appointments I rode two miles and preached in the afternoon. That day the Lord was in the house in power. Tuesday evening we had a glorious prayer meeting. I rode all night around the mountain, and some walked and appeared to be a quarter of a mile off. But the Lord preserved me in the mail stage alone. I adore his name now and I shall for evermore. The preacher in charge arrived the next day after I did, and spent his labors of love among the people. On the Wednesday following he went away and left me in charge of the class, (eight persons) to regulate them, and by the permission of the elder I addressed them. After I had relieved my mind and taken my seat the preacher formed them into a class and appointed a leader, who but three months before, was unconverted; but being so interested for the prosperity of Zion, seemed worthy of the appointment. After this I endeavored to hold prayer meetings through the week; preached twice on Sabbath day and helped to lead class, as the brother was young,—but they were all willing people, and truly it seemed to be the day of God's power among them, and "Peace abided at our House."

At the expiration of three weeks and four days I left them fifteen names on their class book. I then rode a distance of sixty miles over a hard road, hills and mountains, (there being no turn-pike or rail-road on that rout from Wilksbarre to Easton;)—some part of the way there was good sleighing. Through the help of Providence we arrived at Easton about 8 o'clock, P.M. I took supper and lodging in the Hotel, where I was well accommodated; after which I found a small number of colored friends. We had a meeting, and "it was good for us to be there." After this I called at New Hope, thirty-two miles I think from Philadelphia; visited the family I was brought up in, stopped and rested myself, as I felt much exhausted from travelling, so much winter and summer. I preached two or three times. Brother J. B.—was holding a protracted meeting. I gained strength; thank the lord, and then left for home, and arrived in the city the last day of March 1842, having been two years, wanting a few days, almost incessantly travelling. I found my son, together with the rest of my family connections quite well; yet I could hear of the ravages of death, the relentless murderer, who never takes denials; my little grand-daughter, a promising child indeed, was taken with the rest. O! how soon delights may perish, and my heart responds—"The Lord's will be done."

My health being very much impaired, I knew not but that I should be the next one called away, but the Lord spared me for some other purpose, and upon my recovery I commenced travelling again, feeling it better to wear out than to rust out—and so expect to do until death ends the struggle—knowing, if I lose my life for Christ's sake, I shall find it again.

I now conclude—by requesting the prayers of God's people everywhere, who worship in His holy fear, to pray for me, that I ever may endeavor to keep a conscience void of offence, either towards God or man—for I feel as anxious to blow the Trumpet in Zion, and sound the alarm in God's Holy Mount, as ever;—

> Though Nature's strength decay,
> And earth and hell withstand—
> To Canaan's land I'l urge my way,
> At HIS Divine command.

But here I feel constrained to give over, as from the smallness of this pamphlet I cannot go through with the whole of my journal, as it would probably make a volume of two hundred pages; which, if the Lord be willing, may at some future day be published. But for the satisfaction of such as may follow after me, when I am no more, I have recorded how the Lord called me to his work, and how he has kept me from falling from grace, as I feared I should. In all things he had proved himself a God of truth to me; and in his service I am now as much determined to spend and be spent, as at the very first. My ardour for the progress of his cause abates not a whit, so far as I am able to judge, though I am now something more than fifty years of age.

As to the nature of uncommon impressions, which the reader cannot but have noticed, and possibly sneered at in the course of these pages, they may be accounted for in this way: It is known that the blind have the sense of hearing in a manner much more acute than those who can see: also their sense of feeling is exceedingly fine, and is found to detect any roughness on the smoothest surface, where those who can see find none. So it may be with such as I am, who has never had more than three months schooling; and wishing to know much of the way and law of God, have therefore watched the more closely, the operations of the Spirit, and have in consequence been led thereby. But let it be remarked that I have never found that Spirit lead me contrary to the Scriptures of truth, as I understand them. "For as many as are led by the Spirit of God are the sons of God."—Rom. viii. 14.

I have now only to say, May the blessing of the Father, and of the Son, and of the Holy Ghost, accompany the reading of this poor effort to speak well of his name, wherever it may be read. AMEN

P.S. Please to pardon errors, and excuse all imperfections, as I have been deprived of the advantages of education (which I hope all will appreciate) as I am measurably a self-taught person. I hope the contents of this work may be instrumental in leaving a lasting impression upon the minds of the impenitent; may it prove to be encouraging to the justified soul, and a comfort to the sanctified.

Though much opposed, it is certainly essential in life, as Mr. Wesley wisely observes. Thus ends the Narrative of Jarena Lee, the first female preacher of the First African Methodist Episcopal Church.

Bethel at Philadelphia, Penn., United States of America.

8

Nancy Gardner Prince
(1799–?)

■

Introduction

Nancy Gardner Prince is Mary Seacole's U.S.-born counterpart as a female "Black Atlantic" writer. Toward the end of her life, she penned *A Narrative of the Life and Travels of Nancy Prince.*[105] In one critic's view, Prince's narrative is "one of the few surviving autobiographical accounts by a free black woman in the pre-Civil War North. . . . None can match hers for exotic settings and remarkable happenings."[106] Like Seacole, Prince is an explorer who cherishes world-wide physical mobility. In Prince's case, she inherited this love from a variety of male relatives. From an early age until adolescence, she listened to her grandfather and her mother's third husband reciting the history of their ancestors. Several of her male relatives (stepfather, a brother, husband) worked as sailors. During the War of 1812 her second stepfather had been impressed into the British navy.[107]

Prince's wanderlust was fostered by a debilitating domestic life. Overworked and brutalized, she tried to support the family after her mother's health permanently deteriorated. Similar to Harriet Wilson's, but in a different context, Prince's narrative stresses the thin dividing line between servitude and slavery, between brutal employers and brutal owners. As in Jarena Lee's life, Freemasonry also opens up an alternate route to freedom.

Like her male relatives and even more famous eighteenth-century former slave sailors, such as Ottabah Cuguano and Olaudah Equiano, though not in an enslaved status, Prince crisscrosses the globe. She voyages from the North American mainland to Russia, then after several years back again, and thence to Jamaica. She lives out her life in the United States. In many senses, her peripatetic freedom symbolizes the escape from slavery that U.S. slaves described.

■

Biographical Narrative

Nancy Gardner Prince was born in 1799 in Newburyport, on the Massachusetts North Shore, into a family of free African Americans with an admixture of Native American ancestry. A total of 6,500 free African Americans lived in Massachusetts then. Her maternal grandfather, a slave, had fought in the Revolutionary army in the battle of Bunker Hill. The English had enslaved her Indian grandmother. Proud of her heritage, she considered her cultural identity a matter of deep significance.

Nancy's father, Thomas Gardner, died three months after her birth, and the family moved to Boston to live with her maternal grandfather. After her mother remarried and her stepfather died, Nancy and her siblings were moved from one household to another to work. The "grief, poverty, and responsibility, were too much" for Nancy's mother; "she never again was the mother she had been before" (p. 8).

Prince had to stand on her own feet from a very early age. She took care of herself and her siblings, placing them in homes and jobs as best she could. At eight and again at fourteen, with intervals at home, she was an overworked and maltreated domestic servant: "in three months my health and strength were gone" (p.11). On one occasion she rescued her sister Silvia, a sexual victim of their stepfather, from a brothel in Boston.

Prince turned to religion "after living sixteen years without hope," finding comfort there the rest of her life.[108] The minister who baptized her in 1819, the Reverend Thomas Paul, was a leader among Boston's free blacks and a member of the Masonic African Grand Lodge, No. 459, as was her future husband.[109]

In 1824, Nancy Gardner married Nero Prince, a man several years her elder and one of the few black guards in the Russian royal court.[110] He was a founding member of the first black Freemasons' lodge in America, deputy grand Master in 1791, and second grand master in 1807. Beginning in Boston in the 1770s, Freemasonry positively affected the lives of many blacks: "Masonic sermons drew upon the same vocabulary of brotherhood that animated evangelical abolition."[111] After their marriage, the couple left for Russia. In Saint Petersburg, Prince became a seamstress to the ladies of the court, establishing a sewing shop that employed journeywomen and apprentices. She also took in needy children, a gesture in response to her own woeful early years. She was active as well in the Russian Bible Society and in the establishment of various social organizations. As a palace guard, her husband could move with some freedom in the court, an insider circumstance that she could share to some extent. She was in the capital on October 9th, 1824 at the time of the great flood. In 1825, when Alexander I, great-nephew of Catherine the Great, died, she witnessed the attempted military coup—the Decembrist Revolt.

After her husband's death in 1833, Prince returned to the U.S. (On the night she sailed, the proclamation of emancipation was announced in the British Parliament.) Her experiences in Russia made her a sought-after commentator on the Russian aristocracy. She put her celebrity status at the service of the anti-slavery and other reform movements and became acquainted with Lucretia Mott. Steadfast, she nonetheless grew disillusioned with abolition groups and the role that women played in the movement.

Prince decided to go to Jamaica to open a free labor school for impoverished girls in 1840, two years after the apprenticeship system that Britain's Emancipation Act of 1834 had created for former slaves had broken down in that island. Field slaves were to have labored until 1840,[112] but in consequence of the system's inadequacies full emancipation had been proclaimed 1 August, 1838. Missionaries from the United States and Britain flocked to Jamaica.

Prince's missionary efforts were compromised by mercenary and dishonest colleagues, and escalating racial tension dampened prospects of success. Prince did establish a church school there, then left Jamaica the next year.

In the United States she tried to raise funds for the labor school and published *The West Indies: Being a Description of the Islands, Progress of Christianity, Education, and Liberty among the Colored Population Generally.*[113] In 1842, she returned to Jamaica and in 1843 in the *National Anti-Slavery Standard,* attributed not being able to establish a labor school for girls to insufficient support by missionary groups and government.

The West Indies, which covers Prince's life through her Jamaican trips, was reprinted in 1853 and 1856, and also incorporated into *A Narrative of the Life and Travels of Mrs. Nancy Prince* (1850). *A Narrative* relates her anger at injustice, slavery, racism, sex discrimination, and emigration schemes, but curiously, Prince's reservations about emigration are not voiced in public discussion, possibly organized by the Convention Movement or the American Moral Reform Society, founded in 1831 and 1835–1842, respectively, to discuss issues of critical importance to the black community. She omits some important incidents from *A Narrative.* One instance: her role in apprehending a slave catcher after the Fugitive Slave Law was passed. Thomas Hilton applauds Prince's courage in the following account:

> One day between eleven and twelve o'clock, A.M., there was a ripple of excitement in the rear of Smith's Court. Some children had reported that a slave holder was in Mrs. Dorsey's. It being working hours scarcely a colored man was seen in the vicinity; but there were those around that showed themselves equal to the occasion. Among these were Mrs. Nancy Prince, a colored woman of prominence in Boston who, with several others, hurried to the scene. Mrs. Prince had seen the kidnapper before. Only for an instance did [her] fiery eyes rest upon the form of the villain, as if to be fully assured that it was he, for the next moment she had grappled with him, and before he could fully realize his position she, with the assistance of the colored women that had accompanied her, had dragged him to the door and thrust him out of the house. By this time quite a number, mostly women and children had gathered near by, whom Mrs. Prince commanded to come to the rescue, telling them to "pelt him with stones and any thing you can get a hold of," which order they proceeded to obey with alacrity. The slaveholder started to retreat, and with his assailants close upon him ran out of the court. Only once did the man turn in his head-long flight when, seeing them streaming after him terribly in earnest, their numbers constantly increasing and hearing in his ears their exultant cries and shouts of derision he redoubled his speed and, turning the corner was soon lost to view.[114]

At the Fifth National Woman's Rights Convention in Philadelphia in 1854, Prince recounted the experiences described in *A Narrative,* an appearance that was part of her complex politic of class, gender, and race. Divine support, besides, is a constant in *A Narrative.* The 1853 and 1856 editions include further biographical detail about her African ancestry and her economic and emotional struggle to survive.

Prince's whereabouts after 1854 are unknown. A free-born African American who witnessed many historical events, she claimed a new kind of freedom, flouted conventional views of "true womanhood," and pioneered a new genre for black U.S. women.[115] Geographical as well as psychological and political mobility mattered to her. A lecturer and writer, agitator against slavery and for women's rights, hers is one of the most historically important travel narratives of the early nineteenth century. In U.S. cultural history, she epitomized the female "Black Atlantic" world.

■

CHRONOLOGY

1799	Born in Newburyport, Massachusetts, into a family of free black American and Native American heritage.
1799	Father, seaman Thomas Gardner, dies. Upon mother's mental collapse, assumes role of parent. Family lives in Boston with maternal grandmother, who instructs Nancy in religion.
1807	Works as a maidservant in harsh conditions; forced by ill health to return home.
1813	As a domestic servant, is again maltreated, made permanently physically frail.
1816	Rescues sister Silvia from brothel.
1817	Baptized by the Reverend Thomas Paul, Boston black community leader and Freemason, founder of the first Independent African American Church in the North.
1824	Marries Nero Prince, second Grand Master of Prince Hall Grand Lodge of Freemasons, 1807–1809; they travel to Saint Petersburg, where Nero is a guard at the imperial court.
1824–1825	Nancy Prince takes in child boarders; organizes child-care services; is active in Bible study, and operates a sewing business. Witnesses the great flood in St. Petersburg.
1825	Witnesses the unsuccessful Decembrist Revolt.
1833	Returns to the United States after husband's death.
1839	Lectures on Russia.
1840	Observes conditions in post-emancipation Jamaica.
1841	Returns to United States; tries to raise funds for a free labor school. Publishes *The West Indies.*
1842	Returns to Jamaica.
1847	In the United States once again, helps to apprehend a slaveholder trying to catch a runaway.
1850	Publishes *A Narrative of the Life and Travels of Mrs. Nancy Prince;* reprinted in 1853 and 1856 with added biographical information.

1856 Appears before the National Woman's Right Convention. Subsequent whereabouts are unclear.

Date of death is unknown.

■ ■ ■

FROM *A NARRATIVE OF THE LIFE AND TRAVELS OF MRS. NANCY PRINCE*

I was born in Newburyport, September the 15th, 1799. My mother was born in Gloucester, Massachusetts—the daughter of Tobias Wornton, or Backus, so called. He was stolen from Africa, when a lad, and was a slave of Captain Winthrop Sargent; but, although a slave, he fought for liberty. He was in the Revolutionary army, and at the battle of Bunker Hill. He often used to tell us, when little children, the evils of Slavery, and how he was stolen from his native land. My grandmother was an Indian of this country; she became a captive to the English, or their descendants. She served as a domestic in the Parsons family. My father, Thomas Gardner, was born in Nantucket; his parents were of African descent. He died in Newburyport, when I was three months old. My mother was thus a second time left a widow, with her two children, and she returned to Gloucester to her father. My mother married her third husband, by whom she had six children. My stepfather was stolen from Africa, and while the vessel was at anchor in one of our Eastern ports, he succeeded in making his escape from his captors, by swimming ashore. I have often heard him tell the tale. Having some knowledge of the English language, he found no trouble to pass. There were two of them, and they found, from observation, that they were in a free State. I have heard my father describe the beautiful moonlight night when they two launched their bodies into the deep, for liberty. When they got upon soundings, their feet were pricked with a sea-plant that grew under water, they had to retreat, and, at last they reached the shore. When day began to break, they laid down under a fence, as naked as they were born—soon they heard a rattling sound, and trembling, they looked to see what it meant. In a few minutes, a man with a broad-brimed hat on, looked over the fence and cried out, "Halloo boys! you are from that ship at anchor?" Trembling, we answered, yes. He kindly took us by the hand, and told us not to fear, for we were safe. "Jump, boys," said he, "into my cart," which we readily did. He turned about, and soon entered a large yard—we were taken to his house and carried to an apartment, where he brought us clothes and food, and cheered us with every kindness. No search was made for us; it was supposed we were drowned, as many had jumped over-board on the voyage, thinking they could get home to Africa again. I have often heard my step-father boast how brave they were, and say they stood like men and saw the ship set sail with less than half they stole from Africa. He was selling his bamboo baskets, when he was seized by white men, and put in a boat, and taken on board the ship that lay off; many such ships there were! He was called "Money Vose," and his name may be found on the Custom House books in Gloucester. His last voyage was with Captain Elias Davis, in the brig Romulus, belonging to Captain Fitz William Sargent, in whose employ he had been twelve years. During the war, the brig was taken by a British privateer, and he was pressed into their service. He was sick with the dropsy a long while, and died oppressed, in the English dominions. My mother was again left a widow, with an infant six weeks old, and seven other children. When she heard of her husband's death, she exclaimed, "I thought it; what shall I do with these children?" She was young, inexperienced, with no hope in God, and without the knowledge of her Saviour. Her grief, poverty, and responsibilities, were too much for her; she never again was the mother that she had been before. I was, at this time, in Captain F. W. Sargent's family. I shall never forget the feelings I experienced, on hearing of the decease of my father-in-law, although he was not kind to me or my sister; but, by industry a humble home was provided, for my mother and her younger children. Death had twice visited our family, in less than three months. My grandfather died before my father-in-law sailed. I thought I would go home a little while, and try and comfort my mother. The three oldest children were put into families.

My brother and myself stayed at home that Summer. . . . We stayed with our mother until every resource was exhausted; we then heard of a place eight miles out of town, where a boy and girl were wanted. We both went and were engaged. We often went home with our wages, and all the comforts we could get; but we could not approach our mother as we wished. God in mercy took one little boy of seven years, who had been in a consumption one year.

My oldest sister, Silvia, was seventy miles in the country, with the family that brought her up; so were scattered all about. Soon as the war was over, I determined to get more for my labor. I left Essex and went to Salem, in the month of April, 1814, without a friend, without a guide. I first went to

Gloucester, to bid my mother and the family adieu. . . .

In the Spring of 1815, I returned to Salem, accompanied by my eldest sister, and we obtained good places. She took it into her head to go to Boston, as a nursery girl, where she lived a few months and was then deluded away. February 7th, 1816, a friend came to Salem and informed me of it. To have heard of her death, would not have been so painful to me, as we loved each other very much, and more particularly, as our step-father was not very kind to us. . . . My brother George and myself were very desirous to make our mother comfortable; he went to sea for that purpose; the next April, I came to Boston to get a higher price for my labor; for we had agreed to support my mother, and hoped she would take home our little brother and take care of him, who was supported by the town. George came home, and sailed again in the same employ, leaving mother a draw bill for half his wages. My sister returned to Boston to find me, and wished to procure a place to work out. I had just changed my place for one more retired, and engaged my sister with me as a chamber maid; she tried me much. I thought it a needy time, for I had not yielded my heart to the will of God, though I had many impressions, and formed many resolutions; but the situations that I had been placed in, (having left my mother's house at the age of eight,) had not permitted me to do as I wished, although the kind counsels of my dear grandfather and pious teachers followed me wherever I went. Care after care oppressed me—my mother wandered about like a Jew—the young children who were in families were dissatisfied; all hope but in God was lost. I resolved, in my mind, to seek an interest in my Savior, and put my trust in Him; and never shall I forget the place or time when God spake to my troubled conscience. Justified by faith I found peace with God, for forgiveness of sin through Jesus Christ my Lord. After living sixteen years without hope, and without a guide, May 6th, 1819, the Rev. Thomas Paul, baptized myself, and seven others in obedience to the great command. . . .

When winter came, poor mother's health was declining. Little Samuel could do but little; my father-in-law was very cross, his disappointment was very great, for he expected to be supported by my brother George and myself. I could not see my mother suffer, therefore I left my place and went to Salem to watch over her and Samuel, and lived in the Rev. Dr. Bolle's family. In the Spring, I returned to Boston, and took my brother Samuel with me; soon after, my sister Lucy left her place and went to her mother, but was not permitted to stay; my mother wrote to me, requesting me to take care of her. I then determined, in my mind, to bring her to Boston, and if possible, procure a place for her; I then had Samuel and John on my hands; Lucy was not nine, and very small of her age, I could not easily get her a place, but fortunately obtained board for her and Samuel for one dollar a week. My brother John, whom I had boarded, at last got a place where he had wages. Soon the Lord opened the way for little Samuel; Dr. Phelps took him to bring up: so that I was left with one only to sustain; soon my hopes were blasted. John left his place, and was several months on my hands again; finally, he made up his mind to go to sea; I was so thankful that he had concluded to do something, that I took two months' wages in advance to fit him out for Liverpool, in five months he returned without a single thing but the clothes he had on. The ship brought passengers from Ireland. As soon as the vessel arrived, he came to seek me; I went with him for his things; but passengers and all were gone. His wages were small, not enough to make him comfortable: and, had not a friend given him a home, he would again have been dependent on my exertions; another friend took Lucy, with whom she stayed eleven months. She lived in different families until she was about twelve years old; I then put her in the Rev. Mr. Mann's family, at Westminster, for a certain time, thinking it would be best for her; and John I left to fight his own battles. My sister Silvia, was one of my greatest trials. Knowing she was in Boston, my mother, in one of her spells of insanity, got away from her home and travelled to Boston after her; she came where I lived, my employers were very kind to her, she tarried a few days, when I hired a horse and chaise and took them both back to Salem, and returned to my place in 1822, with a determination to do something for myself; I left my place after three months, and went to learn a trade; and after seven years of anxiety and toil, I made up my mind to leave my country. September 1st, 1823, Mr. Prince arrived from Russia. February 15th, 1824, we were married. April 14th, we embarked on board the Romulus, captain Epes Sargent commander, bound for Russia. May 24th, arrived at Elsinore, left the same day for Copenhagen, where we remained twelve days. We visited the king's palace, and several other extensive and beautiful buildings. We attended a number of entertainments, among the Danes and English, who were religious; observed that their manners and customs were similar; they are attentive to strangers; the Sabbath is very strictly observed; the principal religion is Lutheran and Calvinistic, but all persuasions are tolerated. The languages are Dutch, French and English. The Danes are very modest and kind, but like all other nations, they know how to take the advantage. We left Copenhagen the 7th of June, and arrived at Cronstadt on the 19th; left there the 21st for St. Petersburg, and in a few hours, were happy to find ourselves at our place of destination, through the blessing of

God, in good health, and soon made welcome from all quarters. We took lodgings with a Mrs. Robinson, a native of our country, who was Patience Mott, of Providence, who left here in the year 1813, in the family of Alexander Gabriel, the man who was taken for Mr. Prince. There I spent six weeks very pleasantly, visiting and receiving friends, in the manner of the country. While there I attended two of their parties; there were various amusements in which I did not partake, which caused them much disappointment. I told them my religion did not allow of dancing or dice playing, which formed part of the amusements. As they were very strict in their religion, they indulged me in the same privilege. By the help of God I was ever enabled to preserve my stand.

Mr. Prince was born in Marlborough, and lived in families in this city. In 1810 he went to Gloucester, and sailed with Captain Theodore Stanwood, for Russia. He returned with him and remained in his family, and at this time visited at my mother's. He sailed with captain Stanwood in 1812, for the last time. The Captain took with him his son Theodore, in order to place him in School in St. Petersburg. When the Captain sailed for home, Mr. Prince went to serve the Princess Purtossof, one of the noble ladies of the Court. The palace where the imperial family reside is called the court, or the seat of Government. . . .

I learned the languages in six months, so as to be able to attend to my business, and also made some proficiency in the French. My time was taken up in domestic affairs; I took two children to board, the third week after commencing housekeeping, and increased their numbers. The baby linen making and childrens' garments were in great demand. I started a business in these articles and took a journeywoman and apprentices. The present Empress is a very active one, and inquired of me respecting my business, and gave me much encouragement by purchasing of me garments for herself and children, handsomely wrought in French and English styles, and many of the nobility also followed her example. It was to me a great blessing that we had the means of grace afforded us. The Rev. Richard Kennell, was the Protestant pastor. We had service twice every Sabbath, and evening prayer meetings, also a female society, so that I was occupied at all times.

At the time of the inundation, the Bibles and other books belonging to the society were injured. But Mr. Kenell took the liberty to purchase at full price and sell at an advance. In order that the poor might have them, we all agreed to labor for that purpose. I often visited the matron of the Empress' children, and encouraged by her I took some to the Palace, and by this means disposed of many at head quarters. Other friends without the court continued to labor until hundreds and thousands were disposed of. The old Bishop finding his religion was in danger sent a petition to the Emperor that all who were found distributing Bibles and Tracts should be punished severely. Many were taken and imprisoned, two devoted young men were banished; thus the righteous were punished, while evil practices were not forbidden, for there the sin of licentiousness is very common.

I have mentioned that the climate did not agree with me; in winter my lungs were much affected. It was the advice of the best physicians that I had better not remain in Russia during another cold season. However painful it was to me to return without my husband, yet life seemed desirable, and he flattered me and himself that he should soon follow. It is difficult for any one in the Emperor's employment to leave when they please. Mr. Prince thought it best for me to return to my native country, while he remained two years longer to accumulate a little property, and then return—but death took him away. I left St. Petersburg, August 14th, 1833, having been absent about nine years and six months. On the 17th, I sailed from Cronstadt, for New York. Arrived at Elsinore the 25th. Tuesday, 29, left. September the 2d, laid to in a gale. September 18th, made Plymouth, Old English, 19th sailed. Arrived in New York, Oct. 10th. Left there Tuesday 18th, arrived in Boston the 23d. Sabbath, Nov. 9th, I had the privilege of attending service in the old place of worship. On this day I also had the pleasure of meeting with an old friend of my grandfather, nearly one hundred years of age. I found things much changed; my mother and sister Silvia died in 1827, (that I was aware of.) The Rev. T. Paul was dead, and many of my old friends were gone to their long home. The old church and society was in much confusion; I attempted to worship with them but it was in vain. The voyage was of great benefit to me. By the advice of friends I applied to a Mrs. Mott, a female physician in the city, that helped me much. I am indebted to God for his great goodness in guiding my youthful steps; my mind was directed to my fellow brethren whose circumstances were similar to my own. I found many a poor little orphan destitute and afflicted, and on account of color shut out from all the asylums for poor children. At this my heart was moved, and I proposed to my friends the necessity of a home for such, where they might be sheltered from the contaminating evils that beset their path. For this purpose I called a meeting of the people and laid before them my plan: as I had had the privilege of assisting in forming an Asylum for such a purpose in St. Petersburg, I thought it would be well to establish one on the same principles, not knowing that any person had had a thought of anything of the kind. We commenced with eight children. I gave three months of my time.

A board was formed of seven females, with a committee of twelve gentlemen of standing, to superintend. At the end of three months the committee was dispensed with, and for want of funds our society soon fell through.

I passed my time in different occupations and making arrangements for the return of my husband, but death took him from me. I made my home at the Rev. J. W. Holman's, a Free Will Baptist, until I sailed for Jamaica. There had been an Anti-Slavery Society established by W. L. Garrison, Knapp, and other philanthropists of the day. Their design was the amelioration of the nominally free colored people of these States, and the emancipation of the slaves in other States. These meetings I attended with much pleasure. . . .

My mind, after the emancipation in the West Indies, was bent upon going to Jamaica. A field of usefulness seemed spread out before me. While I was thinking about it, the Rev. Mr. Ingraham, who had spent seven years there, arrived in the city. He lectured in the city at the Marlboro' Chapel, on the results arising from the emancipation at the British Islands. He knew much about them, he had a station at a mountain near Kingston, and was very desirous to have persons go there to labor. He wished some one to go with him to his station. He called on me with the Rev. Mr. William Collier, to persuade me to go. I told him it was my intention to go if I could make myself useful, but that I was sensible that I was very limited in education. He told me that the moral condition of the people was very bad, and needed labor aside from any thing else.

I left America, November 16th, 1840, in the ship Scion, Captain Mansfield, bound for Jamaica, freighted with ice and machinery for the silk factory. There were on board a number of handicraftsmen and other passengers. We sailed on Monday afternoon, from Charlestown, Massachusetts. It rained continually until Saturday. Sunday, the 23d, was a fine day. Mr. De Grass, a young colored clergyman, was invited to perform divine service, which he did with much propriety. He spoke of the dangers we had escaped and the importance of being prepared to meet our God, (he died of fever about three weeks after arriving at Jamaica,) some who were able to attend came on deck, and listened to him with respect, while others seemed to look on in derision; these spent the afternoon and evening in cardplaying. About twelve at night a storm commenced; on Monday were in great peril; the storm continued until Friday, the 27th. On that day a sail was seen at some distance making towards us, the captain judging her to be a piratical vessel, ordered the women and children below, and the men to prepare for action. The pirates were not inclined to hazard an engagement; when they saw the deck filled with armed men they left us. Thus were we preserved from the storm and from the enemy. Sabbath, 29th, divine service,—our attention was directed to the goodness of God, in sparing us. . . .

There is in Jamaica an institution, established in 1836, called the Mico Institution. It is named after its founder, Madame Mico, who left a large sum of money to purchase, (or rather to ransom, the one being a Christian act, the other a sin against the Holy Ghost, who expressly forbids such traffic.) Madame Mico left this money to ransom the English who were in bondage to the Algerines; if there was any left, it was to be devoted to the instruction of the colored people in the British Isles.

Besides the Mico establishment, there are in Jamaica twenty-seven church missionary schools, where children are taught gratis. Whole number taught, 952. London Missionary Society Schools, sixteen; the number taught not ascertained. National Schools, thirty-eight. There are also the Wesleyan, Presbyterian and Moravian Schools; it is supposed there are private schools, where three or four thousand are educated in the city of Kingston, and twice the number in the street without the means of instruction. All the children and adults taught in the above named schools, are taxed £1 a year, except the English Church School, this is the most liberal. The Rev. Mr. Horton, a Baptist minister in Kingston, told me he had sent ninety children away from the Baptist school because they did not bring their money. It is sufficient to say they had it not to bring!

Most of the people of Jamaica are emancipated slaves, many of them are old, worn out and degraded. Those who are able to work, have yet many obstacles to contend with, and very little to encourage them; every advantage is taken of their ignorance; the same spirit of cruelty is opposed to them that held them for centuries in bondage; even religious teaching is bartered for their hard earnings, while they are allowed but thirty-three cents a day, and are told if they will not work for that they shall not work at all; an extraordinary price is asked of them for every thing they may wish to purchase, even the Bibles are sold to them at a large advance on the first purchase. Where are their apologists, if they are found wanting in the strict morals that Christians ought to practice? Who kindly says, forgive them when they err. "Forgive them, this is the bitter fruit of slavery." Who had integrity sufficient to hold the balance when these poor people are to be weighed? Yet their present state is blissful, compared with slavery. . . .

I met the Anti Slavery Society at Mrs. Lucretia Motts, who took great interest in the cause. I visited among the friends, and spent my time very pleasantly. August 5th [1841], I started for New York; arrived safely, and staid with an old friend; ascertained that Mr. Ingraham's family were at

Newark, at Theodore Wells'. He died four days after his arrival. I was invited to Mrs. Ingraham's, (his cousin's widow) to spend a week. There I met with much encouragement to labor in the cause. Missionaries were coming and going, and all seemed to be interested in my object. Saturday evening I went to the bath room, where I left my neck ribbon: returning after it, I had the misfortune to fall through an open trap door, down fifteen feet, on hard coal. I had no light with me. I dislocated my left shoulder, and was generally very much bruised; my screams brought the girl to my assistance, and by the help of God she brought me out of the cellar; it was some time before a surgeon could be procured; at last Dr. Josselyn came to my relief, and set my shoulder. I was obliged to remain at Mrs. Ingraham's three weeks; as soon as I was able, I left there for Boston. I intended to have gone by the western boat, but by mistake got on board Captain Comstock's, and was exposed on deck all night in a damp east wind, and when I arrived at the landing I could not assist myself; a sailor, who saw and pitied my situation, kindly took care of me and my baggage, and, on my arrival in Boston, procured a carriage for me. If it had not been for his kindness, I know not how I should have got along.

As soon as I was able, I commenced my task of collecting funds for my Free Labor School in Jamaica. I collected in Boston and vicinity, in New York and Philadelphia, but not sufficient to make up the required sum, and I was obliged to take fifty dollars from my own purse, thinking that when I returned to Jamaica, they would refund the money to me. April 15th [1842], embarked on board the brig Norma, of New York, for Jamaica. I arrived at Kingston May 6th, and found every thing different from what it was when I left; the people were in a state of agitation, several were hanged, and the insurrection was so great that it was found necessary to increase the army to quell it. Several had been hanged. On the very day I arrived a man was hanged for shooting a man as he passed through the street. Such was the state of things that it was not safe to be there.

A few young people met to celebrate their freedom on an open plain, where they hold their market; their former masters and mistresses, envious of their happiness, conspired against them, and thought to put them down by violence. This only served to increase their numbers; but the oppressors were powerful, and succeeded in accomplishing their revenge, although many of them were relations. There was a rule among the slave holders, to take care of the children they have by their slaves; they select them out and place them in asylums. Those who lived with their white fathers were allowed great power over their slave mothers and her slave children; my heart was often grieved to see their conduct to their poor old grand parents. Those over twenty-one. It is well known that at that time, the children, alike with others, received twenty-five dollars a head for their relatives. Were I to tell all my eyes have seen among that people, it would not be credited. It is well known that those that were freed, knowing their children were still in bondage, were not satisfied. In the year 1838, general freedom throughout the British Islands gave the death blow to the power of the master, and mothers received with joy their emancipated children; they no longer looked the picture of despair, fearing to see their mulatto son or daughter beating or abusing their younger brothers and sisters of a darker skin. On this occasion there was an outrage committed by those who were in power. What little the poor colored people had gathered during their four years of freedom, was destroyed by violence; their fences were broken down, and their horses and hogs taken from them. Most of the mulattoes and masters are educated, many of them are very poor, some are very rich; the property is left to the oldest daughter, she divides it with her brothers and sisters; since slavery ended many of them have married; those who are poor, and mean to live in sin, make for New Orleans and other slave States; many of the planters left the island when slavery was abolished. In June, 1841, a number of people arrived from Sierra Leone at Jamaica; these were Maroons who were banished from the island. They were some of the original natives who inhabited the mountains, and were determined to destroy the whites. These Maroons would secrete themselves in trees, and arrest the whites as they passed along; they would pretend to guide them, when they would beat and abuse them as the whites did their slaves; the English, finding themselves defeated in all their plans to subdue them, proposed to take them by craft. They made a feast in a large tavern in Kingston, and invited them to come. After they had eaten, they were invited on board three ships of war that were all ready to set sail for Sierra Leone; many of them were infants in their mother's arms, they were well taken care of by the English and instructed; they were removed about the year 1796—they are bright and intelligent; I saw and conversed with them; when they heard of the abolition of slavery, they sent a petition to Queen Victoria that they might return to Jamaica, which was granted. Several of them were very old when they returned; they were men and women when they left the island, they had not forgot the injuries they had received from the hands of man, not the mercies of God to them, not his judgements to their enemies. Their numbers were few, but their power was great; they say the island, of right, belongs to them. Had there been a vessel in readiness, I should have come back immediately, it seemed useless to attempt to establish a Manual Labor School, as the government was so unsettled that I could not be protected. Some of my former friends were gone as teachers to Africa, and some to other parts of the island. I called on the American Consul to consult with him, he said that although such a school was much wanted, yet every thing seemed so unsettled that I had no courage to proceed. I told him there was so much excitement that I wished to leave the island as soon as he could find me a passage, it seemed useless to spend my time there. As soon as it was known that I intended to return, a movement was made to induce me to remain. I was persuaded to try the experiment for three months, not thinking their motive was bad. Before I left the United States, I got all that was needed, within fifty dollars. The fifty dollars I got from my own purse, expecting they would pay me. It cost me ten dollars for freight, and twenty-five for passage money; these people that I had hoped to serve, were much taken up with the things I had brought, they thought that I had money, and I was continually surrounded; the thought of color was no where exhibited, much notice was taken of me. I was invited to breakfast in one place, and to dine in another, &c. A society was organized, made up of men and women of authority. A constitution was drafted by my consent, by those who were appointed to meet at my rooms. Between the time of the adjournment they altered it to suit themselves. At the time appointed we came together with a spirit apparently becoming any body of Christians; most of them were members of Christian churches. The meeting was opened with reading the Scriptures and prayer. Then said the leader, since our dear sister has left her native land and her friends to come to us, we welcome her with our hearts and hands. She will dwell among us, and we will take care of her—Brethren think of it! after which he sat down, and the constitution was called for. The Preamble held out all the flattery that a fool could desire; after which they commenced the articles, supposing that they could do as they thought best. The fourth article unveiled their design. As we have designed to take care of our sister, we the undersigned will take charge of all she had brought; the vote was called, every person rose in a moment except myself: every eye was upon me; one asked me why I did not vote, I made no answer—they put the vote again and again, I remained seated. Well, said the President, we can do nothing without her vote; they remained some time silent, and then broke up the meeting. The next day the deacon called to see what the state of my mind was, and some of the women proposed that we should have another meeting. I told them no, I should do no more for them. As soon as they found they could not get the things in the way they intended, they started to plunder me; but I detected their design, and was on my guard. I disposed of the articles, and made ready to leave when an opportunity presented. A more skilful plan than this, Satan never designed, but the power of God was above it. It is not surprising that this people are full of deceit and lies, this is the fruits of slavery, it makes master and slaves knaves. It is the rule where slavery exists to swell the churches with numbers, and hold out such doctrines as, obedience to tyrants, is a duty to God. I went with a Baptist woman to the house of a minister of the Church of England, to have her grandchild christened before it died; she told me if she did not have it christened, it would rise up in judgment against her. This poor deluded creature was a class leader in the Baptist Church, and such is the condition of most of the people: they seemed blinded to every thing but money. They are great for trade, and are united in their determination for procuring property, of which they have amassed a vast amount. Notwithstanding I had made over various articles to one of the American missionaries, a Mr. J. S. O. Beadslee, of Clarendon Mountains, I also gave to others, where they were needed, which receipts and letters I have in my possession. Notwithstanding all this, they made another attempt to rob me, and as a passage could not be obtained for me to return home, I was obliged to go to the Mico establishment again for safety, such was the outrage. Houses were broken open and robbed every night. I came very near being shot: there was a certain place where we placed ourselves the first of the evening. A friend came to bring us some refreshments, I had just left the window when a gun was fired through it, by one that often sat with us; this was common in the time of slavery. Previous to vessels arriving, passages were engaged. I disposed of my articles and furniture at a very small profit. On the 1st of August, Capt. A. Miner arrived, and advertised for passengers. The American Consul procured me a passage, and on the 18th of August, myself and nine other passengers embarked for New York.

Before giving an account of the voyage from Jamaica, it may prove interesting to some readers, to have a brief description of the country. With her liberty secured to her, may she now rise in prosperity, morality, and religion, and become a happy people, whose God is the Lord.

West Indies.

A denomination under which is comprehended a large chain of islands, extending in a curve from the Florida shore on the northern peninsula of America, to the Gulf of Venezuela on the southern. These islands belong to five European powers, vis: Great Britain, Spain, France, Holland, and Denmark. An inhabitant of New England can form no idea of the climate and the productions of these islands. Many of the particulars that are here mentioned, are peculiar to them all.

The climate in all the West India Islands is nearly the same, allowing for those accidental differences which the several situations and qualities of the lands themselves produce; as they lie within the tropic of Cancer, and the sun is often almost at the meridian over their heads, they are continually subjected to a heat that would be intolerable but for the trade winds, which are so refreshing as to enable the inhabitants to attend to their various occupations, even under a noonday sun; as the night advances, a breeze begins to be perceived, which blows smartly from the land, as it were from the centre towards the sea, to all points of the compass at once. The rains make the only distinction of seasons on these islands. The trees are green the year round; they have no cold or frost; our heaviest rains are but dews comparatively; with them floods of water are poured from the clouds. About May, the periodical rains from the South may be expected. Then the tropical summer, in all its splendor, makes its appearance. The nights are calm and serene, the moon shines more brightly than in New England, as do the planets and the beautiful galaxy. From the middle of August to the end of September the heat is most oppressive, the sea breeze is interrupted, and calms warn the inhabitants of the periodical rains, which fall in torrents about the first of October.

The most considerable and valuable of the British West India Islands, lies between the 75th and the 79th degrees of west longitude from London, and between 17 and 18 north latitude; it is of an oval figure, 150 miles long from east to west, and sixty miles broad in the middle, containing 4,080,000 acres. An elevated ridge, called the Blue Mountains, runs lengthwise from east to west, whence numerous rivers take their rise on both sides. The year is divided into two seasons, wet and dry. The months of July, August, and September, are called the hurricane months. The best houses are generally built low, on account of the hurricanes and earthquakes. However pleasant the sun may rise, in a moment the scene may be changed; a violent storm will suddenly arise, attended with thunder and lightning; the rain falls in torrents, and the seas and rivers rise with terrible destruction. I witnessed this awful scene in June last, at Kingston, the capital of Jamaica; the foundations of many houses were destroyed; the waters, as they rushed from the mountains, brought with them the produce of the earth, large branches of trees, together with their fruit; many persons were drowned, endeavoring to reach their homes; those who succeeded, were often obliged to travel many miles out of their usual way. Many young children, without a parent's care, were at this time destroyed. A poor old woman, speaking of these calamities to me, thus expressed herself: "Not so bad now as in the time of slavery; then God spoke very loud to *Bucker,* (the white people,) to let us go. Thank God, ever since that they give us up, we go pray, and we have it not so bad like as before." I would recommend this poor woman's remark to the fair sons and daughters of America, the land of the pilgrims. "Then God spoke very loud." May these words be engraved on the post of every door in this land of New England. God speaks very loud, and while his judgments are on the earth, may the inhabitants learn righteousness!

The mountains that intersect this island, seem composed of rocks, thrown up by frequent earthquakes or volcanoes. These rocks, though having little soil, are adorned with a great variety of beautiful trees, growing from the fissures, which are nourished by frequent rains, and flourish in perpetual spring. From these mountains flow a vast number of small rivers of pure water, which sometimes fall in cataracts, from stupendous heights; these, with the brilliant verdure of the trees, form a most delightful landscape. Ridges of small mountains are on each side of this great chain; on these, coffee grows in great abundance; the valleys or plains between these ridges, are level beyond what is usually found in similar situations. The highest land in the island is Blue Mountain Peak, 7150 feet above the sea. The most extensive plain is thirty miles long and five broad. Black River, in the Parish of St. Elizabeth, is the only one navigable; flatboats bring down produce from plantations about thirty miles up the river. Along the coast, and on the plains, the weather is very hot; but in the mountains the air is pure and wholesome; the longest days in summer are about thirteen hours, and the shortest in winter about eleven. In the plains are found several salt fountains, and in the mountains, not far from Spanish Town, is a hot bath of great medicinal virtues; this gives relief in the complaint called the dry-bowels malady, which, excepting the bilious and yellow fevers, is one of the most terrible distempers of Jamaica. The general produce of this island is sugar, rum, molasses, ginger, cotton, indigo, pimento, cocoa, coffees, several kinds of woods, and medicinal drugs. Fruits are in great plenty, as oranges, lemons, shaddocks, citrons, pomegranates, pineapples, melons, pompions, guavas, and many others. Here are trees whose wood, when dry, is incorruptible; here is found the wild cinnamon tree, the mahogany, the cabbage, the palm, yielding an oil much esteemed for food and medicine. Here, too, is the soap tree, whose berries are useful in washing. The plantain is produced in Jamaica in abundance, and is one of the most agreeable and nutritious vegetables in the world: it grows about four feet in height, and the fruit grows in clusters, which is filled with a luscious sweet pulp. The Banana is very similar to the plantain, but not so sweet. The whole island is divided into three counties, Middlesex, Surrey, and Cornwall, and these into six towns, twenty parishes, and twenty-seven villages.

This island was originally part of the Spanish Empire in America, but it was taken by the English in 1656. Cromwell had fitted out a squadron under Penn and Venables, to reduce the Spanish Island of Hispaniola; but there this squadron was unsuccessful, and the commanders, of their own accord, to atone for this misfortune, made a descent on Jamaica, and having arrived at St. Jago, soon compelled the whole island to surrender.

Ever since, it has been subject to the English; and the government, next to that of Ireland, is the richest in the disposal of the crown. Port Royal was formerly the capital of Jamaica; it stood upon the point of a narrow neck of land, which, towards the sea, forms part of the border of a very fine harbor of its own name. The conveniences of this harbor, which was capable of containing a thousand sail of large ships, and of such depth as to allow them to load and unload with the greatest ease, weighed so much with the inhabitants, that they chose to build their capital on this spot, although the place was hot, dry sand, and produced none of the necessaries of life, not even fresh water. About the beginning of the year 1692, no place for its size could be compared to this town for trade, wealth, and an entire corruption of manners. In the month of June in this year, an earthquake which shook the whole island to the foundation, totally overwhelmed this city, so as to leave, in one quarter, not even the smallest vestige remaining. In two minutes the earth opened and swallowed up nine-tenths of the houses, and two thousand people. The waters gushed out from the openings of the earth, and the people lay as it were in heaps: some of them had the good fortune to catch hold of beams and rafters of houses, and were afterwards saved by boats. Several ships were cast away in the harbor, and the Swan Frigate, which lay in the Dock, was carried over the tops of sinking houses, and did not overset, but afforded a retreat to some hundreds of people, who saved their lives upon her. An officer who was in the town at that time, says the earth opened and shut very quick in some places, and he saw several people sink down to the middle, and others appeared with their heads just above ground, and were choked to death. At Savannah above a thousand acres were sunk, with the houses and people in them, the place appearing, for some time, like a lake; this was afterwards dried up, but no houses were seen. In some parts mountains were split, and at one place a plantation was removed to the distance of a mile. The inhabitants again rebuilt the city, but it was a second time, ten years after, destroyed by a great fire. The extraordinary convenience of the harbor tempted them to build it once more, and in 1722 it was laid in ruins by a hurricane, the most terrible on record.

Such repeated calamities seemed to mark out this spot as a devoted place; the inhabitants, therefore, resolved to forsake it forever, and to reside at the opposite bay, where they built Kingston, which is now the capital of the island. In going up to Kingston, we pass over a part of and between Port Royal, leaving the mountains on the left, and a small town on the right. There are many handsome houses built there, one story high, with porticos, and every convenience for those who inhabit them. Not far from Kingston stands Spanish Town, which, though at present far inferior to Kingston, was once the capital of Jamaica, and is still the seat of government.

On the 3d of October, 1780, there was a dreadful hurricane, which overwhelmed the little seaport town of Savannah, in Jamaica, and part of the adjacent country; very few houses were left standing, and a great number of lives were lost; much damage was done also, and many lives lost, in other parts of the island.

In January, 1823, a society was formed in London for mitigating and gradually abolishing slavery, throughout the British dominions, called the Anti-Slavery Society. His Royal Highness, the Duke of Gloucester, was President of the Society; in the list of Vice Presidents are the names of many of the most distinguished philanthropists of the day, and among them that of the never to be forgotten Mr. Wilberforce; as a bold champion, we see him going forward, pleading the cause of our down-trodden brethren. In the year 1834, it pleased God to break the chains from 800,000 human beings, that had been held in a state of personal slavery; and this great event was effected through the instrumentality of Clarkson, Wilberforce, and other philanthropists of the day.

The population of Jamaica is nearly 400,000; that of Kingston, the capital, 40,000. There are many places of worship of various denominations, namely, Church of England, and of Scotland, Wesleyan, the Baptist, and Roman Catholics, besides a Jewish Synagogue. These all differ from what I have seen in New England, and from those I have seen elsewhere. The Baptist hold what they call class-meetings. They have men and women deacons and deaconesses in these churches; these hold separate class-meetings; some of these can read, and some cannot. Such are the persons who hold the office of judges, and go round and urge the people to come to the class, and after they come in twice or three times, they are considered candidates for baptism. Some pay fifty cents, and some more, for being baptized; they receive a ticket as a passport into the church, paying one mark a quarter, or more, and some less, but nothing short of ten pence, that is, two English shillings a year. They must attend their class once a week, and pay three pence a week, total twelve English Shillings a year, besides the sums they pay once a month at communion, after service in the morning. On those occasions the minister retires, and the deacons examine the people, to ascertain if each one has brought a ticket; if not, they cannot commune; after this the minister returns, and performs the ceremony, then they give their money and depart. The churches are very large, holding from four to six thousand; many bring wood and other presents to their class-leader, as a token of their attachment; where there are so many communicants, these presents, and the money exacted, greatly enrich these establishments. Communicants are so ignorant of the ordinance, that they join the church merely to have a decent burial; for if they are not members, none will follow them to the grave, and no prayers will be said over them; these are borne through the streets by four men, the coffin a rough box; not so if they are church members; as soon as the news is spread that one is dying, all the class, with their leader, will assemble at the place, and join in singing hymns; this, they say, is to help the spirit up to glory; this exercise sometimes continues all night, in so loud a strain, that it is seldom that any of the people in the neighborhood are lost in sleep.

After leaving Jamaica, the vessel was tacked to a south-west course. I asked the Captain what this meant. He said he must take the current as there was no wind. Without any ceremony, I told him it was not the case, and told the passengers that he had deceived us. There were two English men that were born on the island, that had never been on the water. Before the third day passed, they asked the Captain why they had not seen Hayti. He told them they passed when they were asleep. I told them it was not true, he was steering south south-west. The passengers in the steerage got alarmed, and every one was asking the Captain what this meant. The ninth day we made land. "By———," said the Captain, "this is Key West; come, passengers, let us have a vote to run over the neck, and I will go ashore and bring aboard fruit and turtle." They all agreed but myself. He soon dropped anchor. The officers from the shore came on board and congratulated him on keeping his appointment, thus proving that my suspicions were well founded. The Captain went ashore with these men, and soon came back, called for the passengers, and asked for their vote for him to remain until the next day, saying that he could by this delay, make five or six hundred dollars, as there had been a vessel wrecked there lately. They all agreed but myself The vessel was soon at the side of the wharf. In an hour there were twenty slaves at work to unload her; every inducement was made to persuade me to go ashore, or set my feet on the wharf. A law had just been passed there that every free colored person coming there, should be put in custody on their going ashore; there were five colored persons on board; none dared to go ashore, however uncomfortable we might be in the vessel, or however we might desire to refresh ourselves by a change of scene. We remained at Key West four days.

September 3d, we set sail for New York, at 3 o'clock in the afternoon. At 10 o'clock a gale took us, that continued thirty-six hours; my state-room was filled with water, and my baggage all upset; a woman, with her little boy, and myself, were seated on a trunk thirty-six hours, with our feet pressed against a barrel to prevent falling; the water pouring over us at every breaker. Wednesday, the 9th, the sun shone out so that the Captain could take an observation. He found himself in great peril, near the coast of Texas. All hands were employed in pumping and bailing. On the eleventh, the New Orleans streamer came to our assistance; as we passed up the river, I was made to forget my own condition, as I looked with pity on the poor slaves, who were laboring and toiling, on either side, as far as could be seen with a glass. We soon reached the dock, and we were there on the old wreck a spectacle for observation; the whites went on shore and made themselves comfortable, while we poor blacks were obliged to remain on that broken, wet vessel. The people were very busy about me; one man asked me who I belonged to, and many other rude questions; he asked me where I was born; I told him Newburyport. "What were your parents' names?" I told him my father's name was Thomas Gardner; his countenance changed; said he, "I knew him well;" and he proved friendly to me. He appeared very kind, and offered to arrange my affairs so that I might return to New York through the States. I thought it best to decline his proposal, knowing my spirit would not suffer me to pass on, and see my fellow-creatures suffering without a rebuke. We remained four days on the wreck; the boxes that contained the sugar were taken out; the two bottom tiers were washed out clean. There were a great many people that came to see the vessel; they were astonished that she did not sink; they watched me very closely. I asked them what they wished. In the mean time, there came along a drove of colored people, fettered together in pairs by the wrist; some had weights, with long chains at their ankles, men and women, young and old. I asked them what that meant. They were all ready to answer. Said they, "these negroes have been imprudent, and have stolen; some of the are free negroes from the northern ship;" "and what," I asked "are they there for?" "For being on shore, some of them at night." I asked them who made them Lord over God's inheritance. They told me I was very foolish; they should think I had suffered enough to think of myself. I looked pretty bad, it is true; I was seated on a box, but poorly dressed; the mate had taken my clothes to a washerwoman; why he took this care, he was afraid to send the cook or steward on shore, as they were colored people. I kept still; but the other woman seemed to be in perfect despair, running up and down the deck, wringing her hands and crying, at the thought of all her clothes being destroyed; then her mind dwelt upon other things, and she seemed as if she were deranged; she took their attention for a few minutes, as she was white. Soon the washer-woman came with my clothes; they spoke to her as if she had been a dog. I looked at them with as much astonishment as if I had never heard of such a thing. I asked them if they believed there was a God. "Of course we do," they replied. "Then why not obey him?" "We do." "You do not; permit me to say there is a God, and a just one, that will bring you all to account." "For what?" "For suffering these men that have just come in to be taken out of these vessels, and that awful sight I see in the streets." "O that is nothing; I should think you would be concerned about yourself." "I am sure," I replied, "the Lord will take care of me; you cannot harm me." "No; we do not wish to; we do not want you here." Every ship that comes in, the colored men are dragged to prison. I found it necessary to be stern with them; they were very rude; if I had not been so, I know not what would have been the consequences. They went off for that day; the next day some of them came again. "Good morning," said they; "we shall watch you like the d—— until you go away; you must not say anything to these negroes whilst you are here." "Why, then, do you talk to me, if you do not want me to say any thing to you? If you will let me alone, I will you." "Let me see your protection," they replied, "they say it is under the Russian government." I pointed them to the 18th chapter of Revelations and 15th verse: "The merchants of these things which were made rich by her, shall stand afar off, for the fear of her torment, weeping and wailing. For strong is the Lord God who judgeth her." They made no answer, but asked the Captain how soon he should get away.

On the 17th, the Captain put eight of us on board the bark H. W. Tyler, for New York; we had about a mile to walk; the Captain was in honor bound to return us our passage money, which we had paid him at Jamaica; he came without it to see if we were there, and went away saying he would soon return with it; but we saw no more of him or our money! Our bark, and a vessel loaded with slaves, were towed down the river by the same steamer; we dropped anchor at the bottom of the bay, as a storm was rising. The 18th, on Sabbath, it rained all day. Capt. Tyler knocked at my door, wishing me to come out; it rained hard; the bulwark of the bark was so high I could not look over it; he placed something for me to stand on, that I might see the awful sight, which was the vessel of slaves laying at the side of our ship! the deck was full of young men, girls, and children, bound to Texas for sale! Monday, the 19th, Capt. Tyler demanded of us to pay him for our passage. I had but ten dollars, and was determined not to give it; he was very severe with all. I told him there were articles enough to pay him belonging to me. Those who had nothing, were obliged to go back in the steamer. Tuesday, the 20th, we set sail; the storm was not over. The 22d the gale took us; we were dismasted, and to save sinking, sixty casks of molasses were stove in, and holes cut in the bulwarks to let it off. All the fowls, pigs, and fresh provisions were lost. We were carried seventy-five miles up the bay of Mexico. The Captain was determined not to pay the steamer for carrying him back to New Orleans, and made his way the best he could.

The 3d of October we arrived again at Key West. The Captain got the bark repaired, and took on board a number of turtles, and a plenty of brandy. Friday, the 7th, set sail for New York; the Captain asked me why I did not go ashore when there in the Comet; "had you," said he, "they intended to beat you. John and Lucy Davenport, of Salem, laid down the first ten dollars toward a hundred for that person who should get you there." The Florida laws are about the same as those at New Orleans. He was very talkative: wished to know if I saw anything of the Creole's crew while at Jamaica. I told him they were all safe, a fine set of young men and women; one dear little girl, that was taken from her mother in Virginia, I should have taken with me, if I had had the money. He said his brother owned the Creole, and some of the slaves were his. "I never owned any; I have followed the sea all my life, and can tell every port and town in your State."

October 19th, 1842, arrived in New York, and thankful was I to set my feet on land, almost famished for the want of food; we lost all of our provisions; nothing was left but sailors' beef, and that was tainted before it was salted. I went at once to those who professed to be friends, but found myself mistaken. I hardly knew what was best. I had put up at Mrs. Rawes'; she did all she could to raise the twenty-five dollars that I must pay before I could take my baggage from the vessel. This seemed hard to obtain; I travelled from one to another for three days; at last I called at the Second Advent office; Mr. Nath'l Southard left his business at once, and took me to Mr. Lewis Tappan, and others; he raised the money, and went with me to the ship after my baggage. It was three o'clock on Saturday afternoon when I called on Mr. Southard; the vessel and Captain belonged to Virginia, was all ready for sea, waiting for a wind; they had ransacked my things. I took from Jamaica forty dollars' worth of preserved fruits; part were lost when we were cast away in the Comet, and some they had stolen. At 8 o'clock on Saturday evening, I made out to have my things landed on the wharf; it was very dark, as it rained hard. My kind friend did not leave me until they were all safely lodged at my residence. I boarded there three weeks, thinking to come home; but it was thought best for me to wait, and see if Capt. Miner came or not, hoping that I might recover my loss through him. I took a room, and went to sewing, and found the people very kind.

February, 1843, the colored men that went back to New Orleans, for the want of passage money, arrived at New York, wearied out. All the white people remained there. I waited in New York until the last of July, when I started for Boston. August 1st, 1843, arrived, poor in health, and poor in purse, having sacrificed both, hoping to benefit my fellow creatures. I trust it was acceptable to God, who in his providence preserved me in perils by land, and perils by sea.

"God moves in a mysterious way
His wonders to perform;
He plants his footsteps on the sea,
and rides upon the storm.

"Deep in unfathomable mines
Of never failing skill,
He treasures up his bright designs,
And works his sovereign will."

Having lost all, I determined, by the help of God, to leave the event; some of my friends in the city sympathized with me, and others took the advantage to reproach me. But in the hands of the Lord there is a cup; the Saviour drank it to the dregs. They gather themselves together; they hide themselves; they mark my steps; they waited for my soul, but the Lord in my defence, the Holy one of Israel is my Saviour. I'll trust him for strength and defence. What things were gain to me, I counted loss for Christ, for whom I have suffered all things; and do count them nothing, that I may win Christ, and be found in him, not having mine own righteousness, which is of the law, but that which is through the faith of Christ, that which is of God by faith, that I may know him, and the power of his resurrection, and the fellowship of his sufferings, being made conformable unto his death, strengthened with all might, according to his glorious power, unto all patience and long-suffering, with joyfulness, thinking it not strange concerning the fiery trials, as though some strange thing happened; for saith the apostle, it is better if the will of God so be that ye suffer for well doing, than for evil; they think it strange that ye run not with them to the same excess of riot, speaking evil of you. If they do these things in a green tree, what shall be done in a dry!

"I hate to walk, I hate to sit
With men of Vanity and lies;
The scoffer and the hypocrite
Are the Abhorrence of my eyes.

God know their impious thoughts are vain,
And they shall feel his power;
His wrath shall pierce their soul with pain,
In some surprising hour."

The first twenty months after my arrival in the city, notwithstanding my often infirmities, I labored with much success, until I hired with and from those with whom I mostly sympathized, and shared in common the disadvantages and stigma that is heaped upon us, in this our professed Christian land. But my lot was like the man that went down from Jerusalem, and fell among thieves, which stripped him of his raiment, and wounding him, departed, leaving him half dead. What I did not lose, when cast away, has been taken from my room where I hired. Three times I had been broken up in business, embarrassed and obliged to move, when not able to wait on myself. This has been my lot. In the midst of my afflictions, sometimes I have thought my case like that of Paul's when cast among wild beasts. "Had not the Lord been on my side, they would have swallowed me up; but blessed be the Lord who hath not given me prey to their teeth."

In 1848 and '49 the Lord was pleased to lay his hand upon me. Some of my friends came to my relief; but the promises of God were neither few nor small; he knows them that trust and fear him. No one has greater reason to be grateful than I. God has preserved me through much suffering and the past winter. I have passed through another furnace of affliction, and may God's dispensations be sanctified to me. The sufferings of this present life are not worthy to be compared with the glory that shall be revealed hereafter. Who shall separate us from the love of Christ? Shall tribulation, or distress, or persecution, or famine, or nakedness, or peril, or sword? Nay, in all these things we are more than conquerors, through him that loved us, and gave himself for us. Soon he will come; here we live by faith; if any one draw back, my soul shall have no pleasure in him.

Truly the promises of God are given for our encouragement; they are yea and amen, in Christ Jesus; they are a covert from the storm, a shelter from the heat, a sure retreat for the weary and way worn traveler.

Many are the trials and temptations to which we are exposed in this vale of tears, but in heaven we shall be free from the bondage of sin. Nothing can enter there to annoy or molest the redeemed ones: the Captain of our salvation was made perfect through suffering; he was despised and rejected of men, a man of sorrows, and acquainted with grief; and that he might sanctify the people with his own blood, suffered without the gate. Let us go forth, therefore, unto him, bearing his reproach. Here we have no continuing city nor abiding place.

I have much to be thankful to God for; for the comforts of this life, and the kind friends who have so kindly bestowed their favors upon me, and while they in this life have an abundance, may they have the presence of God; and when the King shall come, may they have their lamps trimmed and burning: then shall he say, "Come ye blessed of my Father, inherit the kingdom prepared for you from the foundation of the world: for I was hungered, and ye gave me meat, I was thirsty, and ye gave me drink, naked, and ye clothed me, sick, and in prison, and ye visited me. Then shall the righteous answer, saying: when saw we thee and hungered, and fed thee, and thirsty, and gave thee drink, naked, and clothed thee, sick, and in prison, and ministered unto thee, or a strange, and took thee in?" And the King shall answer and say: "Inasmuch as ye have done it unto one of the least of my disciples, ye have done it unto me. The poorest can do something for the cause of Christ; even a cup of cold water, given with a desire to benefit a fellow creature, will be acceptable to God. May the power of God, and the spirit of Christ rule and reign in all hearts. He knoweth them that love and trust in him."

I am a wonder unto many, but the Lord is my strong refuge, and in him will I trust. I shall fear no evil, for thou, O Lord, art ever near to shield and protect thy dependent children. Underneath him is the everlasting arm of mercy; misfortune is never mournful for the soul that accepts it, for such do always see that every cloud is an angel's face; sorrow connects the soul with the invisible.

O Father, fearful indeed is this world's pilgrimage, when the soul has learned that all its sounds are echoes, all its sights are shadows. But lo! a cloud opens, a face serene and hopeful looks forth and saith, "Be thou as a little child, and thus shalt thou become a seraph, and bow thyself in silent humility and pray, not that afflictions might not visit, but be willing to be purified through fire, and accept it meekly."

9

Mary Ann Shadd Cary (1823–1893)

■

Introduction

PARALLELING HARRIET ANN JACOBS'S LIFE, Mary Ann Shadd's life was fundamentally altered by passage of the Fugitive Slave Law in 1850: she moved to Canada and for many years was the outstanding spokeswoman for emigration as a response to slavery.

The process of relocation was not new. The return of slaves to Africa had been proposed in 1714. In the nineteenth century until the Civil War, the American Colonization Society urged members of black communities to emigrate to Liberia.[116] Mexico, Haiti, and South America were among other proposed destinations. The Fugitive Slave Law had sent fifteen thousand slaves and free blacks fleeing north of the border by 1860, a phenomenon known as the "Canadian fugitive slave movement."[117] Cary was an important participant in the agitation that caused the outflow. The debate in print over integration, arms, leadership, and self-reliance was heated and involved both the Refugee Home Society and the American Missionary Association.

An ardent activist, principally by means of editorials but occasionally in sermons, letters, or circulars, Cary did not shy from controversy and always rose to the occasion in public. Crossing ideological borders at will, Cary battled lifelong against suspect emigration schemes and injustice in general.

■

Biographical Narrative

A leading journalist, editor, abolitionist, feminist, and radical activist, Mary Ann Camberton Shadd was born on October 9, 1823, in Wilmington, Delaware. She was the oldest of the thirteen children of Abraham Doras Shadd (b. 1801) and Harriet Parnell Shadd (b. 1806), who were free and prosperous members of the black community. In economic terms, she was much better placed than Jarena Lee, Harriet Jacobs, Harriet Wilson, and Nancy Prince—on a par, perhaps, with the Hart sisters and Mary Seacole. Abraham Shadd, a shoemaker by trade, was an active abolitionist who owned a well-patronized boot and shoe store. Shadd gained prominence as a delegate to the annual meetings of the American Anti-Slavery Society in the mid 1830s; as president of the National Convention of the Improvement of Free People of Color in the United States (1833); and as township councilman in Chatham, Ontario, in the 1850s.[118] He was also a subscription agent for William Lloyd Garrison's *Liberator*. By 1836, the Shadd family had moved to West Chester, Pennsylvania. Their home was said to be a station on the underground railway.

Mary Ann spent six years at a Quaker school in West Chester. Her teacher, Phoebe Darlington, was a delegate to the 1838 Anti-Slavery Convention of American Women. In 1839, at sixteen, Mary Ann Shadd herself began teaching in schools for black children in Wilmington, and then in Norristown, Pennsylvania, New Jersey, and New York City. That early career was disrupted by passage in 1850 of the Fugitive Slave Law, whose provisions entitled any white man to swear that any black person was his runaway slave. Black people had no defenses open to them against chicanery in such a situation; the U.S. commissioners to whom white men often swore false testimony were legally obliged to send blacks caught by deceit into slavery. Hence there occurred a huge exodus of the imperiled to Canada, a particularly favored choice because black people could buy land there, vote, and send their children to school. Mary Anne Shadd's belief in the principle of self-reliance induced her to support emigration to Canada wholeheartedly. In 1849 she published her ideas on black autonomy in the pamphlet "Hints to the Colored People of North America."

Persuaded by his daughter's exhortations, Abraham Shadd settled in Canada. Mary Ann and her brother Isaac established a home in Windsor, Ontario, just across the river from Detroit, in 1851. She chose Windsor in part because it was the first stop on the underground railroad for escapees from Ohio and the West—who often went no farther. Windsor rapidly became home to a large number of black refugees. Shadd was a leader and spokesperson among the community of black refugees in the city. The politics of race was her paramount priority. In Carla Peterson's words:

> She insisted that racial difference must be viewed not as a fundamental biological difference that separates peoples hierarchically but

> simply as a superficial difference of complexion. Refusing to name her own people according to either racial or geographical origin—Negro, African, African American, and so forth—she referred to them in terms of "complexion character" only. She further argued that if biological theories of race are to be abandoned, so must those social constructions which derive from them and which condition the lives of African Americans, categorizing them as intellectually inferior, developmentally retarded, morally depraved.[119]

Mary Ann Shadd was committed to voluntary emigration as a means of combating slavery and implicitly denouncing the United States as a slave–owning society. In 1852, an ambitious forty-four-page pamphlet by Shadd appeared: *A Plea for Emigration; or, Notes of Canada West, in its Moral, Social and Political Aspect.*[120] It extolled Canada as a potential new national home for African Americans and promoted farming—a back to the land argument. The tract was reprinted over several years. Shadd's careful use of statistics rendered her the first black woman to utilize a database for propaganda purposes. *A Plea* established her as a strong voice in the black nationalist movement and was an important contribution to the ongoing debate about the status of black women in activist politics and their right to speak.[121] Shadd resumed her teaching career in an integrated school but in exigent circumstances: no books, desks, or financial support. Eventually she was offered $125 a year by the American Missionary Association, a group founded by abolitionists in 1846 that evangelized through philanthropy.

The school was a political venture; Shadd wanted education available for the colony of escaped slaves. Among them were Josiah Henson, the prototype of Harriet Beecher Stowe's Uncle Tom, and Henry Bibb, editor of the newspaper *Voice of the Fugitive.*[122] Bibb had escaped from slavery in 1837 and become a renowned abolitionist lecturer until passage of the Fugitive Slave Law.

Shadd fearlessly took controversial stands. An especial thorn in the side of her detractors was her attack on the Refugee Home Society, a group that raised funds to settle black people on low-cost land in western Ontario; Bibb was its motor force. Shadd called the project a "begging scheme" because it solicited funds to buy and then sell to refugees when the refugees could purchase government land for less. The refugees were being made dependent rather than self-sustaining. She charged further that donations went straight into Bibb's pocket. The society was self-serving and uncaring.

As a result of her uncompromising position on the Refugee Home Society, Shadd believed, the American Missionary Association withdrew its financial support. In 1852, undaunted, Mary Anne Shadd discussed the possibility of founding a newspaper with Samuel Ringgold Ward, the black abolitionist, in Canada West. The introductory issue appeared in March 1853, with Ward given the title of editor. It was well-known, however, that Mary Ann Shadd was the driving force behind the publication. All correspondence to the *Provincial Freeman*, the paper stated, should be addressed to Mary Ann Shadd of Windsor, Canada West. Its goals were the elevation of people of color and temperance while being non-sectarian. The second issue named Mary Ann Shadd as the "publishing agent." Meanwhile Ward went to Britain, then finally emigrated to Jamaica, never returning to Canada. By October 1854, the *Provincial Freeman* was firmly attached to Mary Anne Shadd's name, and soon emigration became the central debate. Eventually, Mary Anne Shadd fully endorsed the emigration principles of Martin Delany, noted black abolitionist. Shadd undertook a speaking tour of the United States in 1854 to attract support for the newspaper. In the same year, she flouted gender conventions concerning women journalists by stating her name as Mary A. Shadd "as we do not like the Mr. and Esq. by which we are so often addressed." Thus Shadd became the first black woman newspaper publisher and editor in North America. Her sister Amelia and brother Isaac assisted her in the bold venture.

In this era, African American female journalists were still virtually invisible although several were important contributors to a wide range of newspapers. Together, they exemplify the complexity of the experiences of black women in several countries.[123] The first black newspaper was probably *Freedom's Journals*, founded by Samuel Cornish and John Russoun. Black women—among them Sarah Mapps, Francis Ellen Watkins Harper, and Maria Miller Stewart—contributed substantially to a number of abolitionist newspapers, such as the *North Star*, edited by Frederick Douglass, and *The Liberator*, edited by William Lloyd Garrison. The difficulties for black professional women turned out to be overwhelming for Shadd. By 1855 the Rev. William P. Newman had accepted her invitation to be editor. [124]

Although he did not support the emigration movement and agitated for slaves and former slaves to stay in the United States and fight, Douglass supported Shadd.[125] In an editorial on 4 July, 1856, in the *North Star*, he commented favorably on her activities. In particular, he praised but constructively criticized as well her notion, stated below, that whites were exploiting abolition for gain:

> It is a difficult matter for an American to take a liberal view on subjects involving the interests of colored Americans, disconnected from the selfishness of individual gain, personal or pecuniary. The position assumed by the majority who oppose Negro Slavery, is, that it works positive evil to the white classes, and, for our own profit, it should be abolished; the inherent wickedness of the system is lost to sight, but "our" interests as white freemen, may not be subserved by its continuance."[126]

Supportive as Douglass was of women's right to speak at conventions and their equality in the abolition movement, Shadd saw his position on emigration to Canada as ambiguous. In particular, she disliked his comparison of emigration to Canada with emigration to Liberia.[127]

At the 1855 eleventh annual Colored National Convention in Philadelphia, Mary Ann Shad requested to be allowed to speak, an unusually bold act for the time. The status of females was intensely debated, particularly their speaking in public. Shadd did not shy from doing so, and gained the floor on that occasion.

> She at first had ten minutes granted her as had the other members. At their expiration, ten more were granted, and by this time came the hour of adjournment; but so interested was the House, that it granted additional time to her to finish, at the commencement of the afternoon session; and the House was crowded and breathless in its attention to her masterly exposition of our present condition and the advantages Canada opens to colored men of enterprise.[128]

Her speaking style, once described as "nervous, hurried and unfeminine" was often criticized. Nonetheless, she was one of the few and intrepid black women undertaking public speaking in the years before the Civil War.

In 1856, she married Thomas F. Cary, twelve years her senior, who had three children from a previous marriage and ran a barber shop and a bathhouse in Toronto. (Indicative of her intense dedication, less than a week after the ceremony the new Mrs. Cary went on a six-month speaking tour of the Midwest.) Upon her return she took care of his children, Anne, Thomas, Jr., and John. Their daughter, Sarah, was born in 1857; a son, Linton, in 1860. After a business setback, Thomas Cary, in deteriorating health, moved to Chatham, where he died the same year Linton was born. Mary Ann taught there until 1863, when she returned to the United States.

During the Civil War, Cary was officially commissioned a Union Army recruiting agent, recommended by her friend Martin Delaney.[129] Participating in a variety of debates on an African American home place, John Brown's insurrection, and Haitian independence, she opposed the movements for emigration to Africa and Haiti; these places, she considered, were alien, disease-ridden, and economically hostile to black immigrants. From the 1850s to the Civil War, she was one of the few women activists who stood firm in this regard. A courageous and forthright visionary, Mary Ann Shadd Cary fought unceasingly for economic independence for black communities.

■

Chronology

1823	Born in Wilmington, Delaware, oldest of thirteen children, to political activists Harriet and Abraham Shadd, whose home was an underground railroad station. Her father owned a boot and shoe store and was a subscription agent for Garrison's *Liberator.*
1833–1839	Attended Quaker school in West Chester, Pennsylvania. Her teacher, Phoebe Darlington, was a delegate to the 1831 Anti-Slavery Convention of American Women.
1839–1850	Begins teaching in various schools for black children in Wilmington, then in Pennsylvania, New Jersey, and New York.
1851	Leaves for Canada because of the Fugitive Slave Law (1850), after lecturing about benefits of emigration to Canada. Settles in Windsor, Canada West (now Ontario).
1851–1852	Begins teaching; fifty-six pupils, children and adults, first year. Publishes pamphlet, *A Plea for Emancipation: or, Notes of Canada West in its Moral, Social, and Political Aspect.*
January 1853	American Missionary Association withdraws funding for her school.
March 1853–1859	Always the driving force but deferring to gender bias, she formally and informally edited, coedited the *Provincial Freeman,* the first black woman to edit a weekly newspaper in the United States and Canada and the first anti-slavery organ in Canada West. Both her brother Isaac and her sister-in-law Amelia assisted her at various times. The newspaper made a temporary comeback for several years under Isaac Shadd's

	leadership, after Shadd Cary resigned the editorship in 1857. She occasionally contributed.
1855	Despite opposition to a woman speaking in public, in Philadelphia, she addressed the eleventh Colored National Convention on the subject of emigration to Canada.
January 1856	Marries widower Thomas F. Cary, operator of a barber shop and bathhouse in Toronto and father of three children; settles in Chatham; begins six-month tour of the Midwest in Chicago.
August 1857	Sarah Elizabeth Cary born.
1858	Discusses abolition in the United States with John Brown, Thomas Cary, and others, at the home of Isaac Shadd.
1859–1863	Teaches in Chatham, at a school operated by Amelia Freeman Shadd, Isaac Shadd's wife.
1860	Linton Cary born; Thomas Cary dies.
1861	Helps Osborne Anderson record his experiences at Harper's Ferry in *A Voice from Harper's Ferry.* She opposed revived Haitian emigration plans. When war broke out, Martin Delany and some Shadd family members abandoned plans for emigration to Africa and supported war efforts.
c. 1863	Appointed Union Army Recruiting Officer by special order to enlist colored volunteers in the Union Army in Indiana; becomes increasingly interested in black nationalism because of Martin Delany.
1867	Enters Howard University Law Department as a student, the first woman to do so.
1868	Moves to Detroit and earns a Teaching Certificate from Detroit Board of Education.
1869	Gives up teaching in Detroit and moves to Washington, D.C.; speaks at the "Colored Men's Labor Convention" and at a gathering on woman suffrage. Enrolls in the Howard University Law School as an evening student.
1870	Drafts statement to present to the House of Representatives Judicial Committee for the right to vote; one of the few women to vote in federal elections during Reconstruction.

1871	Withdraws from Howard University. Later states that she was refused a law degree because of her sex.
1874	With sixty-three other women, she tries to register to vote in a future D.C. election.
1876	Representing ninety-four black women, writes to the National Women Suffrage Association, asking for their names to be included in a statement demanding franchise.
1878	She addresses the convention of the NWSA.
1880	Organizes the all-Black Colored Women's Progressive Franchise Organization; campaigns for women's rights under its auspices.
1881	Joins National Women's Suffrage Association. Returns to Howard University.
1883	At the age of 60, obtains her law degree, becoming one of the first black women to do so.
1892	Linton Cary dies tragically.
1893	Dies, leaving her family an estate valued at $150.

■ ■ ■

Personal Letter

Windsor, Canada West
December 28, 185

Professor G. Whipple
Dear Sir—

Yours of the 15th has been received for which and the enclosed draft you will please accept my thanks.

I am not at all surprised that your attention should be called to my case, indeed the many assertions made by Mr. and Mrs. Bibb, publicly and privately, of my being "nearly down [now]" with the certainty of a still more dishonorable position, and over all, the confident way in which they expressed themselves, made their dishonorable actions both in supplying Rev. C. C. Foote with falsehoods concern[ing m]e, and in endeavoring to make my residence here an impossibility too apparent. I am surprised though that the Rev. C. C. Foote should accuse me of "outrageous slanders."

Had your letter reached me two weeks before, I would have answered in person and given that gentleman an opportunity of putting before you his evidence that I have slandered him or any person; but as the boats have stopped running, I can give you but an imperfect idea of the matter by letter.

I will proceed to take up Mr. F.'s charges in their order, and in the outset deny ever having written "slanderous letters to abolitionists concerning their society and agents.["] I have written truthful private letters to friends, to which his attention has been called, and which contained just what Rev. C. C. Foote knew to be true. I have not given my opinion merely, but have given facts; when it was a matter of opinion, only, I said nothing.

In "affirming that the fugitives do not need help" there is no slander, but a fact known to every one who knows much about them, and continually insisted upon by fugitives themselves. I will here call your attention to a large meeting held, in this place, by fugitives on this very subject: it was one of a number of the same kind held in different parts of the province. "That they get but little of what is raised" is no slander, but is strictly true, whether it refers to begging for old and new clothes, money &c., or for the Refugees Home Society. Agents of the clothes and money, in most cases give out very little to destitute fugitives, and fugitives in this district, never heard of money being given to them—some have had it taken away. Henry Bibb denied ever having received "one shilling" for fugitives when talking to them, although dollars have been acknowledged through the *Voice* as having been sent for that purpose. It may be asked why publish and then deny the receipts?

'Few take the Voice and its contents are not generally known' is the opinion of many when trying to account for that fact.

Mr. Foote knows that at a subsequent meeting of the R.H.S to the one held Aug. 25th, every agent but himself was discharged for taking too large a percentage; he did not take quite so much as the other, and was therefore [word crossed out] retained. However, that he is solely absorbed in this money question, the points raised by him in the meeting of the 25 Aug., have no doubt. They were 1st: Twenty-five acres were ample, as many who contribute had not more land themselves, and were not willing to give for more acres to others than they possessed. 2nd: If the retention and other objectionable clauses contained in the Constitution were omitted, people would not give.

Again: the name of Hon. Joshua R. Giddings should not be on the Ex. Committee, as many persons who gave, and would give, were opposed to Mr. Giddings and would withhold contributions were he appointed.

I deny ever having said or written that the Society was "got up" for the benefit of the agents, and declare that to be gratuitous on the part of Mr. Foote, as is the assertion of my having sent seven pages of scandal after him. I believe a few of the officers are anti-slavery men and that many who contribute to support it are genuine abolitionists. I do not know that it was gotten up only for the benefit of the agents and officers, but I believe it is for their benefit now only: I know that if the agents have not been benefitted, the black people have not. Let it be "got up" for whatever purpose, it is not at present answering any good one.

The average amount taken by agents has been [53, crossed out] 63 percent; Mr. Foote knows that, and a school boy can tell how much has been collected when told that three thousand and a few hundred dolls., the amount they report make 37 percent of a number.

Theodore Holly, junior editor of the Voice, told me several months since that more than ten thousand dolls. had been receive, and intimated that Henry Bibb was his authority; when told of the fraud, he also said that Horace Hallock and the other members in Detroit, had free access to the funds, by which they carried on extensive business operations, and he was glad a colored man (H. Bibb) could have the same. He said Bibb was the originator of the [same, crossed out] scheme—that Hallock and the rest "stole his thunder," (Mr. B. and wife have told me the same,) and that it was gotten up on the principle that the whites owed the blacks, and would never be done paying them. Mr. George Cary a member of the Ex. Committee told me the agents had acted dishonestly, and made no exception—that he distrusted most of the officers—they were not anti-slavery men; but they insisted on buying lands in one locality, as there were the prospect of increased value from the vicinity of the Great Western Railroad. He said [that] H. Bibb and himself held a Deed of the first two hundred acres purchased, and that they had not transferred it to the Society (though asked to do so) and never would, as from the movements of the men he was convinced they were not honest. The fact is (and I can bring the evidence,) the black men in the Society distrust the white men, and they in turn distrust them. A prominent member of the Ex. Committee (Mr. S. A. Baker) told me I could assure fugitives, that H. Bibb would have nothing to do with the Deeds. C. C. Foote who with E. P. Benham (one of the formerly discharged agents, but now reinstated) counselled the doing away of the Farmington organization, as perfected by H. Bibb, thought "abler hands" might be at the helm. He will recollect of [visits] to a prominent gentleman in Canada, made by himself, to know if the purchasing of lands would not be made by him instead. I know that, then H. Bibb threatened to "blow up" the whole scheme.

That many thousands of dollars have been collected is evident, prominent members of the Ex. Committee say so—they also say that agents took 63 percent—they also say that if the blacks make "a time" about the scheme, they will keep the land; members of the Committee living in Detroit, said so to men who went to inquire about the land, & George Cary of Dawn repeated it in my hearing to fugitives here.

The prominent objections to the Society are: It is not needed at all as Government offers land cheaper and on better conditions: many families of fugitives own farms near the Refugees Home, and not one of whom gave as much per acre as the Society charges; it [arrays] the whites against the blacks, because of the superior political privileges sought to be given to ignorant men, by which in petty elections, black men may control, when the provisions made by Government affect all alike.

It keeps active the begging system, and thus diverts the gifts of benevolent persons from their proper course. By claiming to be a "Missionary Society," funds are diverted from efficient missionary organizations. It fosters exclusive institutions, making a line between black men even. Though one half is said to be applied to educational and religious purposes, fugitives only may be so benefitted, if it can be called a benefit in such a case. Thousands of dollars are collected on the plea that much is being done for fugitives, with them, when the Society's organ, the Voice, actually advertises lots as ready for settlers, so indifferent are the people about them; and of the few lots taken, of the thousand acres now held by the Society, but eight families live thereon, although funds have been accumulating for more than one year. Instead of the settlers being men of "good character," as at Mr. King's, the testimony of respectable fugitives is that they come to [word crossed out] town whenever they can get a few shillings, spend them in the liquor stores for whiskey, and depend upon borrowing a little meal etc., from their neighbors. The Home is looked upon as a lounging place for worthless thriftless men, and is calle[d] "Bibbs plantation," "Nigger quarter" and other names indicative of their hatred of oppression. In calling attention to what he is pleased to call my slanders, Mr. Foote should have said what he knew of the hostility to the Society entertained by fugitives, at whose request I have written such parts of the private letters as touch on the [subject (crossed out)] Home, and also a letter for the Liberator which is in that paper of the 10th inst.—also a letter to the Freeman, not [word crossed out] out. The Editors asked questions after reading the minutes of the meeting held here, and fugitives hold the views expressed in the answer[s].

It is no slander to say that Henry Bibb has hundreds of dollars belonging to fugitives—probably thousands would be nearer the truth. Henry Bibb is a dishonest man, as as such must be known to the world. To expose him is a duty which though painful, involving as it does loss of confidence, in colored men, who assume to be leaders of their people must nevertheless be performed, and that event Rev. C. C. Foote has no power to prevent. True, he may partly [word crossed out] succeed in crushing a mere woman like myself, but I have the certainty that it will be done; and I will here say in passing, that it may be wisdom, but it is certainly not brave neither is it christian-like in Mr. Foote, because of his love of the dollar, to pounce upon one he thought *easy* to crush, and cautiously avoid allusion to able and weighty *men*, whom he knew to be actively opposed to his scheme, and who in reality spoiled his prospects in Philadelphia.

C. C. Foote does not believe Mr. Bibb to be strictly honest, else why not let the purchasing of land remain in his hands? Not one of the Officers of the R.H.S can give a good title to land excepting probably, Mr. Cary, he being the only British subject connected with the society—for according to the laws here aliens cannot hold real estate without a risk. Bibb who is not yet a subject, could have given as good a title as Mr. Foote or those who now give. No, sir Mr. Foote distrusts him, and seeks to get land purchasing out of his hands and succeeds too. Prominent abolitionists in Illinois say that Bibb's appeals for axes, hoes, seminaries, etc., after the passage of the fugitive Law, obtained for him several hundreds of dollars, and there are men *here* who gave to him for that purpose, and who were surprised to learn that fugitives had never heard of the money. Abolitionists in Indiana whose names I have, told fugitives now here, that Henry Bibb had money sent him by them and others for fugitives—that friends sent to him liberally for that purpose, and recommended to them to call on him for funds to start business. They further add their testimony to others of veracity, that he took up collections frequently West, for the fugitives, but he denies it. Within the present year, and during the time he has been asking for "donations" etc. to help him out of difficulty, he has built a house, bought a vessel, bought a house and lots [leased, crossed out] on which he lives, leased another, and Mrs. Bibb has purchased a farm, and there are other business operations I can mention, besides the paper and being in receipt of several hundreds per annum for buildings and lots in Detroit. This is the man who is "making sacrifices" for the fugitives. The man who travels West with toes and elbows out, to create sympathy—who has a smile a prayer or billingsgate ready on the instant, and who at home, wraps up in purple and fine linen by warm fires, and sends from his door naked fugitives, on the pleas that "abolitionists have left it discretionary with him to give or not." Fugitives have come to me to inquire what steps must be taken to secure money given to them by friends in his house and withheld by him, on the pretense that they would not know how to expend it. I have seen the miserably clad fugitive fresh from a southern plantation sent away empty, when in the cellar under our feet were cloth clothes rotting and have helped un-head barrels of new and excellent clothing of all description.

Fifty persons, hereabouts, will testify to flat denial when needy, or abuse and rags. His chickens have been comfortably roosting on good fugitive clothes the entire season, a fact I called his attention to on the evening of Dec. 1[5] and which resulted in their removal from the poles the next day. Within a month I have heard a prominent Western abolitionist (Rev. A. St. Clair) say in the [presence] of several others that it was well understood, by the leading men in Michigan, that Henry Bibb was not to be "trusted in money matters." He and wife are at one in this matter. Under advice from her, appeals can be made to abolitionists to help sustain an objectionable paper, on the pretence of doing much for the fugitives; sacrifices are reported—great pecuniary disadvantages—mortgages etc., when at the same time he and she both, buy and build and carry on more extensive operations by land and water, than any colored people within fifty miles on either side of the river. The "seven pages of scandal" spoken of, was the reply to an article in the Pa. Freeman written too by request of fugitives and in which C. C. Foote's name does not occur; but which was received when Mr. Foote was in the city. I have a letter from Philadelphia dated Dec. 6th which [says, word crossed out] contains this passage: "He (Mr. Foote) bestowed any amount of praise on Bibb and wife—said they were held in universal 'respect in Canada to his certain knowledge:' but you were looked upon in a different light.["]

He also intimated that ambitious motives led "you to Canada, but finding yourself inadequate" to compete with [Mrs.] Bibb, it naturally excited "your ire. Such stuff and much more was let off" by Mr. Foote. I [th]ink I might with truth retort and charge Mr. Foote with slandering me. He has certainly done his best both in Pennsylvania and in New England to give him bad eminence, by saying what he knew was false, but Mrs. Bibb has said the same [just hear] and also that your society would not sustain me. I have no fear that the Refugees' Home Society will succeed—it must ultimately go down. God's approbation may not be looked for of a scheme whose advocates as a last resort, are driven to make a wreck of private character to sustain it.

In conclusion I can only say I have endeavored to do my duty here as your teacher, and have studiously sought to so act as not to bring contempt upon our Lord's cause. I have spoken out of what I and others know of the Refugees' Home society, and of Henry Bibb, but not until silence was no longer safe nor right. Foreseeing what must inevitably result should I remain here, I asked to leave this field last summer, though against the wishes of the people and not in accordance with my desire to serve them. I wished to avoid direct collision with the Bibbs. But you intimate that permanency was desirable, and I made no effort to provide for the future. In doing what I have done I repeat no one has been slandered; facts and statements made by persons of veracity have been given; and I trust the cause of truth has been subserved and the interests of fugitives promoted measurably.

May God and not man decide for you in this matter, that exact justice may be given to all parties. Yours very respectfully,

Mary A. Shadd

P.S. Several officers of the R.H.S. make no pretensions to being anti-slavery men—that is [especially] true of the purchasing committee, as told me by an officer; one cause of complaint against H. Hallock is, that he steadily refuses to give security for the funds entrusted to him.

M. A. S.

■

EDITORIALS FROM THE *PROVINCIAL FREEMAN*

Provincial Freeman (Toronto, Canada West), 25 March 1854

Anti-Slavery Relations

As a new, though humble instrumentality in the anti-slavery field, it is necessary to state clearly the position of the Provincial Freeman, and the relation it holds to the great anti-slavery bodies of America; 1st, that there may be no doubts in the minds of the public as to its real position; and 2d, by way of reply to questions already propounded.

As a matter of curiosity, growing out of the establishment of a paper devoted to the measures it is proposed to advocate, the inquiry has been made by friends in the U.S. as to the "bearings" of the Freeman; "whether towards Garrisonianism, Lewis-Tappanism, Douglassism, Free-Soilism, or what?" In other words, will this journal be committed to the distinguishing doctrines of any one of the above schools exclusively?

No, friends, no! In the United States, the centre of operations of American Slavery, and hitherto the field of active anti-slavery [operat]ions on this continent, circumstances not directly affecting us, have divided abolitionists into several classes; each of which has in its particular way, and with especial deference to the peculiar tenets held, endeavored to lead the growing liberal sentiment of the people. The national relations of abolitionists in the U.S., the peculiarity of the civil religious polity under which they live, and their present local position in the Northern division of the country, no doubt, determine the phase of anti-slavery effort with them; but with Canadians, as with British subjects everywhere, the case is quite different.

Living in a country in which chattel Slavery is not tolerated; in which this man's origin or that man's peculiarities of feature, complexion, &c., are not made subjects of special legislation, and do not militate against him, it is not thought to be either practicable or necessary to insist, solely, upon a political view of the matter.

We wish to help create a sentiment in Canada, and out of Canada, that shall tell against Slavery; and to point out, so far as we can see it, the course that people in this country should pursue to that end.

The matter of political action to affect Slavery should, we think, be left for the consideration of abolitionists, in those communities in which it is legalized; to them properly belongs the right to adopt whatever course of action therein, a knowledge of its practical bearings may suggest. It is not for us to say, Do this or do that to remove the evil from among you; but, Be just and untiring in your efforts to speedily accomplish your object; leaving ourselves the right at the same time to prefer this or that course as a matter of opinion. But we do clam for Canadians the right to say how they will work.

With British subjects, then, whether by birth or adoption, the question assumes and can assume only a moral phase. Having no slaves (the southern U.S. assertion to the contrary notwithstanding), extending to each class the immunities of freeman, it is important to aid in fashioning public opinion on the question of Slavery by insisting on a strictly Scriptural course of conduct between man and man; on the part of governments towards individuals; on the part of individuals to preserve their freedom, that the enormities of a system such as American Slavery and its cognates, Russian despotism and Italian and Austrian oppression, may be clearly understood and destroyed.

The precaution of exposing to the moral, religious and immoral, the immoral, irreligious, revolting features of any system of oppression however mild (?) is indispensable to the preservation of liberty in this country, contiguous as it is, to a powerful nation in various parts of which Slavery is not only invested with the sanctity of lawful protection, and made the distinguishing feature of political preferment; but in which the general polity, is, by contrast with the long tried and approved axioms of the most liberal government of Europe and our own country, suggestive of exciting change; where the deceptive glare made by the cry of "equality! progress! toleration!" obscure the evils inflicted upon all classes, too surely resulting from despotism practiced upon one class.

Our crusade, then must be a moral one. If a sound moral and religious influence, when exerted by individuals, can accomplish great good, surely the influence of large communities, such as this, for instance, in its character of a liberal, powerful, well sustained Province, can do more. If Slavery is better than freedom in its general features, to individuals, it is also in particulars; if better for individuals or classes in a country it is for the people at large. If Slavery is the better condition, the relation is a moral one, its results to the enslaved are elevating, and the idea that freedom is desirable is nothing more than a wild hallucination of disordered intellect. But it is not so. The experience of mankind, whether they will confess it or not, is, that Slavery works positive evil; and, it is not unimportant to observe that the moral sense of mankind, formed, sustained, enforced by Christian teaching and example, is opposed to it. Then, duty requires that it be destroyed; sympathy for those who cannot of themselves break its iron grasp requires it; and as the influence of nations is not sectional but world wide, and as among those of America, our own in preeminently gaining importance, from position, relation to European governments and national origin, it is of the first moment that a strong moral feeling shall be created here.

The British government and people possess a power, determination and influence, hardly equalled by any other nation; and it is very clear that efforts made in this part of Her Majesty's dominions to countenance the despotism in the U.S., at the same time that they deeply injure us, have a direct influence in retarding the period of emancipation. These remarks will, it is hoped, satisfy all that it is neither our duty nor inclination to be the advocate of any particular school; but at the same time that we endeavor to enforce the broad and comprehensive ground of the moral bearings of the question, so firmly insisted upon by British anti-slavery men every where, we shall accept whatever we understand to be anti-slavery, in spirit and tendency, in the views and doctrines held forth by the different schools of the United States.

■

Provincial Freeman (Toronto, Canada West), 27 May 1854

The Humbug of Reform

"This is a great age." we are often told, and undeniably it is; great in moral progress—great in the inventive genius displayed, and great in the facilities it offers to invest vice with the semblance of virtue.

The disposition to make black appear white, is the most prominent feature of the times. It is not confined to projects of doubtful propriety either; but is as true of the most necessary reforms as of other, and less important projects. We pass over the different schemes for this great purpose or the other, which are, in some degree, made to contribute their quota to the general fund of deception, and come at once to the most important movement now engrossing the attention of the people of America—the abolition question. This project which has for its object the emancipation of the slave is not an exception.

It is a difficult matter for an American to take a liberal view on subjects involving the interests of colored Americans, disconnected from the selfishness of individual gain, personal or pecuniary. The position assumed by the majority who oppose Negro Slavery, is, that it works positive evil to the white classes, and, for our own profit, it should be abolished; the inherent wickedness of the system is lost to sight, but *"our"* interests as white freemen, may not be subserved by its continuance.

All around, we hear much of Anti-Slavery. Men now have a measure of glory in being abolitionists, since the thought of security against "any more ebony additions on this continent," is prevailing, the thousands who flock to the standard, are only required to use the Shibboleth abolition, in order to be received into the household of Anti-Slavery faith; such proselytes are not to be relied upon, much less should they be tolerated as orthodox on a subject of such great importance. Some of the most miraculous changes of the present time, have been wrought among them, first, violently in favor of freedom for the poor negro, and as quick, and with no perceptible intermediate change, as decidedly in favor of his expatriation or his continuance in servitude. A man in haste to be popular, sets out with the opinion that Slavery is encroaching upon his rights—at once a love for all men is announced, but, as there is an intervening obstacle in his progress, the brotherhood of the race is a "fixed fact": there is a surplus of affectionate consideration for the black brother; wondrous things are to be done for him, and that in the twinkling of an eye.

In fact, being so blind that he cannot see to advantage, the seeing must be done for him. He cannot hear either, expect that which has first been tried, and found to be safe for his delicate organs; the consequence is, that after many "convictions" and "opinions" a [word illegible] puzzle induced by his decidedly progressive course, in spite of the tutoring and watching he gets, he is thought to be just what his barefaced oppressors have all along asserted of him—"an undesirable part of the free population." The land of his forefathers would be the best country for him, could it only be "fixed up a bit"—say a few missions and some republics; at all events, America is wanted for those whom Sojourner Truth delights in calling the "Shaxon race."

Why is it that many reflecting men will not be influenced by appeals when made to them by popular reformers, but that their true principles will out, although they cautiously try to conceal them? Sensible people will not allow themselves to be caught with the chaff of an empty profession, made by men calling themselves abolitionists, who, in addition to this, wrangle about this trifle or the other, connected with their particular creed, and so lose sight of the shadow of their aim.

We are an abolitionist—we do not want the slave to remain in his chains a second; whether the master gets paid or not, is a point of no importance to us whatever; strictly speaking; however, has has no claim to him and should not, therefore, have pay for that to which ha has no shadow of right!

We go further, we want that the colored man should live in America—should "plant his tree" deep in the soil, and whether he turns white, or his neighbors turn black by reason of the residence, is of no moment. He must have his rights—must not be driven to Africa, nor obliged to stay in the States if he desires to go elsewhere. We confess to their views as objectionable, as we know them to be, but this does not close our eyes against the "humbug" connected with this abolition reform, some phases of which would cause a worm-eating New Hollander to hide his head from very disgust.

■

Provincial Freeman (Toronto, Canada West), 3 June 1854

A Bazaar in Toronto for Frederick Douglass's Paper, &c.

Since writing the remarks to be found in another column, proposing a Bazaar for the Provincial Freeman, we see it announced that Miss Julia Griffiths, an English lady, Secretary to the Rochester Female Anti-Slavery Society, and assistant in the office of Frederick Douglass' Paper, will open a Bazaar in Toronto, about the middle of this month, under the patronage of the Toronto Anti-Slavery Society, to dispose of the unsold English and Irish goods of the Rochester Fair.

A lucky paper, that! The Rochester Bazaar is held every year for its support. It has, we are informed, a paying subscription list, numbering thousands. The first instalment of the Uncle Tom Fund, was given by Mrs. Stowe for its support. It has private patronage incredible, besides, very recently, an addition to its coffers has been made, called the "Thousand Dollar Fund"—a sum contributed by one hundred persons, and gotten up, mainly, we are told, by a great effort on the part of Miss Griffiths, and now, Toronto must pay her golden tribute, by solicitation of the same untiring Miss Griffiths.

Barnum is distanced, and no mistake, in this, succession of brilliant efforts to get the "tin!" But how is it that the wire-workers of a paper opposed to emigration to Canada, are making arrangements to hold a Bazaar for its support in the country? Are the abolitionists to hold a Bazaar for its support in the country? Are the abolitionists of Canada, or, rather of the Toronto Society, opposed to free colored people coming into the Province to settle? and are these the initiatory steps to a public endorsement of Anti-emigration views?

We know that such is the opinion of a portion of the citizen here, but may they not be mistaken? We do not wish to be liable to a silent imputation of mis-representing the great people engaged in this movement—humble as we are, we would like to know more of the facts, as well to satisfy our minds, as to enlighten the public. We have had many inquiries made of us, recently, as to the movements of the Toronto Anti-Slavery Society, not one of which we could answer, of course, not knowing where to find it, to get any information. We think, however, that there is a prospect of its being found about the "middle of June," anxious inquirers will then be able to see and hear to their satisfaction. Should they conclude not to lose a moment in the search, we would suggest an application to the parent Society, in New York City, U.S., through Lewis Tappan, Esq., the great embodiment of Anti-Slavery Society tactics for the States and the Canadas.

The Toronto Anti-Slavery Society have had Rev. Samuel R. Ward in England and other parts of Britain, collecting funds for newly arrived fugitives—because the necessary amount was difficult to raise here in a reasonable time for those needy ones. Now in the name of honor and humanity, what is the state of the case? Are those funds to be lavished on favorites in Yankeedom, because Mr. Ward has unfortunately fallen into disgrace with

Lewis Tappan, Esq., and the right wing of the Toronto Society, for his devotion to the interests of colored Canadians, and his manly determination not to bow down sufficient-low, to please this one or that, who may have the shadow, but not the substance of anti-slavery? Poor fugitives! We trust that you may not have to content yourselves in the coming and future winters with only the crumbs that may be left from the £1500 ($6,000) raised by Mr. Ward for you. And poor people of another class, who blow the trumpet for, and "prostrate yourselves["] at the feet of other people!

Well after all this array of facts and opinions, it may be well to look at the bright side: the coming "elephant" may be but a precursor of the "good time," when "distinguished organ["] of Anti-Emigration in the U.S., will cease its opposition to colored freeman who wish to settle in Canada—will emigrate hither instead of simply coming over to take away the money before our "hard" winter sets in, and pour forth its "clarion notes" as the organ of the Toronto Anti-Slavery Society, until the globe shall be shaken by the "awful sound."

But will not Miss Griffiths leave a few coppers behind? The Underground emigrants come on in great numbers, and may "need" a little of something in the cold weather, besides, we know that the friends of Mr. Ward, and of the Provincial Freeman, talk about holding a Huzza for this paper about the same time!

■

Provincial Freeman (Chatham, Canada West), 5 July 1856

The Emigration Convention

For many, many years the colored men of the United States, have been assembling in Conventions, at stated periods, in order to devise ways and means by which to improve their condition. Calls are issued—in due time, delegates assemble, and after making very many speeches (and some of them very excellent ones too) and passing resolutions of similar tenor, from year to year, they return to their homes with but little hope of any very great amount of good to result from their deliberations; but painfully conscious of a reduction in the pocket. We respect a people who show a disposition to change an uncomfortable position, and we must respect the efforts made by any people, although convinced that the means they use to that end are inadequate to the object, but in so doing, we must not be silent upon the merits of their peculiar theory, much less, must we be expected to endorse their action. The anti-emigrationists of the States, require not only the silence, but the most decided approval, by the people generally, of all they are pleased to advance; now in all kindness we think they require too much. Let them meet Emigrationists on the broad platform of free discussion and inquiry, without bickering, animosity or jealousy, and actuated only by the determination to do NOW for their advancement, what should not be imposed as a brethren upon coming generations, and our word for it, results will follow different, and of higher character for good, than any that we have yet seen. Now, personal interests and party manoeuvres absorb much of the time in meetings and out of them, and the great questions are made of secondary importance. Let men who clamor for free thought, speech and action, from their oppressors, tolerate their brethren in the exercise of these necessary rights, so that when those who do not accept for themselves the old policy of staying at *home* on sufferance, wish to be heard, they may not be made the victims of an opposition for opinion's sake, by a part of their own household, as verily, as the entire people are the victims of the slave power.

The convention to be held in Cleveland in August of the present year, will be held by those who have long since out-grown the policy that has guided the colored people of the States for many years. Emigrationists hold that political elevation, the bone of contention, and which cannot be secured without unnecessary sacrifice of time, energy and means in the land of their birth, can be obtained by removal to foreign and more liberal governments. Their positions on this point, should be examined and not be cried down without investigation. They maintain that by emigration they would not only supersede the necessity of colonization to Africa, so strongly insisted upon, and strangely enough, by some white friends, and many colored anti-emigrationists, but that thereby they would be enabled to do Anti-Slavery work more effectually, instead of, as now, remaining where they must, to be popular with some of their leaders, oppose their best interests (to remove) and when in order to get their "bread and cheese," they must actually support their oppressors, and assist in maintaining the government that is in the hands of their enemies a tower of strength. Look calmly and without prejudice at your position anti-emigration brethren, and you too who are indifferent! Not only are your hands tied against your own redemption from political thraldom, but you encourage a people to remain, and you remain and accumulate wealth, the very taxes upon which are not only put into the United States Treasury, and used to maintain a government cemented with the blood of your brethren, but a portion of which, actually is appropriated by its legislators to send you to Africa; thus you are forced to go, made to pay the expenses of your own expatriation in part, and made to contribute your quota to return the Burnses, the Simses and other brave fellows, who wish to escape from the tender mercies of its supporters, and, to pay the price demanded by the keepers of the blood hounds human and canine, who see the fleeing fugitives. Verily brethren your responsibility is awful! but made more intense by the opposition you show, against those who would reverse this order of things.

Cease to uphold the United States government, if it will, and while it does uphold human slavery. Cease to grapple after the shadow while you disregard the substance. "Come out from" a government that begins its depredations upon the rights of colored men, and ends by destroying the liberties of white men: if they will not regard the members of the household, think you they will listen to you? No verily. Go to the Cleveland Convention, and determine to remove to a country or to countries, where you many have equal rights, and thus be *elevated at once.* Where from the responsibilities of your position as freemen, you will have something else to do, and a higher tone of thought, than to *serve* a class of tyrants for reduced wages, and to speculate upon, and imitate the fashions and follies of people who despise and deride you. Go up to Cleveland on the 26th of August.

■

Provincial Freeman (Chatham, Canada West), 26 July 1856

Intemperance

> A colored man passed under the windows of this office on Saturday, "full of strange oaths," and very indiscreet expressions, the promptings of the god to whom he had been pouring in his libations. We cannot tell whom he may have insulted or even hurt under this influence. There is a law against furnishing drink to Indians, and we cannot but think that a similar restriction applied to the "son of Ham" would be a wholesome protection both to themselves and others. Planet

The Planet gets worse, and worse! Something more than bare assertion of regard for colored people must take place to make the community believe it. We all heard, a few days ago, of the Editors of anti-slavery tendencies, and yet, whenever it can put a word in edge-wise, which will bear unjustly upon colored men it does so. The colored people are not wild Indians, neither do they drink more whiskey than their white friends hereabouts. One colored man passed under your office window drunk, and if he had not "hurt" somebody he might have done so, bah! They must be out of a subject to write about down at that office! Every colored man must be prohibited from drinking because on drank freely. Who patronize the saloons, taverns &c., in this place? Indians and colored men only? No! We believe in passing a strictly prohibitory law that will not only prevent Indians and colored men from getting drunk, but will stop white men from drinking as well and not only the "inferior" classes about Chatham, but a drunken Editor occasionally. But the Editor of the Planet must have too much good sense, must be too much of an abolitionist to propose a regulation of the sort in sober earnest, else he must have forgotten that while to see a drunken colored man is of so rare occurrence as to "call him out" on the subject. Drunken officers, "limbs of the law," a drunken M.P.P., or a drunken Editor of his class is quite common nowadays.

M. A. S. CARY

■

Provincial Freeman (Chatham, Canada West), 6 December 1856

The Presidential Election in the United States

Since the great struggle of parties for the presidential candidacy, which recently agitated the American States, a calm seems to have supervened, which the excited state of the contest would hardly justify if viewed from a surface point. But those acquainted with the minutia—with the great principles involved, discover in the apparent "hush" of the present, a suffocating and unnatural stillness, the precursor of a more terrific storm than has hitherto been witnessed. And, why should there not be a perfect hurricane of sentiment—a whirlwind of startling facts, of bloody deeds such as the contest of despotism against nominal freedom has never before realized? Before the result of Mr. Buchanan's election was announced, the pro and anti-slavery parties joined issue; the one for a dominance secured by a mistaken deference to weakness, at first, and held by unworthy advantage afterwards, the other, to maintain the integrity of free institutions for all men. Since the poll has been decided in favor of despotism, the adherents of that party, not only assume that they have beaten, but expect unyielding submission; unquestioned and unquestioning to their authority; but the genius and spirit of liberty is against them. Had the contest assumed the old form; had the abolitionist of the North, moved only by compassion for the slave, appealed to them to withhold their grasp, a result so decisive might be regarded as probably a quietus to further agitation for a time, only, the genuine abolitionist never giving up entirely; but it is no longer the "nigger in the wood pile." Compassion for the slave in his chains, is but secondary to the great necessity of a decided struggle for his own liberties, by the white man of the country. Instead of a handful of abolitionists, from motives of humanity, the world beholds millions of abolitionists from necessity, and depend upon it there will be hard and bloody work, before the struggle terminate[s]! We heartily deplore the prospect. There is no one so thoroughly depraved! as to love violence for its own sake, but the oppressor of the colored man has forced the necessity. Beginning upon the colored minority and aided in their work without dissent by the North, they went on, and on, until the increasing respect for self, and the opinion of the world, obliged northern men to hesitate—then came the rebound—from the black man to the white, and now we contemplate a great but gory struggle. Bleeding Kansas! Ostracism for opinion's sake. Ruffianism in the Halls of Legislation. Impertinence on the high ways and by ways. Incarceration as in the case of the noble Passmore Williamson—not for speaking, not for acting—but for silence; and lastly, the seal upon all the outrages by the election results. But into the future who can bear to look without a shudder at what must be, judging from the decided and demon-like attitude of the South, and her past history and present aggressions? When we remember that away down under all this mass of outraged humanity, the white men North and South, opposed to the institution from an instinct of self preservation and to slaveholders, because of their tyrannical and dictatorial policy towards them—away down under it all, buried nearly out of sight, lie the prostrate slave, and the miscalled free colored man, devoted to wrongs worse even than ever were experienced in Kansas—not shot because they do not stay away from asserting their rights, but stripped of all rights—things without names, to "go on" bleeding and breeding in body and mind and spirit until the struggle over and around them should have terminated. A fearful thing is the result of that last Presidential election! The opinion expressed by that good woman [word illegible] Esther Moore of the Fugitive Bill, is true of this, "there is no name for it."

■

Provincial Freeman (Chatham, Canada West), 6 December 1856

A Good Boarding House Greatly Needed by the Colored Citizens

It is very desirable that some one acquainted with managing properly a good Boarding House would open one in Chatham, at this time, both for the respectable entertainment of the public and the citizens of this place. A "house of all nations" wherein the essentials, good tables and lodgings, excellent deportment from proprietors and visitors, could be insisted upon, and where the charges would be in keeping with the character of the place. A good temperance house of high tone, and fitted up properly and managed by competent persons, would pay well! At the present time, we do not know of a public boarding house that is not also a drinking house. A most unworthy state of morals! and yet such houses, not "gin palaces" either, are blazoned forth as desirable places of resort. We regard them as degrading in their tendency—as calculated to not only corrupt and demoralize the young, but as dangerous to the physical health of the community as the small-pox or cholera. For it is not only that they hold out the temptation to beastly intoxication—a fact that cannot be denied—the quality of their liquors is so inferior generally, as to facilitate disease and death with greater rapidity than ordinary. Some of our Chatham boarding houses make their own liquors and a "make" they may be supposed to be. While the character of houses here is indifferent so far as we have been informed, the rates for entertainment are enormous. The wants of the travelling community justify better provisions than have been made in this respect, and we sincerely hope some enterprising COLORED Canadian or American will take the matter in hand.

M. A. S. C.

▪

Provincial Freeman (Chatham, Canada West), 31 January 1857

Obstacles to the Progress of Colored Canadians

The colored people of these Provinces live in a land of equal laws—equal rights, and yet, no people that we know of are given to complaint more than they. In certain localities, parties can be found, who, taking advantage of the prevalent ignorance among the colored population, administer the law in a way clearly prejudicial to the interests of the latter; but, how far the former are censurable under the circumstances is with us a question, when viewed in the light of an ordinary transaction for the exact extent of the censure to be attached to the colored people themselves is not quite clear, we are convinced however, that the fault is not all on one side, but that to them belongs to a fair share of blame. We make these remarks with no intention to shield white men from merited blame at all, but that the colored people may not take to themselves complete exemption from rebuke for their great indifference to their interests.

Courts of justice, corrupt judges not any other grievance of which we may complain can injure them a tithe in comparison, with the treachery, want of confidence and down right wickedness one towards the other. In the United States, in slavery, the great aim of their oppressors was to destroy confidence the one in the other—to under-value one another in their person and pursuits; at the same time that they inculcate fear of the master, or the person of white complexion, to make him also the idol, the centre of homage, the one to be looked up to, to be clothed and fed by, although the food to be furnished them, whether moral or other, should poison in the taking. Many in coming to Canada, have but fled from the sting, the bitterness of the dose, the direct result of the relation of master and slave, but not all from these other evils which are as clearly concomitants of the relation.

A well organized insurrection for meeting out to the master his just deserts, must be nipped in the bud by the treachery of some "negro," who more in contempt of his own people than hatred to the actions of the man who trampled upon him, must reveal the plot. He had no confidence in his fellows—there was no fellow feeling—he would save his oppressors at the expense of his suffering brethren.

The case of that slave, brutalized as he is, has many a counterpart in these Provinces, among colored men. Try any community—our own to begin with, and seek out if you can among its teeming hundreds, twenty men who see eye to eye upon the subject of their interests! They cannot be found! While upon one question some may unite, there will be the most rancorous and bitter division, upon others equally clear and conclusive; and rather than yield an opinion for the general good; their entire interests may go by the poor. The vulture now at the vitals of [word illegible] is the aim [one or two lines missing] other words, the desire of a few ignorant colored men to lead the people. To that love of power, and the "pickings and stealings" resulting from it may be traced [to] the greater part of the evils entailed upon us. WE pause just here, to say by the way of parenthesis (that no honest colored man or woman knows the moral condition of the colored people of these Provinces can deny what we say), without telling a falsehood, and yet, for saying this much truth, we know as certainly that,

Tray Blanche and Sweet heart,

and every contemptible cur in the pack will either be growling, snapping, barking, or secretly biting for it.

The time has come to "cry aloud and spare not." Instead of being like the Jews, who unite the more because of oppression, unlike every other people, the more the division the better; and unable to get along beautifully in the work of separation, a free invitation is indirectly given for inroads of the enemy, should he assume the garb of a friend, though not possessing one trait to merit the name. Take a retrospect of the colored people of Canada for the last thirty years. Their institutions—their divisions—the knots and "squads"—their white and colored beggars—begging in public for lands, clothes, schools, churches—the quarrels of these beggars, white and colored—the contentions about their lands—among their churches—the immorality among missionaries white and colored, teachers and preachers, male and female—the caucuses, conventions, resolutions, and after all, the return of the pretended leaders of the people, "Like the dog to his vomit, or the sow to her wallowing in the mire," and that too, after years or weeks or months of sin, and after having before "God and the sun" foresworn for the twentieth time such vile deeds.

And now a good reader, and friend to your race, look at the conditions of the same churches, schools, institutions. Calculate if you can, the vast sums drawn from the benevolent of England and America, enough to have installed an empire; then, too, turn to the "mussy fussy" creatures who have been at this work—this business of degrading an entire people, black almost to their [first] estate, as fast as British law could make men of them, and what do we see? Who are these Atlases upon whose powerful shoulders rest in this colored world? Men generally among the whites, who could not be made available for any good work at home—men of fallen fortunes or of no fortunes, who have chosen this field to replenish empty purses, or to fill purses always empty; and among black men, knavish tools of these first named, or men of great ignorance, conceit and ambition, whose highest recommendation, whose certificate of reputation, is their ability to instal beggars and begging, and to squander the same. Think of it! The destiny of thousands of people to be confided to such keeping. Think of a people who when on the other side, was said by one of the greatest philanthropists of the county to be a "nation of servants," and when under British rule aspire to be a nation of beggars. Having spoken in general, we intend in future, to particularize. Instead of treachery, ignorance[,] servility, we want to see confidence, intelligence, independence and instead of a house of cold refugees formerly bond and free, aiming with might and main to curse their people, with a pro-slavery—yankee training. We shall aim to persuade these "suffering" people, to cease hankering after the "flesh pots of Egypt," and as they have come under British rule from necessity, to become at heart in reality.

M. A. S. C.

■

Sermon

Sunday evening, Apr[il] 6, [1858]

1st business of life[,] to love the Lord our God with heart and soul, and our neighbor as our self.

We must then manifest love to God by obedience to his will—we must be cheerful workers in his cause at all times—on the Sabbath and other days. The more readiness we Evince the more we manifest our love, and as our field is directly among those of his creatures made in his own image in acting as themself who is no respecter of persons we must have failed in our duty until we become decided to waive all prejudices of Education birth nation or training and make the test of our obedience God's Equal command to love the neighbor as ourselves.

These two great commandments, and upon which rest all the Law and the prophets, cannot be narrowed down to suit us but we must go up and conform to them. They proscribe neither nation nor sex—our neighbor may be Either the oriental heathen the degraded Europe and or the Eslaved colored American. Neither must we prefer sex with the Slave mother as well as the Slave-father. The oppress, or nominally free woman of every nation or clime in whose Soul is as Evident by the image of God as in her more fortunate contemporary of the male sex has a claim upon us by virtue of that irrevocable command Equally as urgent. We cannot successfully Evade duty because the Suffering fellow woman be[crossed out] is only a woman! She too is a neighbor. The good Samaritan of this generation must not take for the Exemplars the priest and the Levite when a fellow wom[an] is among thieves—neither will they find their Excuse in the custom as barbarous and anti-christian as any promulgated by pious Brahmin that [word crossed out] they may be only females. The spirit of true philanthropy knows no sex. The true christian will not seek to Exhume from the grave the past [word crossed out] its half developed customs and [offer crossed out] insist upon them as a substitute for the plain teachings of Jesus Christ, and the Evident deductions of a more Enlightened humanity.

There is too a fitness of time for any work for the benefit of God's human creatures. We are told to keep Holy the Sabbath day. In what manner? not by following simply the injunctions of those who bind heavy burdens, to say nothing about the same but as a man is better than a sheep but combining with God's worship the most active vigilance for the resurector from degradation violence and sin his creatures. In these cases particularly was the Sabbath made for man and woman if you please as there may be those who will not [exe(crossed out)] accept the term man in a generic sense. Christ has told us as it is lawful to lift a sheep out of the ditch on the Sabbath day, i[f] a man is much better than a sheep.

Those with whom I am identified, namely the colored people of this country—and the women of the land are in the pit figurat[ively] [speaking(crossed out)] are cast out. These were Gods requirements during the Prophecy of Isaiah and they are in full force today. God is the same yesterday to day and forever. And upon this nation and to this people they come with all their significance within your grasp are three or four millions in chains in your southern territory and among and around about you are half a million allied to them by blood and to you by blood as were the Hebrew servants who realize the intensity of your hatred and oppression. You are the government what it does to [th] you Enslaves the poor whites The free colored people The Example of slave holders to access all.

What we aim to do is put away this Evil from among you and thereby pay a debt you now owe to humanity and to God and so turn from their channel the bitter waters of a moral servitude that is about overwhelming yourselves.

I speak plainly because of a common origin and because were it not for the monster slavery we would have a common destiny here—in the land of our birth. And because the policy of the American government so singularly set aside allows to all free speech and free thought: As the law of God must be to us the higher law in spite of powers principalities selfish priests or selfish people to whom the minister it is important that we assert boldly that no where does God look upon this the chief crimes with the least degree of allowance nor are we justified in asserting that he will tolerate those who in any wise support sustain it.

Slavery American slavery will not bear moral tests. It is [in(crossed out)] Exists by striking down all the moral safeguards to society by—it is not then a moral institution. You are called upon as a man to deny and disobey the most noble impulses of manhood to aid a brother in distress—to refuse to strike from the limbs of those not bound for any crime the fetters by which his Escape is obstructed. The milk of human kindness must be transformed into the bitter waters of hatred—you must return to his master he that hath Escaped, no matter how Every principle of manly independence revolts at the same. This feeling Extends to Every one allied by blood to the slave. And while we have in the North those who stand as guards to the institutions the[y] must also volunteer as [s]hippers away of the nominally free. You must drive fr[om] his home by a heartless [os]tracism to the heathen shores when they fasted, bowed themselves, and spread sack cloth and ashes under them. Made long prayers (&c.) that they might be seen of men, but Isaiah told them God would not accept them. They must repent of their sins—put away iniquity from among them and then should their light shine forth.

But we are or may be told that slavery is only an Evil not a sin, and that too by those who say it was allowed among the Jews and therefore ought to be Endured. Isaiah sets that matter to rest he shows that it is a sin handling it less delicately than many prophets in this generation. These are the sins that we are to spare not the sin of Enslaving men—of keeping back the hire of the laborer. You are to loose the bands of wickedness, to undo the heavy burdens to break Every yoke and to let the oppressed go free. To deal out bread to the hungry and to bring the poo[r] [word missing] speaking. Their cry has long been ascending to the Lord who then will assume the responsibility of prescribing times and seasons [and (crossed out)] [for (word crossed out)] for the pleading of their cause—of and righteous cause—and who shall overrule the voice of woman? Emphatically the greatest sufferer from chattel slavery or political proscription on this God's foot-stool? Nay we have Christs Example who healed the sexes indiscriminately thereby implying an Equal inheritance—who rebuf[f]ed the worldling Martha and approved innovator Mary. [The Him] who respected not persons [two words crossed out] but who imposes Christian duties alike upon all sexes, and who in his wise providence metes out his retribution alike upon all.

No friends we suffer the oppressors of the age to lead us astray; instead of going to the source of truth for guidance we let the adversary guide us as to what is our duty and Gods word. The Jews thought to that they were doing [H]is requirements when they did only that which was but a small sacrifice.

■

Open Letter or Circular from the Vigilance Committee

October 1858

As an agent appointed by our Vigilance Committee, established here to conduct the case growing out of the release of the slave boy spoken of by the New York Tribune, and as an Assistant Secretary of the same, I am authorized, and beg to enlist your pecuniary aid towards defending the suit brought against I.D. Shadd (editor of the Provincial Freeman) [brother of Mary Anne Shadd Cary], J. Sparks, Edward Dotson, Shelby Smith, Wm. Streets, John Goodyear and John Hooper. One hundred and fifty others are also liable to arrest under a similar charge of riot and (indirectly) abduction. The parties, with the exception of Messrs. Goodyear and Hooper, are colored men and poor men. The editor of the Freeman (organ of the fugitives) holding the boy in his care, in spite of pro-slavery officials, is the most responsible party to the Court, yet he, the conductor of a struggling paper, must suspend it to meet the exigencies of the case. There is no other resort than to make a direct appeal to the friends of Freedom through those who stand on the watch tower of Freedom, in order that a part at least, of the heavy expense may be met by the 18th of the present month, at which time the trial will come on at the Assizes. Please assure us of your sympathy by a word of encouragement, and whatever your generosity will prompt you to give or sent. [M. A. S. C.]

■

Open Letter to the *Anglo-African*

Weekly Anglo-African (New York, N.Y.), 28 September 1861

CHATHAM, C[anada] W[est]
Sept[ember] 17, 1861

EDITOR OF THE ANGLO-AFRICAN [Robert Hamilton]
Sir:

It is extremely gratifying to know that the Anglo-African is in circulation once more. When your paper "went out," the hopes of many who had only heard of it, seemed to die out with it; some feared, they felt by intuition, that mischief was brewing, and very soon the evil was upon them in its full extent.

In the interim between the transfer of the Anglo-African to other parties, and its republication, a doubtful scheme, said to be for the benefit of our much injured people, was securely matured and established, (?) and it has been pushed forward since with a vigor, a tact, and a unscrupulousness worthy of the early days of African colonization.

For the first time, since colored men dared to canvass questions relating to their own interests, have they been summarily silenced—forbidden to examine both sides; for the first time have they been ruthlessly thrust out of doors by those loud in their protestations of friendship. Not only is this a part of our sad history, but in the prosecution of the Haytain Colonization scheme we have, singularly enough, all of the old, and worn out, and repudiated arguments, about the extinction of or race—extinction from 20 persons in 1620, to 4,000,000 in 1861—the invincibility of American prejudice, common schools, churches, railroads in 1832, and 1861 in States and Canada, the incongeniality of climate—do we not live as long, and are we not as exempt from disease as the pure Anglo-Saxon? We have, with these, the exhumed relics of the past; the fact that instead of unrelenting Democrats and heartless slaveholders, to push forward this new crusade against the best interests of the free colored man of the North, we have Republican abolitionists,and fugitive-slaves, who "once upon a time" fought bravely against the dogma, and when its now cherished arguments were the pet theme of the fierce negro-hater and the great conservators of slave property.

To be consistent, would it not be well for the new colonizationists to dig up their buried foes, and make haste and repair the damage to this generation by singing in praise of their wise foresight, and their genuine friendship for our poor people?

But not only has another doubtful scheme been "set a going," now said to be in the name of the black man, and for black men, but for the first time in thirty years have our Pennington's, our Delany's, our Smith's and Downing's, been cuffed into silence. Our so-called enemies, the African Colonizationists, never dared to stigmatize as drunkards, "renegade negroes" and snobs, those of our men known to be among the leaders in defence of our rights.

Once upon a time brave men and women, with the bugle-blast of indignation spoke out against wrong when it was perpetrated against black men, at the risk of the halter, I have a dim recollection of one noble man called William Lloyd Garrison in such peril Why cannot there be a strong and manly voice now? There has been a slight murmur down about Boston; why does not somebody speak OUT? Are not you recording the dead and buried? Do not you tell of the disappointments? Are not Mother Holly and John Anthony, and numbers, gone? and have not Mrs. Monroe, Sarah Underwood, Mason, and others spoken?

We are told that only the lazy complain, or tell tales; what must we say of the dead? they tell not tales.

I have spoken of the sins of commission, in the interim of your silence —now for the sins of omission during the same period: The American

Union is one scene of distraction: must we for the same cause be at our wits ends? There never was a time when the colored man could afford to be more calm and collected than now. There are thousands of "contrabands" peering cautiously from your forests, and sulking behind corners in your cities, not knowing in their extremity what way to go, and finally starved into asking the first "massa," though it may be an enemy, "am this Canada?" Has the North Star, the old beacon light, gone out, that these men cannot be encouraged to follow the ONLY safe and long tried road to freedom? It seems to me that the devil is let loose to hound the poor fugitives for a season. From the faith of our people being in God, and the North Star, a James Redpath and a star never before heard of, a South Star, now dazzle with a sort of "foxfire" light, to the neglect of our duty to God, our true interests, and our obligations to humanity.

Who, may I ask, is this James Redpath, in the hollow of whose hand lies trembling the destiny of our people? This man, who by a species of moral jugglery, beyond my stupid comprehension, has succeeded in throwing glamour over the optics of all our friends, and who has made the bitter pill of colonization sophistry long since discarded by them, a sweet morsel to hundred of devotees of the god palm? In all sincerity I ask this question. In a letter to the Planet of our town, Mr. Redpath complains that the Rev. W. P. Newman, whom he calls a "renegade negro," is trying "to destroy whatever influence my anti-slavery service may have given me with Americans of African descent."

What have been and what are the anti-slavery services of Mr. Redpath, upon which he claims to be entitled to influence with—colored Americans of African descent. In the name of common sense and common fairness what are they? When Wm. Lloyd Garrison, Lewis Tappan, Wendell Phillips, Gerrit Smith, and a host of such speak of services rendered, we know what they mean—they have toiled in our cause when it cost something, and their noble sacrifices, crop out into a harvest of gratitude from the entire colored people. But what has Mr. Redpath done?

It is this leading men and women by reason of their ignorance and credulity, to untimely graves in the island of Hayti?

A child, say our wise educators should be at least five years old before he should be instructed in the rudiments; it may that moral precocity entitles Mr. Redpath to some consideration, but keeping in view the fact that John Brown has not been dead three years, and Redpath for all practical anti-slavery purposes, must have been borne since then—I cannot forbear again asking what special labor since he came into being entitles him to teach, to dictate a destiny? and to make of no effect—the work of friendly laborer's who toiled hard heretofore? Who can tell!

Brother Newman tells you we have some excitement here in Canada, so we have, the most of it, is caused by the advocacy of this Haytian scheme about which I write. It is not that the thousands about which you have heard so much, are going to leave and throw off their British allegiance, but that a few agents, using the name of Brown and talking Redpath have, by working upon an imaginative and hitherto overworked people, set afloat stories of genial skies, plenty to eat, and little to do, and have, at the same time, plied vigorously the old story about their attaining to the "greatest height" among the whites; these rigmaroles, which they have been scattering broadcast for a few months, have caused excitement. Before then, our people in Canada, thanked God for this Asylum; they went on adding to their statement, and were surely removing the local obstacles to unbounded progress.

A few have gone to Hayti, a few more will go; a few will go to Jamaica; already some have written back from Hayti who are not too well pleased; some more await further advice. Another record of deaths and they will fall back into their former industrious preserving ways; that is what this new scheme will come to here, and in the meantime, in answer to the question of a good woman in Wisconsin, who writes to know "what to do with the contrabands," we say over here, send them to Canada! Send them over here as you have done thousands before, who now sit in the shade of their own noble forests, with none to disturb them. Canada is just as large as ever, and though they may suffer a little for a time, the people will rally to help them; our government will give them one hundred acres of land, in a region where now she gives the same to Norwegians, Irish, English and Scotch, and where colored men can get it if they will, or they can settle down readily, and do well in this western section, with friends and relatives to help them. Do not let the question be asked what shall we do with them? send them along.

M. A. S. Cary

Notes

■

1. See, for example, Zilpha Elaw, *Memoirs of the Life, Religious Experience, Ministerial Travels and Labours, of Mrs. Zilpha Elaw, an Amerian Female of Colour; Together with Some Account of the Great Religious Revivals in America* [Written by Herself] (1846); reprint in *Sisters of the Spirit: Three Black Women's Autobiographies of the Nineteenth Century,* ed. William L. Andrews (Bloomington: Indiana University Press, 1986), pp. 49–160. Charlotte L. Forten [Grimké], *The Journals of Charlotte L. Forten* (1854–1862) ed. with an introduction by Ray Allen Billington (New York: Dryden Press, 1953; reprint New York: Macmillan, 1961); another edition ed. Brenda Stevenson (New York: Oxford University Press, 1988). Frances Ellen Watkins Harper, *Poems on Miscellaneous Subjects* (1854) (Boston: J. B. Yerrinton and Son, 1854; enlarged Philadelphia: Merrihew and Thompson, 1857). Ann Plato, *Essays: including Biographies and Miscellaneous Pieces in Prose and Poetry* (1841) (Hartford Conn.: n.p., 1841). Sarah Parker Remond, "Sarah P. Remond" (1861); in *Our Exemplars, Poor and Rich; or Biographical Sketches of Men and Women,* ed. Matthew Davenport Hill (London: Cassell, Petter, and Galpin, 1861), pp. 276–286. Maria W. Stewart, *Meditations from the Pen of Mrs. Maria W. Stewart* (1832); in Marilyn Richardson, *Maria W. Stewart: America's First Black Woman Political Writer* (Bloomington: Indiana University Press, 1987), esp. pp. 28–42. Lucy Terry, "Bars Fight" (1746), in *American Women Writers to 1800,* ed. Sharon M. Harris (Oxford: Oxford University Press, 1996), pp. 317–318. Phillis Wheatley, *Poems on Various Subjects, Religious and Moral* (1773) (London: Bell, 1773 [first British edition]; Philadelphia: n.p., 1786 [first American edition]).

For Sojourner Truth's orature, see Carla Peterson's fine volume, *"Doers of the Word": African American Women Speakers and Writers in the North* (1830–1880) (Oxford: Oxford University Press, 1995), esp. pp. 24–55; and Nell Irvin Painter. *Sojourner Truth: a Life, a Symbol* (New York: W. W. Norton, 1996).

2. Oddly enough, no one except for son-in-law John Gilbert in his autobiography, mentions that Barry Conyers Hart, a man from a politically well known white family, was a "man of colour." The Rev. William Box, *Memoir of John Gilbert, Esq. Late Naval Storekeeper at Antigua. To Which Are Appended. A Brief Sketch of His Relic, Mrs. Ann Gilbert by the Rev. William Box, Wesleyan Missionary, and a Few Additional Remarks by a Christian Friend* (Liverpool: D. Marples, 1835), p. 22.

3. No recent book specifically documents the history of Antigua in the decades before emancipation. In her wide-ranging study *Slave Society in the British Leeward Islands at the End of the Eighteenth Century* (New Haven: Yale University Press,

1965). Elsa Goveia furnishes some important history and statistics about slave society. Other information can be culled from the rich variety of often religiously based histories and studies of the island mentioned in these notes.

4. For the right to vote, see Goveia, *Slave Society*, p. 97. See also William A. Green, *British Slave Emancipation: The Sugar Colonies and the Great Experiment*, 1830–1865 (Oxford: Clarendon Press, 1976), pp. 17–22.

5. Goveia, *Slave Society*, p. 91.

6. Ibid., pp. 217, 91–92. For an account of slave societies themselves, see B. W. Higman, *Slave Populations of the British Caribbean, 1807–1834* (Baltimore: Johns Hopkins University Press, 1984), pp. 52–53 and passim. For an account of the earliest master-slave relationships in Antigua, see David Barry Gaspar, *Bondsmen and Rebels: A Study of Master-Slave Relations in Antigua, with Implications for Colonial British America* (Baltimore: Johns Hopkins University Press, 1985).

7. Goveia, *Slave Society*, p. 218.

8. Clement Caines, *Letters on the Cultivation of the Otaheite Cane, the manufacture of sugar and rum, the saving of molasses, the care and preservation of stock, with the attention and anxiety which is due to negroes. To these topics are added a few other particulars analogous to the subject of the letters, and also a speech on the slave trade, the most important feature in West Indian culture* (London, 1801), 1:192; Goveia, *Slave Society*, pp. 35, 141, and passim.

9. G. G. Findlay and W. W. Holdsworth, *The History of the Wesleyan Methodist Society* (London: Epworth Press, n.d.), 2:140.

10. Anne Hart Gilbert, *History of Methodism*, pp. 6–7.

11. Ibid., p. 153; Findlay and Holdsworth, *History*, pp. 30–31.

12. Drescher, *Capitalism and Antislavery*, p. 114.

13. Thomas Coke, *A History of the West Indies . . .* (Liverbool: Nuttall, Fisher, & Dixon, 1908; reprint Miami Fla.: Mnemosyne, 1969), 1:92.

14. Goveia, *Slave Society*, p. 235.

15. Ibid., pp. 122, 143. For another view of slave society, see William A. Green, *British Slave Emancipation: The Sugar Colonies and the Great Experiment, 1830–1865* (Oxford: Clarendon Press, 1976), pp. 22–32.

16. Donald G. Mathews, *Slavery and Methodism: A Chapter in American Morality, 1780–1845* (Princeton: Princeton University Press, 1965).

17. Goveia, *Slave Society*, p. 218.

18. Plantocrats were continually attacking slave testimony and defending slavery. For example, in "The Colonial Empire of Great Britain," *Blackwood's Magazine*, November 1831, pp. 744–764, James Macqueen vitriolically attacks Mary Prince's narrative in minute detail and offers extensive refutation by plantocrats and their supporters. *The Anti-Slavery Reporter* for February 1833 published a long report of

the Reverend Curtin's testimony before a Committee of the House of Lords on the condition and treatment of slaves: "Mr. Curtin could not recollect any instances (with one or two exceptions) of cruel treatment of slaves in Antigua, during his thirty years' experience" (p. 516). The testimony of missionaries also made a difference. Missionary Henry Whiteley, for example, returned to England from Jamaica and wrote an account of the atrocities he had witnessed. Two hundred thousand copies were distributed within two weeks. See C. Duncan Rice, "The Missionary Context of the British Anti-Slavery Movement," in *Slavery and British Society, 1776–1846*, ed. James Walvin (London: Macmillan, 1982), p. 160.

19. For information about Elizabeth Hart, see John Horsford, *A Voice from the West Indies: Being a Review of the Character and Results of Missionary Efforts in the British and Other Colonies in the Caribbean Sea, with Some Remarks on the Usages, Prejudices, etc. of the Inhabitants* (London: Alexander Heylind, 1856), pp. 188, 203–204 and passim. See also Frances Lanaghan, *Antigua and the Antiguans: A Full Account of the Colony and Its Inhabitants from the Time of the Caribs to the Present Day. Interspersed with Anecdotes and Legends. Also, an Impartial View of Slavery and the Free Labour Systems; The Statistics of the Island and Biographical Names of the Principal Families*, 2 vols. (London: Saunders & Otley, 1844), vol.1, pp. 317–319 and passim.

20. For Elizabeth Hart Thwaites's testimony, see Horsford, *A Voice*, pp. 211–212; quotation on p. 212. The exact details of her testimony are unclear because records somewhat conflict. Aside from Horsford, who insists she "held out" and kept silence, there is also commentary in Charles Thwaites's journal that suggests she cooperated because she did not think her answers would harm people. See Charles Thwaites's journal, no. 1, pp. 133–137.

21. Macqueen, "The Colonial Empire of Great Britain," appendix L.

22. The hymns and poem appear in John Horsford, *A Voice from the West Indies: Being a Review of the Character and Results of Missionary Efforts in the British and Other Colonies in the Charibbean Sea, with Some Remarks on the Usages, Prejudices, etc, of the Inhabitants* (London: Alexander Heylin, 1856), chap. 7.

23. This letter to an unidentified male friend was published in Horsford, *A Voice from the West Indies.*

24. Elizabeth Hart Thwaite's correspondence with her cousin, Elizabeth Lynch, regarding the establishment of Sunday schools in Antigua (1809) was published in Horsford, *A Voice from the West Indies.*

25. The *Memoir of John Gilbert, Esq., Late Naval Storekeeper at Antigua, to Which Are Appended a Brief Sketch of His Relic, Mrs. Anne Gilbert, by the Rev. William Box, Wesleyan Missionary, and a Few Additional Remarks by a Christian Friend* (Liverpool: D. Marples, 1835) contains the *Memoir* itself, finished by Anne

Gilbert; "A Brief Sketch," by the Reverend William Box (reproduced in appendix A), and "Additional Remarks on John and Ann Gilbert by a Friend" (see appendix B). A copy is in the British Library, shelf-mark 4903df8.

26. For information on John Gilbert, see Anne Hart Gilbert's *The Hart Sisters*, Moira Ferguson, ed., (Lincoln: University of Nebraska Press, 1993), pp. 76–88.

27. Box, *Memoir*, p. 89.

28. For Anne Hart Gilbert's biography, see the introduction to Ferguson, *The Hart Sisters*, esp. pp. 28–35. Note that the birth and death dates of Anne Hart Gilbert and Elizabeth Hart Thwaites have been revised: Ann was born in 1768; Elizabeth in 1771.

29. From his official travels to oversee the implementation of the Emancipation Act, Joseph Sturge offers a Methodist's retrospective view of Anne Hart Gilbert's charitable work: "We went, also, to see the 'Refuge for Female Orphans'; an interesting and most useful institution, which is dependent on the English 'Ladies' Society.' It was declining for want of attention; its chief support had been Mrs. Gilbert, an excellent lady of colour, now dead." Joseph Sturge and Thomas Harvey, *The West Indies in 1837: Being the Journal of a Visit to Antigua, Montserrat, Dominica, St. Lucia, Barbados, and Jamaica, Undertaken for the Purpose of Ascertaining the Actual Condition of the Negro Population of Those Islands*, 2d ed. (London: Hamilton, Adams, 1838), p. 36.

30. As a case in point, when she explains the remuneration they eventually (and reluctantly) received for Sunday services, she does not stipulate who does the work: "As soon as Sunday work had received a check, we attended the Parish Church" (p. 80).

31. William Andrews, *To Tell a Story: The First Century of Afro-American Autobiography, 1760–1865* (Urbana: University of Illinois Press, 1986), p. 17.

32. Moira Ferguson, *Subject to Others: British Women Writers and Colonial Slavery, 1660–1834* (New York: Routledge, 1992). There is a very large body of controversial research on the history of slavery. Among representative texts by black and white historians, black slaves, former slaves, and their contemporaries are the following: Eric Williams, *Capitalism and Slavery* (Chapel Hill: University of North Carolina Press, 1944), esp, pp. 3–107; C. L. R. James, *The Black Jacobins: Toussaint L'Ouverture and the San Domingo Revolution* (New York: Vintage Books, 1963); E. R. Rich, "The Slave Trade and National Rivalries," pt. 4 of chap. 6, in *The Cambridge Economic History of Europe*, vol. 4 of *The Economy of Expanding Europe in the 16th and 17th Centuries*, ed. E. E. Rich and C. H. Wilson (Cambridge: Cambridge University Press, 1967), pp. 323–338; Peter Fryer, *Staying Power: The History of Black People in Britain* (London: Pluto Press, 1984); David Brion Davis, *The Problem of Slavery in Western Culture* (Ithaca: Cornell University Press, 1966), pts. 1,

2; and Roger Anstey, *The Atlantic Slave Trade and British Abolition, 1760–1812* (Atlantic Highlands, N.J.: Humanities Press, 1975).

33. Ferguson, *Subject to Others*, pp. 117–118. Lord Mansfield's decision was erroneously interpreted to mean that England forbade slavery.

34. Fryer, *Staying Power*, p. 213.

35. *A General Index to the Subjects of Debates*, Session 1830-31, vols. 1, 2, 3, *Hansard Parliamentary Debates*, 3rd series, Commons, s.v. Slavery, in no. 11, n.p.

36. Wilkinson, Henry C., *Bermuda from Sail to Steam: The History of the Island from 1784–1901* (London: Oxford University Press, 1973), vol. 1, p. 23; Hayward, Walter Brownell, *Bermuda Past and Present: A Descriptive and Historical Account of the Somers Islands* (New York: Dodd, Mead and Co., 1911), p. 50. Packwood gives population statistics for 1774: 5,632 whites; 5,023 blacks. A tax was imposed on slave imports in the 1770s to limit the number and in 1785 "a new tax on slaves and free Blacks became law" (p. 79). It is impossible to tell from the text whether or not Prince's parents were first-generation slaves.

37. Packwood, Cyril Outerbridge, *Chained on the Rock: Slavery in Bermuda* (New York: Eliseo Torres; Bermuda: Baxter's Limited, 1975), p. 3; Wilkinson, vol. 1, p. 28. The most important secondary source (quoting directly from the Manchester Papers) about the founding of Bermuda and the original black inhabitants in Wesley Frank Craven, "An Introduction to the History of Bermuda," *William and Mary Quarterly* 17 (April 1937): 176–215; (July 1937): 317–362; (October 1937): 437–465; and 18 (January 1938): 13–63. Information about black settlers ([July 1937]: 358–362) makes it clear that black men were experts and instructed the white colonists in their most important potential industries: pearl diving, the care of sugar cane and of tropical and subtropical plants, and the growing and curing of tobacco; "Francisco, Antonye, and James" are specifically mentioned, pp. 360–361.

38. One, in November 1656, was led by a dozen black men, including Black Tom and Cabilecto. They intended to "distroie . . . the English in the night," but several slaves collaborated; Black Tom was hanged and Cabilecto executed on the gibbet. For details of the 1656 conspiracy, see Packwood, *Chained on the Rock*, p. 142. Michael Craton, *Testing the Chains: Resistance to Slavery in the British West Indies* (Ithaca: Cornell University Press, 1982), pp. 225–226. Another plot erupted seventeen years later at Christmas under the leadership of five slaves, one of whom turned (or more likely was tortured into turning) against the other four. After these outbreaks, Governor John Heydon put strict laws into effect (Packwood, pp. 143–145). Prince was most likely to have heard about the plots devised by slaves that occurred within her parents' lifetimes. Between 1720 and 1730, several remarkable poisoning plots that involved slaves knowledgeable about plants and herbs were uncovered. After the poisoning of several whites, a very old slave named Sarah or

Sally Bassett was burnt at the stake for being a ringleader, thereby attaining legendary status. The poisoning plots, including the central role of Sarah Bassett, are discussed in detail in Packwood, *Chained on the Rock* (pp. 146–149). In 1761, an island-wide plot participated in by more than half the black population led to enactment of a law in 1762 that provided for extensive vigilance of black people, especially at night. Such historical tales would have strengthened the already keen sense of self that Prince's environment guaranteed, *Chained on the Rock* (pp. 149–157). Since many whites thought free black people were responsible for the plots, regulations against them were tightened. "This was the last really big conspiracy, planned by Blacks, during slavery. Well over half of Bermuda's slave population of approximately 4,000, were prepared to rebel against almost 5,000 white inhabitants" (p. 156). See also K. E. Ingram, comp. and ed., *Source for West Indian Studies: A Supplementary Listing, with Particular Reference to Manuscript Sources* (Ag Zug, Switzerland: Inter Documentation, 1983), item 0935, p. 261: "William Popple. 1701–64, Governor of Bermuda, 1745–64. Letter to the Lords Commissioners of Trade and Plantations, [gives] an account of an intended insurrection of Negroes and of the measures taken to suppress it . . . " 28 February, 1762 (date of letter), B.L. Shelfmark BB of.l.a.

39. For information about Antiguan law, see Frances Lanaghan, *Antigua and the Antiguans: A Full Account of the Colony and its Inhabitants From the Time of the Caribs to the Present Day, Interspersed with Anecdotes and Legends. Also, an Impartial View of Slavery and the Free Labour Systems; The Statistics of the Island, and Biographical Notices of the Principal Families,* 2 vols. (London: Saunders & Otley, 1884), vol. 2, pp. 155ff. and passim, in Bryan Edwards, *The History, Civil and Commercial of the British Colonies in the West Indies,* vol, 2, quoted in Goveia, *Slave Society,* pp. 218ff., p. 315, and passim. It is possible that the prevalence of free blacks in Antigua spurred Prince to deeper levels of resistance. Antigua was also the island that boasted two stalwart heroes of slave uprisings, Tacky and Tomboy. See Craton, *Testing the Chains,* pp. 115–124, and David Barry Gaspar, "The Antiguan Slave Conspiracy of 1736: A Case Study of the Origins of Collective Resistance," *William and Mary Quarterly* 35, no. 2 (April 1978): 308–323. The ease with which so many British accepted slavery is evident in the texts of visitors on the island. Take Maria Riddell, *Voyages in the Madeira and Leeward Caribbean Isles: With Sketches of the Natural History of These Islands* (Edinburgh: Peter Hill; London: T. Cadell, 1792), pp. 47–104, for example. Riddell confines her comments about the island's black inhabitants to their breeding of goats, selling of fur, catching of lizards, eating of prickle-pears and cassava, usage of calabashes, and the making of cradles from cabbage trees.

40. *The History of Mary Prince* was published by F. Westley and A. H. David and also by Waugh and Innes in Edinburgh. In "A Supplement by the Editor"

Thomas Pringle, secretary of the Anti-Slavery Society, explains the circumstances of his publishing the narrative: he includes testimony from supporters of Prince and mentions detractors. The text went into a third edition that year. No reviews of the text appeared in such prominent periodicals as the *Athenaeum*, the *Critical Review*, the *Monthly Review*, and the *Edinburgh Magazine*, probably because it had provoked such immediate controversy. In 1830–1831, *Hansard* makes no mention of the *History* either. All references in the text will be to the first edition. Versions of the introduction to this text were read at The Black Woman Writer and the Diaspora Conference, East Lansing, Michigan, 27 October 1985; and at the Women's Studies Colloquia Series at the University of Nebraska-Lincoln, 14 November 1985; the Modern Language Association, San Francisco, December 1987; the University of London, History Workshop Colloquium, July, 1988; and the Hamilton Center for Historical Studies, Bermuda, 17 February 1994.

41. Biographical information about Prince comes from the introduction to *The History*, pp. 1–41. For a discussion of the slave narrative, see eds. Charles T. Davis and Henry Louis Gates, Jr., *The Slave's Narrative*, 2d ed. (New York: Oxford University Press, 1985); Marion Wilson Starling, *The Slave Narrative: Its Place in American History*, 2d ed. (Washington, D.C.: Howard University Press, 1988); Elizabeth Fox-Genovese, "My Statue, My Self. Autobiographical Writings of Afro-American Women," in *Reading Black, Reading Feminist*, ed. Henry Louis Gates, Jr. (New York: Meridian Books, 1990) pp. 176–203. For a solid analysis of Prince and the role of autobiography, see Sandra Pouchet Paquet, "The Heartbeat of a West Indian Slave: *The History of Mary Prince*," *African American Review* 26, no. 1 (spring 1992): pp. 131–146.

42. See *The History*, appendix 1, "Mary Prince's Petition presented to Parliament on 26 June 1829," pp. 116–117.

43. Information about Prince's life comes from the introduction to *The History of Mary Prince*, pp. 1–26.

44. San Domingo's policy, established after the successful revolution in 1791, of receiving and protecting slaves on the run from Turks Island and elsewhere, meant that escape and revolution (with a built-in possibility of success) were common subjects of discussion on Turks Island. See Packwood, *Chained on the Rock*, p. 47.

45. Susanna Strickland, Prince's amanuensis, went on to marry Captain John Moodie, emigrate to Canada, and become one of that country's most important early writers. The narrative of some of her experiences in Canada, *Roughing It in the Bush*, includes an attack on racism that may well be indebted to her knowledge of and friendship with Prince. Moodie mentions Prince on at least three occasions in 1831, two in connection with the manuscript and one on the occasion of Strickland's wedding on 4 April 1831 at which Prince was a guest. See Susanna Moodie,

Roughing It in the Bush: or Life in Canada, ed. Carl Ballstadt (Ottawa: Carleton University Press, 1988), pp. 224–229; *Susanna Moodie; Letters of a Lifetime,* ed. Carl Ballstadt, Elizabeth Hopkins, and Michael Peterman (Toronto: University of Toronto Press, 1985), pp. 57, 60, 61.

46. The British Museum copy (B.L. Shelfmark 8154bbb30) carries the following handwritten dedication on the title page: "The Reverend Mr. Mortimer. With the Editor's best respects." The Reverend Mortimer may be the one mentioned in the *Dictionary of National Biography,* who in 1833 wrote *The Immediate Abolition of Slavery compatible with the safety and prosperity of the colonies* (B.L. Shelfmark, 8156aaa67).

47. See *Reports of Cases Determined at Nisi Prius, in the Courts of King's Bench, Common Pleas, and Exchequer, and on the Northern and Western Circuits, from the Sittings After Michaelmas Term, I Will. IV. 1830, Sittings After Trinity Term, 7 Will. IV. 1836, Inclusive,* ed. William Moody and Frederic Robinson, vol. 1 (London: Saunders & Benning, and J. and W. T. Clarke, 1837), p. 277; and *The English Reports,* vol. 174, Nisi Prius 5 (London: W. Green, Edinburgh, Stevens & Sons, 1929), p. 95. For the earlier case in which Pringle and Cadell participated, see the *Times* (London), 22 February 1833, p. 4, col. B.

48. Macqueen, "The Colonial Empire of Great Britain."

49. *Times* (London), 22 February 1833, p. 4, col. B.

50. See note 47.

51. Because of incomplete records, most dates until 1828 are speculative.

52. For information about slave uprisings in Jamaica, see Craton, *Testing the Chains.* See also George Hunte, *Jamaica* (London: B. T. Batsford, 1976); K. E. Ingram, *Jamaica* (Oxford: Clio Press, 1984).

53. On the Akan-speaking "Coromantees," see Craton, *Testing the Chains,* p. 95 and passim; Isaac Dookham, *A Post Emancipation History of the West Indies* (London: Longman Caribbean, 1975), p. 12.

54. Paul Gilroy, *Black Atlantic: Modernity and Double Consciousness* (Cambridge: Harvard University Press, 1993).

55. Adam Potkay and Sandra Burr, eds., *Black Atlantic Writers of the 18th Century: Living the New Exodus in England and the Americas* (New York: St. Martin's Press, 1995), pp. 1–3.

56. Biographical information about Seacole comes from Ziggi Alexander and Audrey Dewjee, eds., *The Wonderful Adventures of Mrs. Seacole in Many Lands* (Bristol, Eng.: Falling Wall Press, 1984), pp. 9–45. For a historical view of black women nurses in the United States, see Darlene Clark Hine, *Black Women in White: Racial Conflict and Cooperation in the Nursing Profession, 1890–1950* (Bloomington: Indiana University Press, 1989).

57. See the discussion of "mulattoes" in Alexander and Dewjee, *Wonderful Adventures*, p. 10.

58. Ibid., p. 19 and passim.

59. Piers Compton, *Colonel's Lady and Camp Follower: The Story of Women in the Crimean War* (New York: St. Martin's Press, 1970), pp. 131, 145.

60. Seacole, *Wonderful Adventures*, pp. 49–50.

61. Ibid., introduction.

62. For an important analysis of *Wonderful Adventures*, see Sandra Pouchet Paquet, "The Enigma of Arrival: *The Wonderful Adventures of Mrs. Seacole in Many Lands*," *African American Review* 26, no. 4 (winter 1992): pp. 651–663.

63. Carla Peterson, "*Doers of the Word": African-American Women Speakers and Writers in the North* (New York: Oxford University Press, 1995), p. 146.

64. Vernon Parrington, *Main Currents in American Thought*, vol. 2 (New York: Harvest, 1927). Any account of antebellum literature was, in Eric Sundquist's words, "defined along the axes of revolution and slavery." That is, the authors wrote about freedom. See Sundquist, *To Wake the Nation: Race in the Making of American Literature.* (Cambridge: Harvard University Press, Belknap Press, 1993).

65. Frances Smith Foster, *Witnessing Slavery* (Westport, Conn.: Greenwood Press, 1979), p. 62.

66. See ibid., and Foster, "Adding Color and Contour to Early American Self-Portraitures: Autobiographical Writings of Afro-American Women," in *Conjuring: Black Women, Fiction, and Literary Tradition*, ed. Marjorie Pryse and Hortense J. Spillers (Bloomington: Indiana University Press, 1985).

67. Frederick Douglass, *Narrative of the Life of Frederick Douglass, an American Slave. Written by Himself* (Boston: Anti-Slavery Office, 1845); William Wells Brown, *Narrative of William Wells Brown, a Fugitive Slave. Written by Himself* (Boston: Anti-Slavery Office, 1847).

68. Jean Fagan Yellin, *Women and Sisters: The Antislavery Feminists in American Culture* (New Haven: Yale University Press, 1989), pp. 103–105.

69. Ibid., pp. 129–131; Starling, *The Slave Narrative*, pp. 89–90.

70. Jean Fagan Yellin, "Written by Herself: Harriet Jacobs's Slave Narrative," *American Literature* 53, no. 3 (November 1981): 485. Note also that the discovery of a cache of thirty letters that Harriet Jacobs wrote to Amy Post, a Quaker feminist and abolitionist from Rochester, New York, has helped to "authorize" the sometimes challenged authorship of Jacobs. Referring to herself as Hatty, Jacobs began the correspondence with Post in midcentury. After their meeting, Post urged Jacobs in the 1850s to write her autobiography. After an uncomfortable episode with Harriet Beecher Stowe in which Jacobs "felt denigrated as a mother, betrayed as a woman, and threatened as a writer by Stowe's action," she decided to write her personal

narrative alone. See ibid., p. 482. "Poor as it may be," said Jacobs, "I had rather give [the narrative] from my own hand, than have it said I employed others to do it for me" (p. 484). As letters attest, Lydia Maria Child edited the manuscript (p. 484). By lending her name to the book, Child underscores its authenticity and wants to arouse "conscientious and reflecting women at the North to a sense of their duty in the exertion of moral influence on the question of Slavery, on all possible occasions" (p. 92). For biographical information, see also Jean Fagan Yellin, "Texts and Contexts of Harriet Jacobs's *Incidents in the Life of a Slave Girl: Written by Herself*," in Davis and Gates, *The Slave's Narrative*, pp. 262–282. For the text of some of Jacobs's letters, see also Dorothy Sterling, ed., *We Are Your Sisters: Black Women in the Nineteenth Century* (New York: Norton, 1984). For information on slaves and slavery in the United States, see Andrews, *To Tell a Free Story*; Foster, *Witnessing Slavery*.

71. Harriet Jacobs, [Linda Brent], *Incidents in the Life of a Slave Girl. An Authentic Historical Narrative Describing the Horrors of Slavery as Experienced by Black Women*, ed. L. Maria Child (San Diego: Harcourt Brace Jovanovich, 1973). All references will be to this edition. The authoritative edition is now Jean Fagan Yellin, ed., *Incidents in the Life of a Slave Girl Written by Herself* (Cambridge: Harvard University Press, 1987).

72. Jacobs, *Incidents in the Life of a Slave Girl*, p. 42.

73. Yellin, *Incidents in the Life of a Slave Girl Written by Herself*, p. xvii. For a names "key," see pp. xv–xvi.

74. Hilary Beckles, Barbara Bush, and Lucille Mathurin discuss the issue of sexual abuse and the courageous resistance of female slaves. See Beckles, *Black Rebellion in Barbados: The Struggle Against Slavery in 1627–1833* (St. Michael, Barbados, W.I: Antilles Publications, 1984); Bush, *Slave Women in Caribbean Society, 1650–1838* (Kingston: Heinemann; Bloomington: Indiana University Press, 1990); Mathurin, *The Rebel Woman in the British West Indies During Slavery* (Jamaica, W.I.: Institute of Jamaica, 1975), pp. 250ff. Sexual abuse and "systems of concubinage" are discussed at length in Goveia, *Slave Society*, and Richard B. Sheridan, *Doctors and Slaves: The Medical and Demographic History of Slavery in the British West Indies, 1680–1834* (Cambridge: Cambridge University Press, 1985). Sheridan quotes tellingly from William Taylor's testimony before the Select Committee on the Extinction of Slavery in 1832. Frances Smith Foster also discusses rape and abuse in "Adding Color and Contour to Early American Self-Portraitures," p. 31, and in *Witnessing Slavery*, pp. 108–109. Whether evangelical men and women knew of the constant rebellions, particularly by female slaves, is an open question. Would they have known, for example, that the Barbados Council declared "black ladies . . . have rather a tendency to the Amazonian cast of character" (Mathurin, *The Rebel*

Woman, p. 15), or that 1,782 women compared with 941 men were punished between 1824 and 1826, or that "the black female spitfire was a plague on the lives of drives, overseers, and managers" (ibid., p. 13)? Could they have been aware of a ditty (likely of questionable morality in evangelical eyes) sung by black women in the Caribbean that suggested why they felt empowered to revolt?

> And while he palaver and preach him book
> At the negro girl he'll winkie him yeye
> "Hi! de Buckra, hi!" (Beckles, *Black Rebellion,* p. 16)

We do know, however, that the legal cases of such abused and exploited female slaves as Killy Hilton, Grace, and Kate had become notorious causes célèbres through the propaganda of the *Anti-Slavery Reporter.* Female petitioners such as the slave Polly (mentioned in Quaker anti-slavery correspondence) also added to the composite profile of rebelling women. See also Sander L. Gilman, "Black Bodies, White Bodies: Toward an Iconography of Female Sexuality in Late Nineteenth-Century Art, Medicine, and Literature," in *"Race," Writing, and Difference,* ed. Henry Louis Gates, Jr. (Chicago: University of Chicago Press, 1985), pp. 223–261.

75. Foster, *Witnessing Slavery,* pp. 58–59.

76. Yellin, *Women and Sisters,* p. 91.

77. Ibid., p. 485.

78. Yellin, *Incidents,* p. xviii.

79. Information about Jacobs is available in the comprehensive introduction to Yellin, *Incidents.* Supplementing that information is Yellin, "Written by Herself," pp. 479–486. Note, too, that several earlier personal documents written around the mid-nineteenth century frequently stress the spiritual dimension; see ed., William L. Andrews, *Sisters of the Spirit. Three Black Women's Autobiographies and the Nineteenth Century* (Bloomington: Indiana Univeristy Press, 1986).

80. See note 70.

81. Sundquist, *To Wake the Nation,* p. 29.

82. Barbara A. White, "'Our Nig'" and the She-Devil: New Information about Harriet Wilson and the 'Bellmont' Family," *American Literature* 65, no. 1 (March 1993): 21–52. New information about the Hayward family, following the groundbreaking path of Henry Louis Gates, Jr., comes from White's data. See also David Ames Curtis and Henry Louis Gates, Jr., "Establishing the Identity of the Author of *Our Nig,*" in *Wild Women in the Whirlwind: Afra-American Culture and the Contemporary Literature Renaissance,* ed. Joanne M. Braxton and Andrée Nicole McLaughlin (New Brunswick: Rutgers University Press, 1990), pp. 48–69.

83. *Our Nig: or, Sketches from the Life of a Free Black, in a Two-Story White*

House, North. Showing That Slavery's Shadows Fall Even There (New York: Random House, 1983). For information about Harriet E. Wilson and her text, see the introduction to *Our Nig* by Henry Louis Gates, Jr., pp. xi-lix. For the issue of discontinuities, see particularly, Hortense J. Spillers, "Cross-Currents, Discontinuities: Black Women's Fiction," in *Conjuring: Black Women, Fiction, and Literary Tradition,* ed. Marjorie Pryse and Hortense J. Spillers (Bloomington: Indiana University Press, 1985), pp. 249–261. See also Kari J. Winter, *Subjects of Slavery, Agents of Change: Women and Power in Gothic Novels and Slave Narratives, 1790–1865* (Athens: University of Georgia Press, 1992), esp. pp. 34–35.

84. See Wilson, *Our Nig,* pp. xi–lix. For a discussion of fiction as a weapon for authentic voicing, see Richard Yarborough, "The First Person in Afro-American Fiction," in *Afro-American Literary Study in the 1990s,* ed. Houston A. Baker, Jr., and Patricia Redmond (Chicago: University of Chicago Press, 1989), pp. 111, 124, and passim.

85. Wilson, *Our Nig,* preface.

86. For Harriet Beecher Stowe's bigotry, see Yellin, "Written by Herself," p. 482.

87. Mary Dearborn, *Pocahantas's Daughters: Gender and Ethnicity in American Culture* (New York: Oxford University Press, 1986), p. 32. See also note 85.

88. Carla Peterson, *"Doers of the Word,"* p. 169.

89. Marilyn Richardson, *Maria W. Stewart: America's First Black Woman Political Writer* (Bloomington: Indiana University Press, 1987), esp. pp. 24–42.

90. C. Eric Lincoln and Lawrence H. Mamiya, *The Black Church in the African American Experience.* (Durham: Duke University Press, 1989), p. 47. For slaveholding practices and new taboos, see also William Warren Sweet, *Methodism in American History* (New York: Methodist Book Concern, 1933), p. 233.

91. Daniel Payne, *History of the African Methodist Episcopal Church* 1: 4–5 (Nashville: A.M.E. Church, 1891, reprinted New York, 1968). See also eds. Rosemary Skinner Keller, Louise L. Queen, and Hilah F. Thomas, *Women in New Worlds* (Nashville: Abingdon, 1982), pp. 278, 279, 284, 445, and George Eaton Simpson, *Black Religions in the New World* (New York: Columbia University Press, 1978), pp. 1–20.

92. Sharon Harley, *The Timetable of African American History* (New York: Simon & Schuster, 1995), p.78.

93. See Peterson, *"Doers of the Word,"* for a brilliant appraisal of Lee's activities, esp. pp. 73–87.

94. For a careful evaluation of the genre of spiritual autobiography and Lee's role, see Frances Smith Foster, *Written by Herself: Literary Production by African American Women 1746–1897* (Bloomington: Indiana University Press, 1993), p. 58.

95. Ibid.

96. Ibid., p. 70.

97. Andrews, *Sisters of the Spirit*, p. 33.

98. Potkay and Burr, *Black Atlantic Writers*, p. 15. For black Freemasonry, see W. H. Grimshaw, *Official History of Freemasonry Among the Colored People in North America* (New York: Negro University Press, 1903); and Donn A. Cass, *Negro Freemasonry and Segregation: An Historical Study of Prejudice Against American Negroes as Freemasons, and the Position of Negro Freemasonry in the Masonic Fraternity* (Chicago: Ezra A. Look, 1970).

99. Andrews, *Sisters of the Spirit*, p. 40. See also Mary G. Mason and Carol H. Green, eds., *Journeys: Autobiographical Writings by Women* (Boston: G. K. Hall, 1979), pp. 73–87; and Bert J. Loewenberg and Ruth Bogin, eds., *Black Women in Nineteenth-Century American Life: Their Words, Their Thoughts, Their Feelings* (University Park: Pennsylvania State University Press, 1976), pp. 136–141.

100. *The Life and Religious Experience of Jarena Lee* (1836) and *Religious Experience and Journal of Mrs. Jarena Lee* (1849).

101. Andrews, *Sisters of the Spirit*, p. 6.

102. Foster, *Written by Herself*, pp. 74–75.

103. Andrews, *Sisters of the Spirit*, p. 47.

104. Foster, *Written by Herself*, pp. 73.

105. Nancy Prince, *A Black Female's Odyssey Through Russia and Jamaica: The Narrative of Nancy Prince*, introd. Ronald G. Walters (New York: Markus Wiener, 1990). Most of the biographical facts, unless otherwise noted, come from this edition. See also Loewenberg and Bogin, *Black Women*, pp. 201–218.

106. Prince, *A Black Female's Odyssey*, p. ix.

107. Ibid., p. xi.

108. Ibid., pp. xii, 12.

109. See *Encyclopedia of African-American Religion*, ed. Larry G. Murphy et al. (New York: Garland, 1993).

110. For Nero Prince, see Allison Blakely, *Russia and the Negro: Blacks in Russian History and Thought* (Washington, D.C.: Howard University Press, 1986), pp.15–19.

111. Potkay and Burr, *Black Atlantic Writers*, p. 15. For further information about the black community in Boston, see James Oliver Horton, and Lois E. Horton, *Black Bostonians: Family Life and Community Struggle in the Antebellum North* (New York: Holmes & Meier, 1979).

112. Prince, *A Black Female's Odyssey*, p. xviii.

113. Nancy Prince, *The West Indies, Being a description of the Islands, Progress of Christianity, Education and Liberty Among the Colored Population Generally* (Boston: Dow & Jackson, 1841).

114. Thomas Hilton, quoted in Sterling, *We Are Your Sisters*, p. 222. See also *Collected Black Women's Narratives*, Introd. Anthony G. Barthelemy (New York, Oxford: Oxford University Press, 1988), p. xxxvii.

115. Hazel Carby points out that the concept of true womanhood excluded black women because of the equation constantly made between black women and clandestine sexuality. Hence at some level, women like Mary Seacole and Nancy Prince felt freer to be itinerant, but always within some prescribed boundaries. Hazel V. Carby, *Reconstructing Womanhood: The Emergence of the Afro-American Woman Novelist* (Oxford: Oxford University Press, 1987), pp. 17, 23–34.

116. Rodger Streitmatter, Mary Ann Shadd Cary, *Raising Her Voice, African American Women Journalists Who Changed History* (Lexington, Ky.: University Press of Kentucky, 1994), p. 25.

117. Ibid., p. 26.

118. *The Black Abolitionist Papers,* vol. 2. Canada 1830–1865, ed. C. Peter Ripley (Chapel Hill: University of North Carolina Press, 1986). For information on Mary Ann Shadd Cary, see also Jim Bearden and Linda Jean Butler, *Shadd: The Life and Times of Mary Shadd Cary* (Toronto: NC Press, 1977).

119. Peterson, *"Doers of the Word,"* pp. 99–100.

120. Bearden and Butler, *Shadd*, p. 57 and passim.

121. Jane Rhodes, "Mary Ann Shadd Cary and the Legacy of African-American Women Journalists," in *Women Making Meaning: New Feminist Directions in Communication,* ed. Lana F. Rakon (New York: Routledge, 1992), p. 214.

122. For Henry Bibb, see Bearden and Butler, *Shadd*, pp. 60–68; see also *The Black Abolitionist Papers*, vol. 2. Canada 1830–1865, ed. C. Peter Ripley (Chapel Hill: University of North Carolina Press, 1986), pp. 109–110 n, 170–175.

123. Rhodes, "Mary Ann Shadd Cary and the Legacy," pp. 210–224.

124. Ibid., p. 213.

125. Ibid., p. 214.

126. The *Provincial Freeman*, 27 May 1854, quoted ibid., p. 215.

127. Peterson, "*Doers of the Word,*" p. 110.

128. Ibid., p. 102.

129. Sterling, *We Are Your Sisters*, p. 257.

Selected Bibliography

■

Primary Sources

Mary Anne Shadd Cary

"Hints to the Colored People of North America." 1849.

A Plea for Emigration, or *Notes of Canada West, in its Moral, Social, and Political Aspect: with Suggestion respecting Mexico, W. Indies and Vancouver's Island for the Information of Colored Emigrants.* Detroit: George W. Pattison, 1852.

Provincial Freeman. March 1854–September, 1857. University of Pennsylvania Library, Philadelphia.

Ripley, C. Peter, ed. *The Black Abolitionist Papers.* Vol. 2, *Canada, 1830–1865.* Chapel Hill: University of North Carolina Press, 1986. Esp. pp 245–309.

Anne Hart Gilbert

Box, The Rev. William. *Memoir of John Gilbert. Esq., Late Naval StoreKeeper at Antigua, to Which are Appended a Brief Sketch of His Relic, Mrs. Anne Gilbert, by the Rev. William Box, Wesleyan Missionary, and a Few Additional Remarks by a Christian Friend.* Liverpool: D. Marples, 1835.

Ferguson, Moira, ed. *The Hart Sisters.* Lincoln: University of Nebraska Press, 1993.

Harriet Ann Jacobs

Incidents in the Life of a Slave Girl, Written by Herself. [as Linda Brent] Edited by L. Maria Child. Boston: n.p., 1861.

———. *Incidents in the Life of a Slave Girl, Written by Herself.* [as Linda Brent] Introduced by Jean Fagan Yellin. Cambridge: Harvard University Press, 1987.

———. *Collected Black Women's Narratives.* Introduced by Anthony G. Barthelemy. Schomburg Library of Nineteenth-Century Black Women Writers, ed. Henry Louis Gates, Jr. New York: Oxford University Press, 1988.

Jarena Lee

The Life and Religious Experience of Jarena Lee, A Coloured Lady, Giving an Account of Her Call to Preach. Philadelphia, 1836.

Religious Experience and Journal of Mrs. Jarena Lee, Giving an Account of Her Call to Preach the Gospel. Philadelphia, 1849.

Mary Prince

The History of Mary Prince, A West Indian Slave, Related by Herself. London, 1831. Reprint, edited by Moira Ferguson. London: Pandora Press, 1987; Ann Arbor: University of Michigan Press, 1992; rev. 2nd ed. 1997.

Nancy Gardner Prince

A Black Woman's Odyssey through Russia and Jamaica: The Narrative of Nancy Prince. Introduced by Ronald G. Walters. New York: Marcus Weiner, 1990.

A Narrative of the Life and Travels of Mrs. Nancy Prince, Written by Herself. Boston: Published by the author, 1850. Reprint, Second Edition. 1853. In *Collected Black Women's Narratives,* ed. Henry Louis Gates, Jr., introduced by Anthony G. Barthelemy, Schomburg Library Series, 1988.

The West Indies: Being a Description of the Islands, Progress of Christianity, Education, and Liberty among the Colored Population Generally. Boston: Dow & Jackson Printers, 1841.

Mary Jane Grant Seacole

Wonderful Adventures of Mrs. Seacole in Many Lands. Edited by Ziggy Alexander and Audrey Dewjee. London, 1857. Reprint, Bristol, Eng.: Falling Wall Press, 1984.

Elizabeth Hart Thwaites

Ferguson, Moira, ed. *The Hart Sisters.* Lincoln: University of Nebraska Press, 1993.

Harriet E. Adams Wilson

Our Nig; or, Sketches from the Life of a Free Black, In A Two-Story White House, North. Showing That Slavery's Shadows Fall Even There. By "Our Nig." Boston: Printed by Geo. Rand & Avery, 1859. Reprint, with introduction and notes by Henry Louis Gates, Jr.. New York: Random House, Vintage Books, 1983.

Secondary Sources

Books

Andrews, William L. *To Tell a Free Story: The First Century of Afro-American Autobiography, 1760–1865.* Urbana: University of Illinois Press, 1986.

———. *Sisters of the Spirit: Three Black Women's Autobiographies of the Nineteenth Century.* Bloomington: Indiana University Press, 1986.

Ashcroft, Bill, Gareth Griffiths, and Helen Tiffin. *The Empire Writes Back: Theory and Practice in Post-Colonial Literatures.* London: Routledge, 1989.

Astley, Sir John D. *Fifty Years of My Life.* 2 vols. London: Hurst & Blackett, 1894.

Atwood, Thomas. *The History of the Island of Dominica. Containing a description of its situation, extent, climate, mountains, rivers, natural productions, &c. &c. Together with an account of the civil government, trade, laws, customs, and manners of the different inhabitants of that island. Its conquest by the French, and restoration to the British Dominions.* London: Printed for J. Johnson, 1791. Reprint, London: Frank Cass, 1971.

Baker, Houston A., and Patricia Redmond, eds. *Afro-American Literary Study in the 1990s.* Chicago: University of Chicago Press, 1992.

Baker, Rachel. *The First Woman Doctor.* London: Harrap, 1946.

Bamfield, Veronica. *On the Strength: The Story of the British Army Wife.* London: Charles Knight, 1974.

Baylen, J. O., and A. Conway, eds. *Soldier-Surgeon: The Crimean War Letters of Dr. Douglas A. Reid, 1855–1856.* Knoxville: University of Tennessee Press, 1968.

Bearden, James, and Linda Jean Butler. *Shadd: The Life and Times of Mary Shadd Cary.* Toronto: NC Press, 1977.

Bell, Bernard W. *The Afro-American Novel and Its Tradition.* Amherst: University of Massachusetts Press, 1987.

Bell, Roseann P., Bettye J. Parker, and Beverly Guy-Sheftall, eds. *Sturdy Black Bridges: Visions of Black Women in Literature.* Anchor Books, New York, 1979.

Blackwell, Elizabeth, M.D. *Pioneer Work in Opening the Medical Profession to Women. Autobiographical Sketches.* London: Longmans, 1895.

Blackwood, Lady Alicia. *A Narrative of Personal Experiences and Impressions during a Residence on the Bosphorus throughout the Crimean War.* London: Hatchard, 1881.

Blain, Virginia, Patricia Clement, and Isobel Grundy. *The Feminist Companion to Literature in English.* New Haven: Yale University Press, 1990.

Blakely, Allison. *Russia and the Negro: Blacks in Russian History and Thought.* Washington D.C.: Howard University Press, 1986.

Box, The Rev. William. *Memoir of John Gilbert, Esq. Late Naval Storekeeper at Antigua. To Which Are Appended. A Brief Sketch of His Relic, Mrs. Anne Gilbert. by the Rev. William Box, Weslyan Missionary, and a Few Additional Remarks by a Christian Friend.* Liverpool: D. Marples, 1835.

Brackenbury, George. *The Campaign in the Crimea.* London: Colnaghi, 1856.

Bragg, George F. *Heroes of the Eastern Shore.* Baltimore: G. F. Bragg, 1939.

Brathwaite, Edward Kamau. *The Development of Creole Society in Jamaica, 1770–1820.* Oxford: Clarendon Press, 1971.

Braxton, Joanne M. *Black Women Writing Autobiography: A Tradition Within a Tradition.* Philadelphia: Temple University Press, 1989.

Buck, Claire, ed. *The Bloomsbury Guide to Women's Literature.* New York: Prentice Hall, 1992.

Buckley, Roger Norman. *Slaves in Red Coats: The British West India Regiments 1795–1815.* New Haven: Yale University Press, 1979.

Bush, Barbara. *Slave Women in Caribbean Society, 1650–1838.* Bloomington: Indiana University Press, 1990.

Caines, Clement. *Letters on the Cultivation of the Otaheite Cane, the manufacture of sugar and rum, the saving of molasses, the care and preservation of stock, with the attention and anxiety which is due to negros. To these topics are added a few other particulars analogous to the subject of the letters, and also a speech on the slave trade, the most important feature in West Indian culture.* Vol. 1. London, 1801.

Carby, Hazel V. *Reconstructing Womanhood: The Emergence of the Afro-American Woman Novelist.* New York: Oxford University Press, 1987.

Carmichael, Mrs. A. C. *Domestic Manners and Social Condition of the White, Coloured and Negro Population of the West Indies.* 2 vols. London: Whittaker, Treacher, 1833. Reprint, Westport Conn.: Greenwood Press, n.d.

Carter, Violet Bonham, ed. *Surgeon in the Crimea.* London: Constable, 1968.

Caulfield, James E. *One Hundred Years' History of the Second Battalion West India Regiment, from the date of raising, 1795 to 1898.* London: Forster Groom, 1899.

Chatoyer, Joseph. "The Declaration of Joseph Chatoyer, Chief of the Chariabs," in *An Account of the Black Chariabs in the Island of St. Vincents: with the Chariab Treaty in 1773, and other original documents.* Compiled for the papers of the late Sir William Young, London of Sewell, 1795.

Chesney, Kellow. *A Crimean War Reader.* London: Severn House, 1975.

Child, Lydia Maria. *The Freedmen's Book.* Boston: Ticknor & Fields, 1865.

Christian, Barbara. *Black Feminist Criticism: Perspectives on Black Women Writers.* New York: Pergamon Press, 1985.

Clarkson, Thomas. *The History of the Rise, Progress, and Accomplishment of the Abolition of the African Slave-Trade by the British Parliament.* Vol. 1. London: Longman, Hurst, Rees, & Orme, 1808.

Coke, Thomas. *A History of the West Indies, containing the Natural, Civil, and Ecclesiastical History of each Island; With an Account of the Missions instituted in those islands, from the commencement of their civilization: but more especially of the Missions which have been established in that Archipelago by the Society Late in Connexion with the Rev. John Wesley.* 3 vols. Vol. 1. London: Printed for the Author 1811; reprint Miami, Florida: Mnemosyne, 1969.

Compton, Piers. *Colonel's Lady and Camp-Follower: The Story of Women in the Crimean War.* London: Robert Hale, 1970.

Cornelius, Janet Duitsman. *"When I can read my title clear": Literacy, Slavery, and Religion in the Antebellum South.* Columbia: University of South Carolina Press, 1991.

Cracknell, Basil E. *Dominica.* Newton Abbot, England: David & Charles; Harrisburg, Penn.: Stackpole Books, 1973.

Craton, Michael. *Testing the Chains: Resistance to Slavery in the British West Indies.* Ithaca: Cornell University Press, 1982.

Cundall, Frank. *Historic Jamaica.* London: Institute of Jamaica, 1915.

Curtin, Phillip D. *Two Jamaicas: The Role of Ideas in a Tropical Colony, 1830–1865.* Cambridge, Mass.: Harvard University Press, 1955.

Davies, Carole Boyce. *Black Women, Writing and Identity: Migrations of the Subject.* New York: Routledge, 1994.

Davis, Angela Y. *Women, Race, and Class.* New York: Random House, 1981.

Davis, Charles T., and Henry Louis Gates, Jr., eds. *The Slave's Narrative.* 2d ed. New York: Oxford University Press, 1985.

Davy, John. *The West Indies Before and Since Slave Emancipation. Comprising The Windward and Leeward Islands' Military Command; founded on notes and observations collected during a three years' residence.* London: W. & F. G. Cash, 1854. Reprint, London: Frank Cass, 1971.

Dearborn, Mary V. *Pocahantas's Daughers: Gender and Ethnicity in American Culture.* Oxford: Oxford University Press, 1986.

Delany, Martin R. *The Condition Elevation, Emigration and Destiny of the Colored People of the United States.* Published by the Author. Philadelphia, 1852. New ed. Arno Press, New York Times, New York, 1968.

Drescher, Seymour. *Capitalism and Antislavery: British Mobilization in Comparative Perspective.* London: Macmillan, 1986.

Dull, Steven Ray. "The Life of Mary Ann Shadd Cary." Master's thesis, San Francisco State University, 1990.

Dunlop, Alexander. *Notes on the Isthmus of Panama.* London, 1852.

Edwards, Paul, and David Dabydeen, eds. *Black Writers in Britain, 1769–1890.* Edinburgh: Edinburgh University Press, 1991.

Ellis, A. B. *The History of the First West India Regiment.* London: Chapman & Hall, 1885.

Equiano, Olaudah. *The Interesting Narrative of the Life of Olaudah Equiano or Gustavus Vassa, the African. Written by Himself.* Vol. 1. London: printed and sold by the author, 1789. Reprint, *Equiano's Travels. His Autobiography. The Interesting Narrative of the Life of Olaudah Equiano or Gustavus Vassa the African.* Edited by Paul Edwards. London: Heinemann, 1967.

Eyre-Todd, George, ed. *The Autobiography of William Simpson, R.I.* London: Unwin, 1903.

Fanon, Frantz. *Black Skin: White Masks.* New York: Grove Press, 1967; London: Pluto Press, 1986.

Farwell, Byron. *For Queen and Country.* London: Allen Lane, 1981.

Fenton, Roger. *Photographer of the Crimean War.* Edited by A. and H. Gernsheim. London: Secker & Warburg, 1954.

Ferguson, Moira. *Subject to Others: British Women Writers and Colonial Slavery, 1660–1834.* New York: Routledge, 1992.

Findlay, G. G., and W. W. Holdsworth. *The History of the Wesleyan Methodist Missionary Society.* Vol. 2. London: Epworth Press, n.d.

Fortescue, Sir John W. *A History of the British Army.* 13 vols. London and New York: Macmillan, 1899–1930.

Forty, G., and A. Forty. *They Also Served.* Kent: Midas, Tunbridge Wells, 1979.

Foster, Frances Smith. *Witnessing Slavery: The Development of Ante-bellum Slave Narratives.* Westport, Conn.: Greenwood Press, 1979.

———. *Written by Herself: Literary Production by African American Women, 1746–1892.* Bloomington: Indiana University Press, 1993.

Fox-Genovese, Elizabeth. *Within the Plantation Household: Black and White Women of the Old South.* Chapel Hill: University of North Carolina Press, 1988.

Fryer, Peter. *Staying Power: The History of Black People in Britain.* London: Pluto Press, 1984.

Gaspar, David Barry. *Bondmen and Rebels: A Study of Master-Slave Relations in Antigua, with Implications for Colonial British America.* Baltimore: Johns Hopkins University Press, 1985.

Gates, Henry Louis, Jr., ed. *Schomburg Library of Nineteenth-Century Black Women Writers.* New York: Oxford University Press, 1988.

George, Carol V. R. *Segregated Sabbaths: Richard Allen and the Emergence of Independent Black Churches, 1760–1840.* New York: Oxford University Press, 1973.

Giddings, Paula. *When and Where I Enter: The Impact of Black Women on Race and Sex in America.* New York: Morrow, 1984.

Gilroy, Paul. *The Black Atlantic: Modernity and Double Consciousness.* Cambridge: Harvard University Press, 1993.

Goodman, Margaret. *Experiences of an English Sister of Mercy.* London: Smith, Elder, 1862.

Goveia, Elsa V. *Slave Society in the British Leeward Islands at the End of the Eighteenth Century.* New Haven: Yale University Press, 1965.

Green, William A. *British Slave Emancipation: The Sugar Colonies and the Great Experiment, 1830–1865.* Oxford: Clarendon Press, 1976.

Grieve, Symington. *Notes Upon the Island of Dominica (British West Indies) Containing Information for Settlers, Investors, Tourists, Naturalists, and Others with statistics from the official returns, also regulations regarding crown lands and import and export duties.* London: Adam & Charles Black, 1906.

Griffith, Cyril E. *The African Dream: Martin R. Delany and the Emergence of Pan-African Thought.* University Park: Pennsylvania State University Press, 1975.

Grimshaw, William H. *Official History of Freemasonry among the Colored People in North America: Tracing the Growth of Freemasonry from 1717 Down to the Present Day.* New York: Negro University Press, 1969.

Gwin, Minrose C. *Black and White Women of the Old South: The Peculiar Sisterhood in American Literature.* Knoxville: University of Tennessee Press, 1985.

Hall, Douglas. *A Brief History of the West India Community.* Barbados: Caribbean Universities Press, 1971.

Handler, Jerome S. *The Unappropriated People: Freedmen in the Slave Society.* Baltimore: Johns Hopkins University Press, 1974.

Hankison, Alan. *Man of Wars: William Howard Russell of the Times.* London: Heinemann, 1982.

Hayward, Walter Brownell. *Bermuda Past and Present: A Descriptive and Historical Account of the Somers Islands.* New York: Dodd, Mead and Co., 1911.

Henriques, F. *Children of Caliban.* London: Secker & Warburg, 1974.

Harris, Wilson. *Tradition: The Writer and Society.* London: New Beacon Books, 1967.

Higginson, General Sir George. *Seventy-One Years of a Guardsman's Life.* London: John Murray, 1916.

Higman, B. W. *Slave Population and Economy in Jamaica, 1807–1834.* Cambridge: Cambridge University Press, 1976.

Hine, Darlene Clark, Elsa Barkley Brown, Rosalyn Terborg-Penn. *Black Women in America: An Historical Encyclopedia.* 2 vols. Bloomington: Indiana University Press, 1993.

Hine, Darlene Clark, Wilma King, Linda Reed. *We Specialize in the Wholly Impossible: A Reader in Black Women's History.* Brooklyn, NY.: Carlson, 1995.

Hine, Darlene Clark, *Black Women in United States History.* 16 vols. Brooklyn, New York: Carlson, 1990.

Hoetink, H. *The Two Variants in Caribbean Race Relations.* Oxford: Oxford University Press, 1967.

Honychurch, Lennox. *The Dominica Story: A History of the Island.* Lennox Honychurch, 1975; Roseau, Domenica Institute, 1984.

hooks, bell. *Ain't I a Woman: Black Women and Feminism.* Boston: South End Press, 1981.

Horton, James Oliver, and Lois E. Horton. *Black Bostonians: Family Life and Community Struggle in the Antebellum North.* New York: Holmes & Meier, 1979.

Hulme, Peter. *Colonial Encounters: Europe and the Native Caribbean, 1492–1797.* New York: Methuen, 1986.

Huxley, Elspeth. *Florence Nightingale.* London: Weidenfeld & Nicholson, 1975.
Jahn, Janheinz. *A History of Neo-African Literature.* Translated by Oliver Coburn and Ursula Lehrburger. London: Faber & Faber, 1968.
James, C. L. R. *The Black Jacobins: Toussaint L'Ouverture and the San Domingo Revolution.* New York: Vintage Books, 1963.
James, Edward T., and Janet W. James, eds. *Notable American Women.* Cambridge: Harvard University Press, 1971.
James, Lawrence. *Crimea, 1854 to 1856.* New York: Van Nostrand Reinhold, 1981.
Jones, Jacqueline. *Labor of Love, Labor of Sorrow: Black Women, Work, and the Family from Slavery to the Present.* New York: Vintage Books, 1990.
Jordan, Winthrop D., *White over Black: American Attitudes Toward the Negro, 1550–1812.* Chapel Hill: University of North Carolina Press, 1968.
Kelly, James. *Voyage to Jamaica.* Belfast: Wislon, 1838.
Kelly, Mrs. Tom. *From the Fleet in the Fifties.* London: Hurst & Blackett, 1902.
Kinglake, A. W. *The Invasion of the Crimea: Its Origin, and an Account of its Progress down to the Death of Lord Raglan.* Reprint, 4th ed. 4 vols. New York: Harper & Brothers. 1863.
Kolchin, Peter. *Unfree Labor: American Slavery and Russian Serfdom.* Cambridge: Belknap Press, Harvard University Press, 1987.
Lanaghan, Frances. *Antigua and the Antiguans: A Full Account of the Colony and Its Inhabitants from the Time of the Caribs to the Present Day, Interspersed with Anecdotes and Legends. Also, an Impartial View of Slavery and the Free Labour Systems: The Statistics of the Island and Biographical Names of the Principal Families.* 2 vols. London: Saunders & Otley, 1844.
Lerner, Gerda, ed. *Black Women in White America: A Documentary History.* New York, Pantheon Books, 1973.
Lincoln, C. Eric, and Lawrence H. Mamiya. *The Black Church in the African American Experience.* Durham: Duke University Press, 1990.
Litwack, Leon F. *North of Slavery: The Negro in the Free States, 1790–1860.* Chicago: University of Chicago Press, 1961.
Loewenberg, Bert James, and Ruth Bogin, eds. *Black Women in Nineteenth-Century American Life: Their Words, Their Thoughts, Their Feelings.* University Park: Pennsylvania State University Press, 1976.
Loggins, Vernon. *The Negro Author: His Development in America.* New York: Columbia University Press, 1931.
Long, Edward. *The History of Jamaica.* 3 vols. London, 1774.
Macherey, Pierre. *A Theory of Literary Production.* Translated by Geoffrey Wall. London: Routledge & Paul, 1978.
Maclean, Charles, M.D. *An Analytical View of the Medical Department of the British Army.* London, 1810.

MacMunn, Sir George Fletcher. *The Crimea in Perspective.* London: Bell, 1935.

Marks, Elaine, and Isabelle de Courtivron, eds. *New French Feminisms: An Anthology.* New York: Schocken Books, 1981.

Martineau, Harriet. *England and Her Soldiers.* London, 1859.

Mary Aloysius, Sister. *Memories of the Crimea.* London: Burns & Oates, 1897.

Mason, Mary Grimley, and Carol Hurd Green, eds. *Journeys: Autobiographical Writings by Women.* Boston: G. K. Hall, 1979.

Mathieson, William Law. *British Slavery and Its Abolition, 1823–1838.* New York: Octagon Books, 1967.

McMahon, Jean, ed. *Gifts of Power: The Writings of Rebecca Jackson, Black Visionary, Shaker Eldress.* Amherst: University of Massachusetts Press, 1981.

Mitra, S. M. *The Life and Letters of Sir John Hall.* London: Longmans, 1911.

Moodie, Susanna. *Letters of a Lifetime.* Edited by Carl Ballstadt, Elizabeth Perkins, and Michael Peterman. Toronto: University of Toronto Press, 1985.

Moritz, Theresa and Allen. *The Pocket Canada: A Complete Guide to the World's Second Largest Country.* Toronto: Van Nostrand Reinhold, 1982.

Morris, Helen. *Portrait of a Chief.* Cambridge: Cambridge University Press, 1938.

Nasta, Susheila. *Motherlands: Black Women's Writing from Africa, the Caribbean and South Asia.* New Brunswick: Rutgers University Press, 1991.

Nelson, Dana D. *The Word in Black and White: Reading "Race" in American Literature, 1638–1867.* New York: Oxford University Press, 1993.

Nugent, Lady Maria. *A Journal of a Voyage to and Residence in the Island of Jamaica, from 1801 to 1805.* 2 vols. London, 1839.

Nussbaum, Felicity A. *The Autobiographical Subject. Gender and Ideology in Eighteenth-Century England.* Baltimore: Johns Hopkins University Press, 1989.

Nutting, M. A., and L. L. Dock. *A History of Nursing.* 4 vols. New York: Putnam, 1907.

Packwood, Cyril Outerbridge. *Chained on the Rock: Slavery in Bermuda.* New York: Eliseo Torres; Bermuda: Baxter's Limited, 1975.

Painter, Nell Irvin. *Sojourner Truth: a Life, a Symbol.* New York: W. W. Norton, 1996.

Patterson, Orlando. *The Sociology of Slavery.* London: Hutchinson, 1967.

Payne, Daniel Alexander. *History of the African Methodist Episcopal Church.* Edited by C. S. Smith. Nashville: Publishing House of the A.M.E. Sunday School Union, 1981.

Pemberton, W. Baring. *Battles of the Crimean War.* London: Batsford, 1962.

Peterson, Carla L. *"Doers of the Word": African American Women Speakers and Writers in the North* (1830–1880). New York: Oxford University Press, 1995.

Potkay, Adam, and Sandra Burr, eds. *Black Atlantic Writers of the 19th Century:*

Living the New Exodus in England and the Americas. New York: St. Martin's Press, 1995.

Prince, Mary. *The History of Mary Prince. A West Indian Slave. Related by Herself.* Edited by Moira Ferguson. London: Pandora, 1987; Ann Arbor: University of Michigan Press, 1993; rev. 2d ed., 1997.

Prochaska, F. K., *Women and Philanthropy in Nineteenth-Century England.* Oxford: Clarendon Press, 1980.

Ragatz, Lowell Joseph, *Absentee Landlordism in the British Caribbean, 1750–1833.* London: Bryan Edwards Press, n.d.

Rakow, Lana, ed. *Women Making Meaning: New Feminist Directions in Communication.* New York: Routledge, 1992.

Ramchand, Kenneth. *The West Indian Novel and Its Background.* New York: Barnes & Noble, 1970.

Richardson, Marilyn, ed. *Maria W. Stewart, America's First Black Woman Political Writer: Essays and Speeches.* Bloomington: Indiana University Press, 1987.

Robinson, H. *Phillis Wheatley and Her Writings.* New York: Garland, 1984.

Rogers, J. A. *World's Great Men of Color.* London: Macmillan, 1972.

Romaine, Suzanne. *Pidgin and Creole Languages.* New York: Longman, 1988.

Rout, Leslie B. *The African Experience in Spanish America: 1502 to the Present Day.* Cambridge: Cambridge University Press, 1976.

Russell, Sir William H. *The British Expedition to the Crimea.* London: 1858.

———. *The Great War with Russia.* London: 1895.

Said, Edward. *Orientalism.* New York: Vintage Books, 1979.

Schiebinger, Londa. *Nature's Body: Gender in the Making of Modern Science.* Boston: Beacon Press, 1993.

Scott, Michael. *Tom Cringle's Log.* Paris, 1829; reprint, Everyman Library, London: J. M. Dent, 1969.

Sekora, John, and Darwin T. Turner, eds. *The Art of Slave Narrative.* Macomb, Illinois: Western Illinois University Press, 1982.

Sheldon, George. *A History of Deerfield, Massachusetts.* Greenfield, Mass.: Press of E. A. Hall, 1895–1896.

Shockley, Ann Allen, ed. *Afro-American Women Writers, 1746–1933: An Anthology and Critical Guide.* Boston, G. K. Hall, 1988.

Shyllon, F. O. *Black Slaves in Britain.* London: Oxford University Press, 1974.

———. *Black People in Britain, 1555–1833.* London: Oxford University Press, 1977.

Simpson, William. *The Seat of the War in the East.* London: Colnaghi, 1856.

Smith, Jessie Carney, ed. *Notable Black American Women.* Detroit: Gale Research, 1992.

Smith, Valerie. *Self-Discovery and Authority in Afro-American Narrative.* Cambridge: Harvard University Press, 1987.

Soyer, Alexis. *Soyer's Culinary Campaign.* London: G. Routledge, 1857.

Stanton, Elizabeth Cady, Susan B. Anthony, and Matilda Joslyn Gage. *History of Woman Suffrage.* Vol. 1. 1881. Reprint, New York: Arno, 1969.

Starling, Marion Wilson. *The Slave Narrative. Its Place in History.* 2d ed. Washington, D.C.: Howard University Press, 1988.

Sterling, Dorothy, ed. *We Are Your Sisters: Black Women in the Nineteenth Century.* New York: Norton, 1984.

Stetson, Erlene, ed. *Black Sisters: Poetry by Black American Women, 1746–1980.* Bloomington: Indiana University Press, 1981.

Streitmatter, Rodger. *Raising Her Voice: African American Women Journalists Who Changed History.* Lexington, Ky.: University Press of Kentucky, 1994.

Sturge, Joseph, and Thomas Harvey. *The West Indies in 1837: being the Journal of a Visit to Antigua, Montserrat, Dominica, St. Lucia, Barbadoes, and Jamaica: undertaken for the purpose of ascertaining the actual condition of the Negro Population of those islands.* London: Hamilton, Adams & Co., 1838.

Summers, Anne. *Angels and Citizens: British Women as Military Nurses, 1854–1914.* London: Routledge Kegan Paul, 1988.

Taylor, Fanny. *Eastern Hospitals and English Nurses.* 2 vols. London: 1856.

Thomas, Hilah F., and Rosemary Skinner Keller, eds. *Women in New Worlds.* Nashville: Abingdon, 1981.

Todorov, Tzvetan. *The Conquest of America.* New York: Harper & Row, 1984.

Trollope, Anthony. *The West Indies and the Spanish Main.* London: 1859. Reprint, Gloucester: Alan Sutton, 1985.

Turner, Mary. *Slaves and Missionaries. The Disintegration of Jamaican Slave Society, 1787–1834.* Urbana: University of Illinois Press, 1982.

Vicars, Hedley. *Walking with God before Sebastopol.* London, 1855.

Walker, Clarence E. *A Rock in a Weary Land: The African Methodist Episcopal Church During the Civl War and Reconstruction.* Baton Rouge: Louisiana University Press, 1982.

Walvin, James. *The Black Presence.* New York: Schocken Books, 1971.

Warner, Phillip, ed. *The Fields of War: A Young Cavalryman's Crimea Campaign.* London: John Murray, 1977.

Washington, Mary Helen. *Invented Lives: Narratives of Black Women, 1860–1960.* New York: Doubleday, 1987.

White, Deborah Gray. *Ar'n't I a Woman? Female Slaves in the Plantation South.* New York: Norton, 1985.

Wilkinson, Henry C. *Bermuda from Sail to Steam: The History of the Island from*

1784–1901. London: Oxford University Press, 1973.

Williams, Cynric R. *A Tour Through the Island of Jamaica from the Western to the Eastern End in the Year 1823*. London, 1826.

Williams, Eric. *Capitalism and Slavery*. New York: Capricorn Books, 1944.

Williams, Jane, ed. *The Autobiography of Elizabeth Davis, a Balaclava Nurse*. London, 1857.

Winks, Robin W. *The Blacks in Canada: A History*. New Haven: Yale University Press, 1971.

Winter, Kari J. *Subjects of Slavery, Agents of Change: Women and Power in Gothic Novels and Slave Narratives, 1790–1865*. Athens: University of Georgia Press, 1992.

Woodham-Smith, Cecil. *Florence Nightingale, 1820–1910*. London: Constable, 1950.

Woodson, Carter G., and Charles H. Wesley. *The Negro in Our History*, Washington, D.C.: Associated Publishers, 1932.

Work, Monreo. *A Bibliography of the Negro in Africa and America*. 1928. Reprint, New York: Octagon Books, 1970.

Wortley, Lady Emmeline Stuart. *Travels in the United States of America during 1849 and 1850*. 3 vols. London, 1851.

Yee, Shirley J. *Black Women Abolitionists: A Study in Activism, 1828–1860*. Knoxville: University of Tennessee Press, 1992.

Yellin, Jean Fagan. *Women and Sisters: The Antislavery Feminists in American Culture*. New Haven: Yale University Press, 1989.

Articles

Alonzo, Andrea Starr. "A Study of Two Women's Slave Narratives: *Incidents in the Life of a Slave Girl* and *The History of Mary Prince*." In *"We Specialize in the Wholly Impossible": A Reader in Black Women's History*. Edited by Darlene Clark Hine, Wilma King, Linda Reed. Brooklyn, New York: Carlson, 1995, pp. 143–146.

Bolster, W. Jeffrey, "'To Feel Like a Man': Black Seamen in the Northern States, 1800–1860." *Journal of American History*. Forthcoming.

Cooper, Afua. "The Search for Mary Bibb, Black Woman Teacher in Nineteenth Century Canada West." In *"We Specialize in the Wholly Impossible" A Reader in Black Women's History*. Edited by Darlene Clark Hine, Wilma King, Linda Reed. Brooklyn, New York: Carlson, 1995, pp. 171–185.

Davies, Carole Bryce, and Elaine Savory Fido, eds. "Introduction: Women and Literature in the Caribbean: An Overview." *Out of the Kumbla: Caribbean Women and Literature*. Trenton, N.J.: Africa World Press, 1990, pp. 1–22.

Doriani, Beth Maclay. "Black Womanhood in Nineteenth-Century America: Subversion and Self-Construction in Two Women's Autobiographies." In *"We Specialize in the Wholly Impossible": A Reader in Black Women's History.* Edited by Darlene Clark Hine, Wilma King, Linda Reed. Brooklyn, New York: Carlson, 1995, pp. 373–392.

Ernest, John. "Economics of Identity: Harriet E. Wilson's *Our Nig.*" *PMLA 109,* no. 3 (May 1994), pp. 424–438.

Foreman, P. Gabrielle. "The Spoken and the Silenced in *Incidents in the Life of a Slave Girl* and *Our Nig.*" *Callaloo* 13, no. 2 (Spring 1990), pp. 313–324.

Foster, Frances Smith. "Adding Color and Contour to Early American Self- Portraitures: Autobiographical Writings of Afro-American Women." In *Conjuring: Black Women, Fiction, and Literary Tradition,* edited by Majorie Pryse and Hortense J. Spillers. Bloomington: Indiana University Press, 1985, pp. 25–38.

Fox-Genovese, Elizabeth. "My Statue, My Self. Autobiographical Writings of Afro-American Women." In *Reading Black. Reading Feminist. A Critical Anthology,* edited by Henry Louis Gates, Jr. New York: Meridian, 1990, pp. 176–203.

Gates, Henry Louis, Jr., and David Ames Curtis, "Establishing the Identity of the Author of *Our Nig.*" In *Wild Women in the Whirlwind: Afra-American Culture and the Contemporary Literature Renaissance,* edited by Joanne M. Braxton and Andrée Nicole McLaughlin, New Brunswick: Rutgers University Press, 1990, pp. 48–69.

Gilman, Sander L., "Black Bodies, White Bodies: Toward an Iconography of Female Sexuality in Late Nineteenth-Century Art, Medicine, and Literature," in *"Race," Writing, and Difference,* ed. Henry Louis Gates, Jr. (Chicago: University of Chicago Press, 1985), pp. 223–261.

Gwin, Minrose C. "Green-eyed Monsters of the Slavocracy: Jealous Mistresses in Two Slave Narratives." In *Conjuring: Black Women, Fiction, and Literary Tradition,* edited by Majorie Pryse and Hortense J. Spillers. Bloomington: Indiana University Press, 1985, pp. 39–52.

Henderson, May Gwendolyn. "Speaking in Tongues: Dialogues, Dialectics, and the Black Woman Writer's Literary Tradition." In *Reading Black, Reading Feminist: A Critical Anthology,* edited by Henry Louis Gates, Jr. New York: Meridian, 1990, pp. 116–142.

Hine, Darlene Clark. "*Lifting the Veil, Shattering the Silence: Black Women's History in Slavery and Freedom.*" In *The State of Afro-American History: Past, Present, and Future.* Edited by Darlene Clark Hine. Baton Rouge: Louisiana University Press, 1986, pp. 223–249.

Hite, Roger W. "Voice of the Fugitive: Henry Bibb and Antebellum Black Separatism." *Journal of Black Studies* 4 (March 1974), pp. 269–284.

Hunter, William R. "Do Not Be Conformed Unto This World: An Analysis of Religious Experiences in the Nineteenth-Century African American Spiritual Narrative." *Nineteenth Century Studies* 8 (1994), pp. 75–88.

Kellow, Margaret M. R. "The Divided Mind of Antislavery Feminism: Lydia Maria Child and the Construction of African American Womanhood," In *Discovering the Women in Slavery: Emancipating Perspectives on the American Past,* edited by Patricia Morton. Athens: University of Georgia Press, 1996.

Macqueen, James. "The Colonial Empire of Great Britain." *Blackwood's Magazine,* November 1831, pp. 744–764.

Painter, Nell Irvin. "Sojourner Truth in Life and Memory: Writing the Biography of an American Exotic." In *"We Specialize in the Wholly Impossible" A Reader in Black Women's History.* Edited by Darlene Clark Hine, Wilma King, Linda Reed. (Brooklyn, New York: Carlson, 1995), pp. 359–371.

Paquet, Sandra Pouchet. "The Enigma of Arrival: *The Wonderful Adventures of Mrs. Seacole in Many Lands.*" *African American Review,* 26, no. 4 (winter, 1992), pp. 651–663.

———. "The Heartbeat of a West Indian Slave: *The History of Mary Prince.*" *African American Review* 26, no. 1 (spring, 1992), pp. 133–146.

Reddock, Rhoda E. "Woman and Slavery in the Caribbean: A Feminist Perspective," In *"We Specialize in the Wholly Impossible" A Reader in Black Women's History.* Edited by Darlene Clark Hine, Wilma King, Linda Reed. (Brooklyn, New York: Carlson, 1995), pp. 127–141.

Rhodes, Jane. "Mary Ann Shadd Cary and the Legacy of African-American Women Journalists." In *Women Making Meaning: New Feminist Directions in Communication,* edited by Lana F. Rakow. New York: Routledge, 1992, pp. 210–224.

Robinson, Amy. "Authority and the Public Display of Identity: *Wonderful Adventures of Mrs. Seacole in Many Lands.*" *Feminist Studies* 20, no. 3 (fall 1994), pp. 537–557.

Spillers, Hortense. "Cross-Currents, Discontinuities: Black Women's Fiction." In *Conjuring: Black Women, Fiction, and Literary Tradition,* edited by Marjorie Pryse and Hortense J. Spillers. Bloomington: Indiana University Press, 1985, pp. 249–261.

Spivak, Gayatri Chakravorty. "Three Women's Texts and a Critique of Imperialism." In *"Race," Writing, and Difference,* edited by Henry Louis Gates, Jr. Chicago: University of Chicago Press, 1985, pp. 262–280.

Tate, Claudia. "Allegories of Black Female Desire; or, Rereading Nineteenth-Century Sentimental Narratives of Black Female Authority." In *Changing Our Own Words,* edited by Cheryl A. Wall. New Brunswick: Rutgers University Press,

1989, pp. 98–126.

Washington, Mary Helen. "Meditation on History: The Slave Narrative of Linda Brent." *Invented Lives: Narratives of Black Women, 1860–1960.* New York: Doubleday, 1987, pp. 3–15.

Yarborough, Richard, "The First Person in Afro-American Fiction," in *Afro-American Literary Study in the 1990s,* ed. Houston A. Baker, Jr., and Patricia Redmond. Chicago: University of Chicago Press, 1989, p. 247, pp. 105–121.

Yellin, Jean Fagan. "*Written by Herself:* Harriet Jacobs' Slave Narrative." *American Literature. A Journal of Literary History, Criticism and Bibliography,* vol. 53, no 3 (November, 1981), pp. 479–486.

_______. "Text and Contexts of Harriet Jacobs's *Incidents in the Life of a Slave Girl: Written by Herself.*" In *The Slave's Narrative.* Charles T. Davis and Henry Louis Gates, Jr. New York: Oxford University Press, 1985, pp. 262–282.

Index